From
Gentleman's Club
to
Professional Body

Copyright © 2008 William Palmer
All rights reserved.

ISBN: 1-4392-1048-9
ISBN-13: 9781439210482

Visit www.booksurge.com to order additional copies.

From
Gentleman's Club
to
Professional Body

The Evolution of the History Department
in the United States, 1940–1980

William Palmer
Department of History
Marshall University

Table of Contents

Acknowledgements .... vii–viii

Introduction .... ix–xxviii

Chapter One: Harvard Leads the Way 1–26

Chapter Two: The Crisis of the Harvard History Department 27–50

Chapter Three: Yale: Keeping Up With Harvard 51–86

Chapter Four: Princeton: Teaching the Young Gentlemen 87–124

Chapter Five: Berkeley: The Great Battle 125–158

Chapter Six: Wisconsin: History as a Calling 159–188

Chapter Seven: Chicago: The Serious Place 189–220

Chapter Eight: Columbia: Reinventing a Department 221–250

Conclusion 251–260

Illustrations 261–270

Bibliography 271–281

Acknowledgements:

    Many people have helped me during the course of writing this book, and it is a pleasure to thank them. First, there are the roughly seventy people, listed in the bibliography, who I interviewed for the book and without whom it could not have been written. Every one of them was courteous and helpful, but I would like to single out Ed Ayers, Jim Banner, Tom Barnes, Gene Brucker, Caroline Bynum, the late Gordon Craig, Dave Cronon, David Davis, David Donald, Rich Fox, John Gillis, Charles Gillispie, Richard Hellie, David Hollinger, Kenneth Jackson, Morton and Phyllis Keller, Stanley Kutler, David Landes, William Leuchtenburg, Pauline Maier, John Merriman, Edmund Morgan, Gary Nash, William Sewell, John Shy, Stephan Thernstrom, Bob Tignor, and Jim Wilkinson, for help beyond the normal call of academic duty. Several of the above group also read parts of the manuscript much to my benefit, saving me from several errors. The errors that remain are mine alone.

    Second, I am grateful to Ann Lage of the Bancroft Library at the University of California at Berkeley for making available to me transcripts of the interviews she conducted with faculty members from the Berkeley history department and for many courtesies during my visit to Berkeley. I am also grateful to librarians and archivists at the Sterling Library, Division of Manuscripts and Archives, at Yale University, for helping me with the papers of George Pierson and C. Vann Woodward. I would also like to thank the various persons from each of the institutions considered here for responding to my requests for photographs of key figures in the story. Jeremy Ramsier of Marshall University's Computing Services cheerfully and skillfully helped me with the technical problems that came up with the manuscript.

Lastly, my greatest debt is to my family. They listen to my favorite anecdotes and tales from the archives, tolerate my absences, help me with my more than occasional computer confusions, and are a joy to be around. This book is for them, with my love.

Introduction

From Gentleman's Club to Professional Body:
The Evolution of the History Department at Leading Universities in the United States, 1940–1980

So perfect was the order as the Yale history department sat down for lunch in the Branford College dining hall in the fall of 1940 that it resembled an academic great chain of being. The Branford dining hall itself embodied Yale in all its Gothic glory, with stained glass windows, elegant wood paneling, and a great Burgundian fireplace transported to New Haven from its original European castle. Sherry was served in the hour before lunch, and seating was assigned. At the center of a long table sat the department chair, flanked to his immediate right and left by the senior full professors, who were, in turn, flanked by the associate professors. At the ends of the table and sometimes at a separate table, depending on the size of the turnout, were the junior faculty, who, in accordance with tradition, did not address the senior faculty by their first names.[1]

While the department had several distinguished members, such as Samuel Flagg Bemis, Wallace Notestein, and Hajo Holborn, it was also a gentleman's club, very waspish, and very much an extension of Yale itself as it stood in 1940. All the department members were male, most of them held Yale degrees, and there were no blacks or Jews. There were also several faculty, known as "dollar a year men," who took only a nominal salary from the university while supporting themselves and their families primarily from their trust funds. The department was also highly Anglo-centric, with its greatest concentration of faculty in English history, amounting to over a third of the department. Most of its members were extremely conservative. Sam Bemis and Wallace Notestein thought Franklin Roosevelt was the devil incarnate.[2] Most of the teaching followed the lecture format, providing a narrative history of the critical political events and processes of the rise of western civilization from the Greeks to World War I, a narrative very relevant to the lives of the young gentleman of wealth and privilege seated in Yale's classrooms.

By the 1980s the shape of the department had been dramatically altered. In 1940 the Yale history department had about twenty faculty; in 1982 it had seventy-one. By 1982 the department's faculty included Jews, Africans, more than a dozen women, and they held degrees from universities around the world, including Oxford, U.C.L.A., Sao Paulo, SUNY Albany, and the University of Kentucky. Fewer than half its members held Yale Ph.D.s. There were no longer any "dollar a year men." While the Yale department retained an anglophile quality, the percentage of English historians had been reduced from over thirty to less than ten, and there were now six historians teaching Asian history, six specializing in Africa and African American history, and even a specialist in the Hispanic peoples of the United States.

Thus, Yale department had ceased in large measure to be a gentleman's club; like history departments at other elite universities, it had become a body of serious professionals. No longer could anyone enter its ranks on the basis of social position. And no longer could anyone receive a permanent place in it without surviving the most rigorous scrutiny. In most cases, junior faculty could not expect to advance without the publication of two major books, favorably reviewed. And there was no respite for the weary. Those who had been granted admission into the temple of the tenured found that the expectations in terms of scholarly production rose even higher.

The social milieu of the department had also changed. While the department continued to have regular lunches, its hierarchical traditions were fading. Seating was no longer ordered to reflect the power structure. Indeed, younger faculty mingled with senior members, and sometimes appeared in the most casual attire. When Richard Fox arrived at Yale as a new faculty member in 1976, he left the great Vann Woodward speechless by appearing at the pre-lunch, "sherry hour," in long hair, no socks, and sandals.[3]

This book is a study of how the change from gentleman's club to modern department evolved at Yale, and at six other history departments in the United States, including Harvard, Princeton, the University of California at Berkeley, Wisconsin, Chicago, and Columbia. It is then, by definition, a study in academic modernization, a process by no means entirely completed and one not easily undertaken in any case.

The choice of these seven departments is based on two admittedly subjective criteria. The first is that these were the departments most frequently mentioned by the subjects of my research when I asked about which departments were most highly regarded, and the second is that there was a significant body of information about them. My selection of course is not intended to suggest that these are the only departments worthy of study, only that they provide a reasonable sample from which we can view change across time. There will undoubtedly be readers who will wish that other departments be included, but few would contest the ones that have been chosen.

In any event, change in higher education is a complex subject. Academics are notoriously uncomfortable with it and prefer that their curricula, research agendas, and value systems stay as fixed and immutable as the institutional stone of the campus buildings. But time pushes forward, devotion to custom and tradition recedes, and new generations arrive on campus with energy and vision, impatient with the calcified ways of their elders.

In many cases the changes that occurred in history departments reflected changes going on in other departments across the university. Comparable patterns of professionalization, for example, occurred in English departments. Universities themselves, and, ultimately history departments, were affected by the emergence of a series of structural forces, particularly demographic and cultural, from which they at times both benefited and suffered from, and, over which they had little control.

The first seismic jolt to the traditional history department came immediately after World War II and followed the lead of Harvard President James B. Conant who built Harvard's reputation by waging a relentless campaign to make publication and scholarly reputation the most desirable qualities in a faculty member.[4] Harvard exerts considerable influence on other institutions, and its standards were gradually adopted elsewhere and were by no means limited to history departments. Many departments in a variety of disciplines at elite universities in the 1950s began recruiting new faculty more on the basis of their promise for scholarly achievement rather than for their devotion to undergraduate teaching, their pedigree, or their agreeable companionship at lunch. Gifted undergraduate teachers continued to be valued, but scholarly production was increasingly becoming the coin of the realm by which departments were evaluated.

The appointments in the Yale history department of Edmund Morgan in 1955, John Morton Blum in 1957, and C. Vann Woodward in 1961 were prime examples of hires based upon scholarly achievement. Morgan and Blum especially were fine undergraduate teachers and all three were good company at lunch, but they were hired mainly for the excellence of their scholarship and the luster it would bring to the department.

However progressive they might be, Yale's appointments and those at most other history departments at leading universities, were still accomplished in the most old-fashioned, aristocratic manner. Democratic faculty governance was still a long way off. Most history departments and most academic departments generally at such universities were run by men raised and indoctrinated in the conviction that there was an intellectual and social elite to which they belonged by virtue of their birth or education. This elite believed that it was entitled to make most decisions on academic matters by themselves in or in consultation with a select group of others of similar temperament and experience.

Two of the greatest initiators of change in the fifties, George Pierson at Yale and Joseph Strayer at Princeton, operated in this manner. They knew what they wanted, and, on the basis of long experience with their departments and universities, assumed what they wanted would be best for their departments; they made appointments with a few phone calls and consultation with carefully selected senior colleagues.

When David Potter left Yale for Stanford in 1961, Morgan and Blum went to Pierson, a thorough New England aristocrat and a descendent of one of Yale's founders, and informed him that the only person who could replace Potter was Vann Woodward, then teaching at Johns Hopkins. Pierson thought about it for a moment and then immediately telephoned Woodward, offering him a Sterling Professorship, Yale's most prestigious chair. The consultation involved three people, and the deliberation took less than five minutes.[5]

Building a more professional history department in the fifties referred to three main developments. It meant hiring faculty based upon their scholarly achievement or potential, the appointment of qualified Jews, and the expansion of the curriculum into areas outside of Europe and the United States. Teaching ability played relatively little role in hiring decisions. Several departments, most notably those at Princeton and Wisconsin, were quite concerned with the teaching ability of the faculty they hired. But faculty in other departments believed, along with Harvard's Conant, believed that good teaching was a function of good scholarship.

The appointment of faculty on the basis of their scholarship and the hiring of qualified Jews were closely linked. By the fifties leading figures in several departments had come to the realization that any department that aspired to be the best must be willing to hire Jews. While the Harvard history department had two Jews on its history faculty in the early twentieth century, it did not hire another one until Oscar Handlin was appointed to a junior position in 1940 and its next Jewish hire was not until the early fifties. But, in 1958, in a move that had clear social implications, the department replaced its celebrated American colonial historian, Samuel Eliot Morison, a man of impeccable New England pedigree, with Bernard Bailyn, a Jew.

The willingness to appoint Jews reflected changes in progress in the academic world for some time. Anti-Semitism was commonplace, even rampant, in American universities before World War II. As David Hollinger has noted, "Jews were suspect in academia partly because many Anglo-Protestants thought them socially crude and aggressive, and politically radical." The history departments at Columbia and Wisconsin were both quite late in hiring Jews in part because of the anti-Semitism of their long-time chairs, Carleton J.H. Hayes at Columbia and Paul Knaplund at Wisconsin. In the early sixties, when Staughton Lynd visited Yale to interview for a position there, he was warned by one of his hosts to avoid buying a house in a particular section of New Haven because that was "where the sons of Abraham reside."[6]

But in the post-war world, even the gentlemanly anti-Semites of the American academy were horrified by the Nazi treatment of the Jews. Moreover, Jews had been admitted for some time into graduate programs in leading history departments, and, it was clear that many of them were persons of exceptional ability. Anti-Semitism by no means vanished from American universities, but, in several cases, as we shall see, the desire to become a department of greatness overcame prejudice.

Despite lingering anti-Semitism on the campus, the most rapid infusion of Jewish faculty occurred at Berkeley. The German medievalist Ernst Kantorowicz was hired just before World War II, and in 1950 the department hired the Asianist Joseph Levenson, but the real explosion came later. By the end of the decade the department was hiring large numbers of Jews. Its appointments included David Landes in economic history, Thomas Kuhn in the history of science, Carl Schorske in European intellectual history, Lawrence Levine in American history, and Hans Rosenberg in modern European history. By 1964, several others, including Gerald Feldman in German history, Sheldon Rothblatt in modern Britain, Henry Rosovsky in economic history, and Leon Litwack in American history, along with many others, had been added.

At the same time, growing awareness of the need to know more about other parts of the world also affected history departments. Before World War II, most departments embraced a curriculum heavily tilted toward the histories of England, Europe, and the United States. By the fifties, it was becoming increasingly clear that these curricula were obsolete in the face of a new and threatening world. World War II had exposed American ignorance about Asia, and, by the fifties, it was evident that Americans were going to have to become more knowledgeable about other areas of the world. The rise of Communist superpowers and their perceived threat to American democracy made a deeper understanding of their history and culture imperative. Moreover, from the arms race to war in Korea, and the desires of peoples in Africa, Latin America, the Middle East, and Southeast Asia to be liberated from colonial oppressors, it became clear that an America that remained ignorant of what was transpiring around the world was destined to become a prisoner of it.

It was at this point that several departments began seriously to expand their offerings in non-western areas. Harvard was ahead of the curve in terms of most American departments, having hired Clarence Haring in Latin American history in 1918, John King Fairbank in Chinese history in 1939 and Richard Frye in the history of the Middle East shortly after the end of World War II. Several departments had Latin Americanists, and Latin America was one of the strengths of the Berkeley department.

But the first real advances in coverage of non-western areas did not come until the fifties. Most departments added East Asian specialists, and, if they didn't already have them, Latin

Americanists as well. Princeton made some significant advances in appointing faculty in non-western areas in the decade or so after 1950, hiring Stanley Stein in Latin America, Marius Jansen in Japan, Fritz Mote in Asia, and Robert Tignor in Africa.

Hiring in non-western areas was also important because many leading universities prided themselves on their mission to provide the nation with people who possessed the expertise needed to govern or to advise those who did on the histories and politics of the developing world. In 1954 Clarence Haring retired at Harvard, and, as late as 1961 he had not been replaced. McGeorge Bundy, previously Dean of the Faculty of Arts and Sciences at Harvard, had been appointed John F. Kennedy's chief of staff. Shortly after his appointment, Bundy wrote a letter to Franklin L. Ford, his successor as dean, scolding him for allowing the Latin American position to go unfilled. Latin America, said Bundy, was emerging as one of the most troubled and dangerous areas of the world. How was Bundy supposed to conduct foreign policy in the region without a Harvard man to advise him?[7]

This does not mean that the expansion of the curriculum into non-western areas was accomplished easily. It proved particularly controversial when adding a non-western position required sacrificing one in a traditional area; things moved more smoothly when non-western areas could be funded through grant money or by cobbling funds from several different sources. Non-western fields were established only with great difficulty at Wisconsin, where many of the senior Americanists derisively referred to it as "swamp history." It was only through the tireless efforts of Philip Curtin that non-western courses made it into Wisconsin's curriculum. One of the most dedicated advocates of non-western history, John King Fairbank of Harvard, came to despair of his colleagues' unwillingness to recognize the need for more positions in Asian history.[8]

The post-war expansion of the American economy had a mixed impact on history departments. On one hand, almost everyone benefited from an economy that was growing at an average rate of 3.5 percent a year between 1945 and 1970. During the same period the gross national product rose from around $200 billion to close to $1 trillion. Moreover, under the Serviceman's Readjustment Act of June, 1944, commonly known as the G.I. Bill, and later supplemented by additional measures, more than $13.5 billion was appropriated between 1945 and 1955 to provide education for veterans stampeding into colleges and vocational schools. At the same time, returning veterans, eager to make up for time lost to military service, also married in large numbers and started families. In 1940 2.5 million children were born. By 1950 the total increased to 3.5 million. Between 1950 and 1980, the American population increased by fifty percent.

Among the results was a sharp and continuous increase in the number of people going to college and in the funds available for higher education. To accommodate the demand, the size and quality of faculties in almost all departments increased between 1950 and 1970. Between 1950 and 1969 the size of the Berkeley history department increased from 25 to 65 faculty members. The rate of expansion was also rapid at the University of Wisconsin. Wisconsin had between six and nine faculty members before World War II, but had over sixty by the mid-sixties. State universities especially benefited from legislatures that had more money to spend than they knew what to do with. Times were so flush that at Berkeley, when the department was deadlocked between two candidates for one position, it was often permitted to hire both of them.[9]

The expansion of universities meant a pressing need for more faculty, and departments scrambled to train graduate students to meet the demand. By the late sixties, the University of Wisconsin had 650 registered graduate students, though not all of them were on campus, and, at one point, the department was awarding over sixty Ph.D.s a year. Several Wisconsin faculty were supervising thirty or forty doctoral students at one time. In the eleven years he spent as a faculty member in the Wisconsin department, William Appleman Williams directed thirty-seven completed dissertations. While Wisconsin's graduate program was exceptional, the production of Ph.D.s grew at other elite institutions as well.[10]

On the other hand, the expansion of state universities posed problems for the private ones. For the first time the biggest state universities could offer competitive salaries, lighter teaching loads, and more research support than private universities. The possibility now existed for state universities to lure faculty away from places like Harvard, Yale, and Princeton. In the late sixties, the University of Michigan, for example, lured John Shy and David Bien away from Princeton, even though both held tenured positions there. In 1969 when Harvard enticed William Bouwsma away from Berkeley, he only stayed for two years before returning to Berkeley.

Yet another seismic jolt came in the sixties. In *People of Plenty*, published in 1954, the historian David Potter predicted that a new generation of Americans, raised in relative affluence and comfort as well as by more permissive standards of child rearing, would begin to question the values of its elders. By the sixties, there were new prophets in the land to encourage the young to challenge authority, experiment with drugs and sex, and generally reject the values of the generation that raised them.[11]

In 1959 Norman O. Brown published *Life Against Death: The Psychoanalytical Meaning of History*, in which he argued that, despite all of society's efforts to deny it, whether it be through parental discipline, religious injunction, or social and educational indoctrination, human beings remained pleasure seeking animals. The book, popular with college students in the sixties, seemed to be one of several manifestos proclaiming that what passed as values were simply artificial barriers erected by society to deny the basic humanity of human beings.[12]

At the same time the civil rights movement exposed fundamental injustices in American society, and the war in Viet Nam seemed to have no strategic purpose other than to enhance the profits and powers of the perceived military/industrial complex. An emerging new left offered unflattering explanations for the pervasive racism and militarism of American society and encouraged students to challenge traditional forms of authority. Moreover, the massive expansion of American higher education in the 1960s had led to the creation of the "multiversity," by which the university had become a hopelessly impersonal institution, mired in bureaucracy and operating like a large corporation.

By the early seventies every university whose history department is considered here faced some kind of student upheaval, some of them violent. While student protests turned out to be somewhat ephemeral, indirectly they had an impact on history departments. Students demanded more say in curricular matters, and almost every university reduced its requirements at some level. Students also wanted to break with traditional white, male, heavily western course offerings. These attitudes led to yet another seismic jolt to the traditional history departments in the late sixties and early seventies whereby courses in African and African American history, women's history, and working class history were added.

Not only were new classes offered in black and women's history, but blacks and, especially, women entered the profession in increasing numbers. Several institutions hired their first black faculty in the sixties and early seventies. Most were in African-American history, including Nathan Huggins at Harvard, John Blassingame at Yale, William Brown at Wisconsin, and Waldo Martin at Berkeley. A significant exception was the medievalist William Chester Jordan, hired at Princeton in 1967.

The entrance of women into the profession bears striking resemblance to the entrance of Jews in the fifties. There were a few women faculty members in history departments before the fifties, although they were mostly in large state universities like the University of Illinois, rather than in the eastern private schools. But, like Jews, women had been admitted, if often grudgingly, to graduate programs for some time. It was clear that many of them had extraordinary abilities and deserved faculty positions in leading departments.

But old prejudices died hard. Male faculty who wished to retain the gentleman's club atmosphere, found many reasons to oppose hiring women, including the assumption that, once hired, women would just get married, have children, and leave the department high and dry. "Why should I take you on?" William B. Hesseltine snapped at a woman who wished to work with him at the University of Wisconsin in the thirties. "All you are going to do is get married, and I will have wasted all this time having you work with me for a Ph.D."¹³ At the same time other male faculty complained that a department that hired women would lose its cohesion because men wouldn't be able to talk with each other freely in the presence of women; still others argued that if women were hired, they would start sleeping with the male faculty.

In most cases, women were hired only with reluctance. The appointment of Mary Wright at Yale in 1959, as well as that of several others, was loaded with ambiguity. After declaring that a woman would teach in the Yale history department only over his dead body, George Pierson was instrumental in her appointment as the first female faculty member in the Yale history department. Adrienne Koch was hired at Berkeley in 1958 and was granted tenure, but left in 1965. In the discussion concerning Nancy Weiss's appointment at Princeton in 1969, Joseph Strayer said, with a wink, "we should hire her; she's a good man." And, while Harvard had several female faculty in the junior ranks in the late sixties and seventies, it did not appoint a woman to a senior position until it hired Angelike Laiou in 1983.¹⁴

Change in history departments also operated in institutional contexts where several intersecting worlds could collide. Each institution studied here, for example, holds a unique conception of itself which in turn shapes its attitudes toward internal reform. Harvard believes it is the world's greatest university and expects to hire nothing less than the best faculty available, but also struggles with the idea that people good enough to teach there actually exist; Yale suffers from a compulsion to keep up with Harvard, but not with anyone else; Princeton takes pride in its devotion to undergraduate teaching and relatively small graduate program; and Wisconsin reveres the memory of its noble tradition in historical studies dating back to Frederick Jackson Turner. Sometimes those self-images change over time. Before 1960 at Berkeley, the history faculty were deeply concerned about the department's mediocre image; by the mid-sixties they relished their reputation as an outstanding department. Both Columbia and Chicago believe that they are more serious and less concerned with pedigree and social position than Harvard, Yale, and Princeton.

Institutions are also combinations of individual leadership at different levels and bureaucratic structures through which departmental change must be mediated. In several cases, college presidents played significant roles in setting the agenda for their universities as a whole, perceiving their mission to be constructing a better university by recruiting better faculty. Conant at Harvard and Kingman Brewster at Yale were examples of presidents who took the initiative to improve the quality of their faculties generally, and change in history departments mirrored changes occurring across the university.

In other cases, change was promoted initially by ambitious department chairs, eager to elevate the reputations of their departments. In the 1950s most departments were small, where persons with strong personalities, vision, political skills, and institutional connections could determine the direction of a department. George Pierson and Joseph Strayer are two examples of department chairs who led by the power of their leadership and political skills. They were both classic insiders, who were undergraduates at the universities where they taught (Pierson also held a Yale Ph.D.) and closely tied to their university's power structures. Because their institutional loyalty was unquestioned, they could be trusted, even by those clinging to the old traditions, to keep change from exceeding the boundaries of permitted institutional aspiration. When an outsider, such as Carl Bridenbaugh at Berkeley in the fifties, tried to effect change, the road was considerably bumpier.

Moreover, chairs, such as Pierson and Strayer, by knowledge of the rules (at Princeton in the fifties appointments at the instructor and assistant professor level came within the exclusive purview of the chair) and winning the support of two or three other senior faculty, could control most appointments. In addition, because they were responsible for making most of the hires, they were able to build up a body of loyal retainers, thereby making it easier to maintain their control of departmental matters.

By the sixties and seventies, however, scholarly reputation and ability to recognize the latest historical fads and fashions, began to outweigh institutional connection. The most formidable reformer of the sixties, Lawrence Stone at Princeton, a powerful personality to be sure, was able to push that department to still higher levels in part because of his international reputation as a scholar and his ability to see the future of the discipline.

By the seventies departments also faced another set of problems. Communities like Cambridge, Massachusetts, New Haven, Connecticut, or Berkeley, California, which were once small, highly attractive places to live, where faculty could live close to campus in affordable housing with good schools and cultural opportunities nearby, were victims of changing demographics. The flight to the suburbs, inflation, crime, high cost of housing, declining tax bases, and crumbling schools were just a few of the factors affecting university communities.

Where Harvard or Yale could once simply crook their fingers at prospective faculty and feel confident they would come, they now found themselves having to work at recruiting. It was necessary to convince prospective faculty that in addition to the privilege of teaching at a great university, they could find affordable housing, good schools for their children, and an agreeable lifestyle away from the university.

At the same time, a new demographic type appeared on the scene, the academic couple. In the fifties, with a few exceptions, candidates for faculty positions were usually men with a wife who did not work outside the home and who required no extra accommodation. By the seventies, not only were there more women applying for jobs, but candidates of both sexes often had a spouse with career ambitions which would require accommodation.

By 1980, then, a more broadly based, professional department had emerged, but its emergence introduced new problems as well as solving old ones. The very size of new departments made it hard to find direction. Moreover, where the faculties of the fifties had a fair amount common ground in their training, social backgrounds, and teaching or professional interest, departments were now so diverse and so specialized that faculty in them might as well have been in different disciplines rather than different subfields. Writing about the ways in which the American historical profession regarded the concept of objectivity, Peter Novick entitled his chapter on the eighties, "There was no King in Israel," suggesting that the profession had lost a common purpose and direction.[15]

There were other reasons why that it was unlikely that the dramatic changes in history departments of earlier periods could be repeated. In addition to the size and diversity of departments, by 1980 democratic faculty governance and affirmative action had taken over. In the late sixties, Alvin Kernan, then the acting provost at Yale, commissioned Bart Giamatti, then a young assistant professor in the English department, who would later become Yale's president, to rewrite Yale's faculty handbook. Giamatti spent a summer working on it; Kernan was satisfied with his work, and copies were sent to the Yale faculty who uttered scarcely a peep. Kernan later noted ruefully that had he allowed a faculty member to rewrite the faculty handbook without running it through several committees and faculty leaders a few years later, the entire campus would have been turned upside down.[16]

An administrative change of any significance now needed the approval of involved parties at numerous steps along the way. At the department level, decisions about how positions should be defined, what processes would be followed, who would be interviewed, and who would be hired were now matters for the entire department or at least an appointments committee. The days when George Pierson could pick up the phone and hire Vann Woodward were long gone.

At the same time, while a more professional department emerged by the eighties, the process was still by no means complete. While women had entered into the halls of the great gentleman's departments, that transition was still difficult, and the number of women hired in history departments was still less than the percentage of women receiving Ph.Ds.

Moreover, while there was an exciting period of hiring at

the senior level in the eighties, the profession also faced serious problems. The post-war economic boom had come to an end. There were fewer jobs for historians, state universities faced major budget cuts, and private ones were forced to lift tuition to undreamed of levels. The search for outside sources of funding reached crisis levels at almost every elite university.

A few words should be said about the methods used in writing this book. I wrote my first book on Oliver St. John, a seventeenth century lawyer and parliamentary radical during the English Civil War. St. John left a tiny paper trail, consisting of a few speeches and a carefully deceptive, self-serving *apologia*. Most of his story had to be sifted through chance remarks in other documents. Getting information about him proved difficult as did gaining a sense of the kind of person he was. I moaned frequently to my friends about how nice it would be to have more direct evidence or to even talk to someone who actually knew him.

In the writing of this book, I faced exactly the opposite problem. The evidence available for this book was an embarrassment of riches. While several key persons involved in the process of creating the more professional department were dead, I could talk to people who knew them quite well, and to almost anyone among the living who was involved. I could even pose to my subjects the exact questions I wished to ask. I also discovered quickly that not only do most historians have very good memories, but those who also served as deans have even better ones. Additionally, several institutions had made serious efforts to preserve the historical record. Yale and Wisconsin have substantial collections of the papers of their eminent historians. For the last decade or so, the Bancroft Library at Berkeley has been engaged in developing an oral history collection of interviews with Berkeley faculty from all disciplines, including over a dozen history faculty from the fifties and sixties.

But the profusion of material proved to be almost as problematic in this case as the lack of it had been in the case of St. John. It was no easier writing a book with copious information than one with limited amounts. Most of this book is based on interviews with people who served in history departments between 1940 and 1980. I did some of the interviews in the mid-nineties for an earlier book, *Engagement with the Past: The Lives and Works of the World War II Generation of Historians,* published in 2001; some of the interviews were done by others and already accessible in print or repository; but most I did myself directly for this book.

Not surprisingly, the interviews came in all sizes and shapes, several of which pose problems for the historian. The first problem was that there were differing points of view even, and sometimes especially, within the same department. While there are significant exceptions, leading history departments, I discovered, were not always cheerful places. The burden of unwritten volumes haunts almost everyone. The junior faculty are often demoralized. At more than one elite institution, the pecking order jokingly, but not inaccurately, could be described as senior faculty at the top, followed by undergraduate students, graduate students, and, at the bottom, the junior faculty. Of course there are numerous variations. The senior faculty member who is an ogre to the junior faculty member whose tenure they opposed, is an angel to the junior faculty member whose tenure they supported.

Even for those who hold tenure in an elite department, nagging doubts remain. Others may hold a higher position in the eyes of the administration, make more money, or exert more influence. At Harvard and several other institutions considered here, salaries are negotiated between an individual faculty member and a dean of the faculty. Theoretically, no one knows what anyone else makes, but word does leak out, and the disparities can be wide. The question of "mirror, mirror, on the wall, who is the most brilliant of us all?" often rears its head.

Moreover, while most of my subjects were extremely cooperative, there was a guarded nature to some of their remarks. Several insisted that their particular department was harmonious, a true community of scholars with no rivalries, power struggles, or unseemly scandals. Such attitudes were hardly unexpected. In addition to cherishing a possibly exaggerated sense of harmony, the interviewees may have insisted on their department's essential harmony in part because they were aware that there remained people at the institution whose feelings could be hurt, friends whose reputations, even after death, needed to be preserved, and old wounds that could be reopened if they spoke too freely.

This is a problem because much of the argument here concerns decisions made about appointments and promotions. History departments at most leading universities guard their gates tenaciously, knowing that considerable attention within the profession will be riveted on who they admit and who they turn away. I made 1980 the cut-off date for the study partly in the hope that after a quarter of a century, some of the controversy and bitterness over some of these decisions had subsided. In some cases this was not true. There was more than one moment when the voice on the other end of the line said, "I better not say any more," on a decision made decades ago.

Happily, some level of closure was possible in other cases. At Berkeley, for example, the most bitter controversies in the department as it emerged as a noteworthy body concerned hiring of William Bouwsma in 1956 and the promotion of Thomas Kuhn in 1962. By 2005 it was no problem at all to get the surviving participants to talk freely about both episodes, and, no problem, I think, for me to understand what happened and why with a fair amount of clarity. But openness and clarity were not always possible at other institutions, and even in the example of the Berkeley, despite the emerging consensus about what happened, it was still largely the winners who got to put their case forward.

Given the discretion of some of my sources, I made it a point to try to talk not just to those who had thrived in their departments, but to the outlyers, those who had left, both by choice or by decree. Here I sometimes confronted the reverse of the original problem. While many retained some affection for the institution that scorned them, some of my interview subjects were so embittered that they would scarcely concede that anything good was happening in the department while they were there.

The problems in source material reflect the dilemma of the

contemporary historian. When you write about dead subjects, you have only reviewers and colleagues to worry about. But, when you work in part with live subjects, you face a dilemma. The amount of material that you can draw out of people depends in large measure on your ability to establish a working rapport with them. Had I probed too deeply into sensitive matters, such as controversial tenure decisions and personal rivalries, I might have failed to gain that rapport or to gather much of the information I got in the book. On the other hand, it was necessary to ask unpleasant questions about such things as the entry of women and Africans into the profession, the feelings in the department concerning the student difficulties, and why certain people had failed to get tenure.

In the end there was no obvious way to resolve the difficulties in source material. As C. Vann Woodward noted many years ago, oral history is perhaps no different than any other kind of history. The historian asks questions, reads, selects, analyzes, interprets, and attempts to impose some level of order on the material. But in the face of conflicting testimony, there is no obvious scientific or testable principle to ascertain the truth. In the last resort, historical interpretation comes down to the weighing of evidence and the historian's best judgment of where the truth lies.

With a few important exceptions, we, as historians, have not been good about charting the institutional history of our profession. We are very good about charting its intellectual currents and changes in fashion, but less attention has been paid to the evolution of the profession itself. This book, hopefully, will serve as a first step in addressing that problem.

---

[1] William Palmer, *Engagement with the Past: The Lives and Works of the World War II Generation of Historians* (Lexington, Ky., 2001), pp. 101-2.

[2] Idem, "Interview with Hannah Gray," December 8, 2005.

[3] Idem., "Interview with Richard Fox," July 18, 2005.

[4] Morton and Phyllis Keller, *Making Harvard Modern: The Rise of*

America's University (Oxford, 2001), pp. 15-26.

5 John Morton Blum, *A Life with History* (Lawrence, Kan., 2004), p. 157.

6 David Hollinger, *Science, Jews, and Secular Culture: Studies in Mid-Twentieth Century American Intellectual History* (Princeton, 1996), p. 25; Staughton Lynd, "Academic Freedom: Your Story and Mine," *Columbia Forum* (Fall, 1967): 23-8. (In the George Pierson Papers, Yale University Department of Manuscripts and Archives, Sterling Library)

7 Palmer, "Interview with John Womack" March 25, 2005

8 John King Fairbank, Chinabound: A Memoir (New York, 1980), p. 393; Philip Curtin, On the Fringes of History (Athens, Ohio, 2005), pp. 127-34.

9 For details on Berkeley, see Gene Brucker, "History at Berkeley," in Brucker, Henry F. May, and David Hollinger, *History at Berkeley: A Dialog in Three Parts* (Berkeley, 1998), pp. 6, 9.

10 Palmer, "Interview with David Cronon," February 8, 2005.

11 David Potter, *People of Plenty: Economic Abundance and the American Character* (Chicago, 1954).

12 Norman O. Brown, *Life Against Death: The Psychoanalytical Meaning of History* (Hanover, N.H., 1959).

13 Kenneth Stampp, "Historian of Slavery, the Civil War, and Reconstruction, University of California at Berkeley, 1946-1983," An oral history conducted in 1996 by Ann Lage (Regional Oral History Office, the Bancroft Library, University of California at Berkeley, 1996), p. 15.

14 Blum, *Life with History*, p. 157; Henry F. May, "Comments," in Brucker, May, and Hollinger, *History at Berkeley*, p. 28; Palmer, "Interview with James Banner," February 26, 2005.

15 Peter Novick, *'That Noble Dream': The Objectivity Question and the American Historical Profession* (Cambridge, Mass., 1987).

16 Kiernan, *In Plato's Cave*, p. 151.

Chapter One
Harvard Leads the Way

Academic modernization in the Harvard history department was ahead of the curve in terms of other universities. The department began taking decisive steps to improve the quality of its faculty in the 1920s. At the beginning of the decade, the history department already possessed some famous names, including Albert Bushnell Hart, Archibald Cary Coolidge, Edward Channing, Samuel Eliot Morison, and Frederick Jackson Turner. But its critical step was probably the appointment of Arthur Schlesinger, Sr., in 1924. Schlesinger's initial appointment came about when, Morison, who was going to Oxford for a year, recommended Schlesinger as his replacement on a temporary basis. Schlesinger made such a good impression during his time at Harvard that he was invited to stay after Morison returned.[1]

Schlesinger's appointment was critical because he was perhaps the preeminent social historian of his time and a cutting edge scholar within the discipline. As a student at Columbia, Schlesinger had been greatly influenced by James Harvey Robinson and "the New History." Uncomfortable with the traditional emphasis on political and diplomatic narrative, Robinson sought a redefinition of history that encompassed all aspects of human behavior and incorporated the social sciences and their methodologies into historical study. His goal, no less than that of the French

Annalistes, was the creation of a unified approach that would explore connections between politics, economics, religion, culture, the family, and ideas. Schlesinger was perhaps the scholar who best embodied "the New History."[2] His books, *Colonial Merchants and the American Revolution* (1918), *New Viewpoints in American History* (1922), and *The Rise of the City, 1878-1898*, (1933) reflected its influence and marked him as an innovative scholar. *New Viewpoints in American History* even contained a perceptive essay on the role of women in American history.

Other appointments made in the department around this time included William Langer in central Europe, William Scott Ferguson in ancient history, Frederick Merk in the history of the American West, and Gaetano Salvemini, an able historian of modern Europe and an anti-fascist who had fled from Mussolini. Harvard also had faculty in areas that would have been considered unusual at the time, such as Clarence Haring in Latin American history, and in Russian and East European history, where Michael Karpovich taught Russian history, Robert Howard Lord taught Slavic history, and Langer also taught Eastern Europe.[3] Even in the thirties, the department possessed only a few of the gentleman teacher types so prevalent at other elite institutions.

The department was quite distinguished. All told, seven past or future presidents of the American Historical Association graced the corridors of the Harvard history department in the 1930s.[4] At the same time, the department offered many specializations that transcended conventional time periods and geographic boundaries. In addition to the social history taught by Arthur Schlesinger, Sr., there was also intellectual history taught by Crane Brinton, and economic history taught Abbott Payson Usher.

Students had the opportunity to explore many different interdisciplinary connections. Medieval studies was particularly strong, possessing Charles Homer Haskins, the premier American medievalist of his time, as well as E.K. Rand in classics and George Sarton, the historian of medieval science. When Oscar Handlin arrived in Cambridge in the fall of 1934 to begin his graduate studies, his original intention was to study medieval history.[5]

There were many other options. From History and Literature, Perry Miller dispensed a beguiling mixture of literature, history, and religion. Joseph Schumpeter, a European émigré, combined economics and sociology, and, within the department, Crane Brinton was a pioneer in historical sociology and comparative method.

Despite its brilliance, the department still had a group of waspy faculty at its core. Morison's aristocratic pedigree was impeccable, and he and Roger Merriman were two of several faculty who were independently wealthy. Merriman's social position was a key factor in his selection as an early master of Eliot House, the most preppy of Harvard's residential houses. Other faculty were wedded to patrician rituals. Mason Hammond, another department member of private wealth and a specialist in Roman history, regularly served afternoon tea to interested students. And, while Jewish graduate students began entering the department in the twenties and thirties, there were no full-blooded Jews on the history faculty, although two, Charles Gross and Julius Klein, had served earlier, and Arthur Schlesinger, Sr. was partly descended from German Jews.

Moreover, in the 1930s Harvard did not yet enjoy a reputation as one of the world's foremost universities. Edwin O. Reischauer, the great scholar of Japan, who arrived in Cambridge for graduate study in 1932, recalled that Harvard was "still an aristocratic, parochially New England institution…heavily centered on the undergraduate college, which was populated largely by preppies… a few bright New York Jews and Middle Westerners were tolerated, but not really welcomed."[6]

Some steps toward change when taken in the 1920s under the leadership of A. Lawrence Lowell, president of the university from 1908 to 1933 and a true New England Brahmin. When asked by his successor, James Bryant Conant, what his salary was, Lowell replied that he had no idea; he always returned it to the university. As president, Lowell initiated many reforms in undergraduate education, such as specific concentrations, required courses, tutorial instruction, based on the Oxford model, and the construction of residential houses.

But several of his policies betrayed his position as a member of the New England aristocracy. He opposed aid for graduate students on the ground that such a policy would attract more students from the lower classes. He was a member of the review committee that upheld the death sentences of Sacco and Vanzetti, and he tried to restrict the number of Jews admitted to Harvard as well as to keep black freshmen out of Harvard housing.[7]

The most decisive steps toward change were taken by the chemist James Bryant Conant, who succeeded Lowell as president in 1933, and was in many ways his antithesis. Conant was a Bostonian who could trace his ancestry back to the Pilgrims, but he was no Brahmin. He grew up in working-class Dorchester, where his father was a photoengraver and part-time construction contractor. Conant, however, soon revealed many signs of academic promise. He was the first person in his family to go to college, where he displayed enough brilliance as a chemist to earn a Harvard Ph.D. and an appointment in the Harvard chemistry department. As a faculty member, he quickly established a reputation as an excellent chemist and able administrator.[8]

Conant's selection as president testified to his upward mobility. The favored candidate, Kenneth B. Murdock, possessed the lordly social position expected in a Harvard president; he was the Dean of Arts and Sciences and the son of a prominent Boston banker. Moreover, Conant had other obstacles beyond his class to overcome. As chair of the chemistry department, he had clashed repeatedly with Lowell, and relations between the two were decidedly icy. But Conant's ability was undeniable, and he was eventually chosen.

Conant's aim as president was to transform Harvard into a meritocracy by which he meant that Harvard's goal should be to recruit students and faculty on the basis of their ability and achievements rather than their social position. Such lofty goals meant that Harvard should abandon its traditional role as the educator of the New England elite and endeavor to attract the ablest students and faculty from across the social, religious, and geographic spectrums of the country. Conant further believed that excellence in research was the most desirable quality for a Harvard faculty member.[9]

In many ways, the history department already came fairly close to matching Conant's vision. Normally, modernizing history departments are characterized by three things: increasing emphasis on research, appointments in areas outside western Europe and the United States, and the appointment of Jews to the faculty. All three were present in the Harvard history department in the thirties. First, the emphasis on research is evident in the scholarly production of Schlesinger, Langer, Morison, and several of the others. Second, it was during this time that the great Asianists, John King Fairbank and Edwin O. Reischauer, began their Harvard careers. Finally, in 1940, the department appointed Oscar Handlin, the first Jew to become a member of the Harvard history faculty since Julius Klein in the twenties, to a junior position.

The department was also, generally speaking, a harmonious place. Department cohesion was sustained through regular Thursday lunches where Morison regularly appeared in riding breeches. History faculty and others from related disciplines, competed in hotly contested, late afternoon games of fistball, a variant of volleyball, in the dingy women's gymnasium. Despite the variety of approaches to history among the department members, a general climate of harmony prevailed. William Langer, one of the department's most distinguished members, could not recall "any fundamental difference of opinion or effort at factional conflict."[10]

Despite Harvard's reverence for pedigree and position, the department was staffed to a significant degree by talented young men from the provinces, and several of its leading figures had relatively modest backgrounds by institutional standards. Merk and Schlesinger, perhaps the department's stars, had been undergraduates at state universities. Schlesinger did not hold a Harvard degree, nor did Turner, Haskins, Ferguson, or Karpovich. Merk had only come to Harvard for graduate study because Turner, his Wisconsin mentor, came to Harvard late in his career and brought Merk with him. Paul Buck, author of a Pulitzer Prize winning book on the American South, was, like Schlesinger and

Merk, a native of the Middle West, that vast, amorphous mass of land west of the Hudson River, condescendingly referred to by Edward Channing as "Transappalachia."[11]

Not everyone celebrated the department's recruiting practices. Elliott Perkins, who was one of several in the department who owed his appointment to social position, was probably referring to the department's preference for scholarship over pedigree when he wrote Wallace Notestein in 1940 that "if Archie Coolidge and Haskins could see this place now, they would have a fit."[12]

The appointment of Jews was another important step in establishing the meritocracy and breaking down the gentleman's club atmosphere. Anti-Semitism was a fact of American academic life in the 1930s. Harvard openly discriminated against Jews in its admission policies in the 1920s and remained for the most part a college of white, Anglo-Saxon, Protestants whose fathers, uncles, and grandfathers had gone there. The Jews who were admitted to Harvard were often discouraged from pursuing certain career paths. When John Morton Blum, who entered Harvard as a freshman in 1939, was trying to decide between a career in history or in law, he was advised by Elliott Perkins to pursue a legal career. "You better go to law school," Perkins advised. "Hebrews can't make it in history." At that point, Blum elected to pursue an academic career.[13]

The prevailing anti-Semitism at Harvard makes Oscar Handlin's appointment as a junior faculty member in 1940 even more remarkable. Handlin was many of the things that would normally count against someone who aspired to join the Harvard faculty. While he did hold a Harvard Ph.D., he was Jewish, had no pedigree or "old boy" network connections, and he had been an undergraduate at Brooklyn College, a classic "street-car" college in the phrase of the time, for the lower classes. Handlin might as well have come from Mars as far as Harvard was concerned. But his brilliance was almost universally acknowledged, and brilliance rather than pedigree was increasingly the standard for faculty appointments in the history department.

Despite the shifting of emphasis toward research and graduate education, undergraduate teaching remained the department's primary mission. All of the senior faculty taught undergraduate courses and often left memorable impressions on their students. For many students, Frederick Merk, the historian of the westward movement, was the ideal Harvard lecturer. Organized, lucid, and obviously impassioned by his subject, Merk could hold a room full of even the most indifferent Brahmin gentlemen on the edge of their seats, as he explained how the west was won.[14]

Equally compelling, although for different reasons, was Charles McIlwain, a distinguished scholar of English constitutional law. McIlwain was not a showman; he simply talked. But, like Merk, he could have a class enthralled with his brilliant analyses of the critical documents in English history. Several generations of Harvard students could recall McIlwain's magnificent elucidation of the meaning of the Magna Carta, meticulously examining the text almost word by word, and, lingering particularly over article 24 of the charter, where he pondered the possible meanings of the Latin "vel…vel." Did the conjunctions mean "either" or "both?" In McIlwain's view the entire interpretation of the Magna Carta hinged on the answer to this question.[15]

In the eyes of Barbara Tuchman, a Radcliffe undergraduate in the thirties who took McIlwain's class, McIlwain was "conducting a passionate love affair with the laws of the Angles and the articles of the charter, especially Article 39. Like any person in love, he wanted everyone to know how beautiful was the object of his affections." Years later, Tuchman could not remember the details of Article 39, only the blaze in McIlwain's blue eyes as he discussed them, and that, when it came to the final examination, half the questions were in Anglo-Saxon, a curiosity that McIlwain had neglected to mention. He gave them all A's anyway.[16]

Perhaps the most memorable teacher in the department was Roger B. "Frisky" Merriman, one of Harvard's great patrician characters. A crusty, opinionated instructor of the old school, Merriman taught History 1, a whirlwind tour of the history of Western Europe from its ancient origins right through the Treaty of Versailles. Theodore H. White, a Harvard undergraduate in the late thirties, called History 1 with Merriman "vaudeville in thirty-six acts." Always pacing, sometimes whispering, sometimes shouting, and determined to capture the full sweep and majesty of his subject, Merriman was outrageous, full of prejudice, but never dull. He closed every lecture with the call of "unity, gentlemen, unity."[17]

Teaching at Harvard could be highly individualized. The most memorable experience of Carl Schorske's education was an in-depth tutorial with the classicist William Scott Ferguson he received while beginning his graduate study. Schorske was not a classicist, but had been advised by Langer to take courses in as many different areas as possible. Meeting for two hours every Sunday afternoon at Ferguson's house, Schorske explored a variety of approaches to the ancient world and began to see the possibilities of what a dedicated teacher could do for an engaged student as well as for the integrated cultural analysis that later characterized his own work.[18]

In addition to lectures, Harvard undergraduates also enrolled in tutorials, small group classes, usually taught by recent Harvard Ph.D.s and advanced graduate students. The idea behind them was that instead of simply taking courses, the Harvard undergraduate would also have an experienced teacher to guide them and give coherence to the experience. Many Harvard undergraduates who later became distinguished historians received some of their best teaching here. John Blum had Carl Schorske as a discussion leader and was rewarded with an experience as unforgettable as the one Schorske had with William Scott Ferguson. Blum had another memorable tutorial with the medievalist Barnaby Keeney, who later became president of Brown University, but in 1941 was a graduate student teaching Harvard tutorials.[19]

In the late thirties Theodore H. White was a Harvard undergraduate assigned to the young John Fairbank for his tutorials. Fairbank later became one of the world's greatest China scholars, but at the time, he was a junior faculty member trying to prove himself. He was already engaged in a grim battle with the Sinologists of Harvard's Oriental Studies Department, some of whom insisted that the history of China ended with the Ch'ien-lung dynasty in 1799; everything after that was journalism. Fairbank contended that history was also about understanding the present and was probably the only person in Cambridge in the thirties to recognize the importance of Mao's Long March.

As a tutor, Fairbank devoted himself to developing White's historical vocation by giving him regular assignments beyond his classroom work. The assignments he gave White were often not about China. Under Fairbank's direction, White read works by St. Thomas Aquinas and Alfred North Whitehead's *Science and the Modern World*. For White, it was all valuable, and Fairbank somehow made even the hardest work seem delightful and absorbing.[20]

If students are the standard by which the success of a department should be judged, the Harvard history department was extraordinarily successful. Harvard will of course produce outstanding students during any period. But during the 1930s it produced a group of students that seem to be exceptional even by its standards, including such outstanding undergraduates as Barbara Tuchman, Daniel Boorstin, Edmund Morgan, and Arthur Schlesinger, Jr. As a freshman, Schlesinger was one of 613 students who submitted an essay for the Le Baron Russell Briggs prize. His essay won. He was later chosen for the Society of Fellows, Harvard's unique organization for students considered too bright to be bothered with the tedium of doctoral study. Like Schlesinger, Daniel Boorstin was an intellectual prodigy, entering Harvard at sixteen. During his senior year, Boorstin was editor of the Harvard *Crimson*, won the Bowdoin Prize for his essay on Edward Gibbon's *Decline and Fall of the Roman Empire*, and was awarded a Rhodes Scholarship.[21]

But many of the history department's sterling undergraduates in the 1930s found their greatest stimulation not from history, but from the History and Literature Program, and from the dynamic teaching of Perry Miller and F.O. Matthiessen. For the next quarter century, Miller and Matthiessen formed a combination that dazzled many of Harvard's ablest undergraduates. In the thirties an air of excitement swirled about them as they were working on what would become their seminal works, Miller's *The New England Mind* and Matthiessen's *American Renaissance*. Their approaches to history and literature, however, were quite different, and their relationship was often tense. "Perry, you alleged that you might want to read a sentence in this book. Perhaps you can use the rest for kindling," Matthiessen caustically inscribed the copy of one of his books that he gave to Miller. Other figures of distinction in History and Literature included Howard Mumford Jones from the English Department and Ralph Barton Perry from Philosophy.

But it was Miller and Matthiessen who provided the most electrifying experience. Edmund Morgan entered Harvard as a freshman in 1933, intending to concentrate on English history and literature, until he took a course in American Literature in which Miller was one of the lecturers. Morgan was captivated by Miller's enthusiasm and engagement with his subject. He quickly changed his major to American history so he could have Miller as a tutor.

He was also charmed by Matthiessen, but for different reasons. Miller was dynamic and charismatic, if sometimes profane and intemperate, teaching by the power of his intellect and personality. Matthiessen, by contrast, was quieter, more serious, more forgiving about student lapses, but equally inspiring.[22]

But roses do have thorns, and the situation was less ideal in graduate education. Despite Harvard's increasing emphasis in this area, many graduate students in the history department found the experience desultory. The most frequent complaints concerned snobbery and anti-Semitism among the history faculty. "Faculty members at Harvard," J.H. Hexter, who received a Ph.D. from Harvard in 1937, once recalled, "were not much addicted to speaking to graduate students in the good old days." H. Stuart Hughes found advanced study at Harvard dispiriting and that the Harvard lecture style "exuded staleness and desiccation." John Hope Franklin, a black graduate student at Harvard in the late thirties, did not experience racism, but he did discover anti-Semitism among his fellow graduate students and watched with dismay as faculty verbally abused students and on one occasion failed a graduate student because he did not look like a Harvard Ph.D. While Franklin himself felt well-treated at Harvard, when he left in the spring of 1939, he knew that he did not wish spend even another day there.[23]

George Mosse experienced the best and the worst of being a Harvard graduate student in the years before 1950. Soon after arriving in Cambridge in the fall of 1941, he and his fellow graduate students were informed by Arthur Schlesinger, Sr. that the department had no obligation to find them jobs; its only duty was to train them. Mosse was also dismayed to find evidence of faculty members sniping at each other, and his oral examination, despite Langer's claim of a perfectly harmonious department, was more about departmental rivalries and politics than Mosse's performance.

On the other hand, he admired and respected his principal mentor, McIlwain. Not only was McIlwain's learning impressive, but he cared deeply about his students, personally as well as professionally. He was the inspiration for Mosse's dissertation, *The Struggle for Sovereignty*, which also became his first book. David Owen, a historian of modern Britain, was also a compassionate teacher, encouraging Mosse to publish a paper written for his seminar and instrumental in finding him his first teaching job.[24]

Oscar Handlin's experience at Harvard is particularly revealing about the largely self-directed and somewhat chaotic nature of graduate study during this period. Handlin graduated from Brooklyn College at age nineteen and decided to study medieval history at Harvard. Undeterred by his street-car college roots, Handlin decided to visit Cambridge on his own. In 1934 $3.50 purchased a round-trip, New York to Boston, train ticket. Handlin arrived in Cambridge unannounced, but with a letter to Michael Karpovich, then an assistant professor of Russian history. At 8:30 in the morning Handlin rang the bell of Karpovich's house on Trowbridge Street home and offered his letter. Karpovich, in his robe and pajamas, initially seemed confused by Handlin's appearance, but quickly offered to take him on a tour of the campus. The high point of the tour was a visit to the Widener Library where

Handlin gazed in awe at the breath-taking array of volumes laid out before him and the marvel of open stacks. Karpovich was open and friendly. The two talked about Harvard and history all morning. Karpovich was, however, not certain of the details of admission into the graduate school, and Crane Brinton, who knew them thoroughly, was out of town until the next day.[25]

Handlin decided to stay over, and, the next day, met Brinton, who proved to be as engaging and friendly as Karpovich. Brinton took him to see the dean of the graduate school, who chatted amiably with Handlin for a few minutes and then admitted him, without any supporting documents, such as letters of recommendation or undergraduate transcripts.

With the success of his visit, Handlin returned to Harvard in the fall with great expectations which, unfortunately, were dashed. His dream of studying medieval history crumbled quickly. Haskins was seriously ill; Rand did only classics, and Sarton was buried in his own work. Even Brinton was a bit distant, suggesting that his Enlightenment course was for undergraduates and too superficial for Handlin, and left Handlin to his own devices. With no restriction on the number of courses he could take and no additional tuition involved, Handlin signed up for five courses and completed language requirements in Latin, French and German, although he received mostly mediocre grades.

Despite this inauspicious beginning, he quickly became a Harvard legend, disdaining to take notes at lectures and constantly hectoring even Harvard's most distinguished faculty. To William Langer, he "seemed to seize upon every occasion to differ." Graduate students normally challenge senior faculty at their own peril, and for Handlin, a Brooklyn Jew at patrician Harvard, the risks of defiance seemed even greater. Handlin believed that he escaped the repercussions of anti-Semitism largely because he made no attempt to conceal his identity. Occasionally he heard jokes from peers and faculty with references to Brooklyn and the Dodgers, delivered in "Toid Avenue" accents. If there was an anti-Semitic connotation to them, Handlin chose to ignore it. In any event, the faculty with the most exalted pedigrees, Morison, Murdock, and Eliot Perkins, went out of their way to be helpful. Handlin's dazzling performance on his comprehensive examinations established him as a student of unquestioned brilliance, destined for greatness in the profession.[26]

For his dissertation, Handlin chose Arthur Schlesinger, Sr., whom he admired greatly, as a supervisor. Schlesinger suggested that he study the role of Boston's immigrants, a topic abandoned by another student, as a subject for his dissertation. The suggestion proved to be enormously fruitful. Handlin's doctoral thesis, supported by a Sheldon Fellowship to pursue his research in Dublin and London, allowed him to receive his Ph.D. in 1940. He published the dissertation as *Boston's Immigrants*, and, after a year of teaching at Brooklyn College, returned to Harvard as an instructor.

Over the next decade the department appointed a new cluster of promising faculty, including Fairbank, Handlin, and Schlesinger, Jr., a harvest almost as impressive as its appointments in the 1920s. In several cases, the department benefited from the presence of the Society of Fellows, the body created by Lowell to spare exceptional students the drudgery of graduate school. Several of its junior fellows, including Schlesinger, Jr., and Crane Brinton, became department members.

During the thirties Conant also introduced the "up or out" principle of faculty appointments at Harvard. Before Conant, Harvard had many faculty who had served for years on temporary appointments. Fearing that problems might arise for the permanent faculty if they were surrounded by embittered drones who would never receive permanent appointments, Conant introduced a rigid system of appointments. The positions of lecturer and instructor were reserved for fixed term appointments; theoretically, there was no possibility of advancement. A more promising appointment was that of assistant professor, where the appointee received a five-year contract. By December of his fourth year, the appointee came up for review by the department, which either recommended him for promotion to associate professor, a rank that carried tenure, or declined to do so. The rejected candidate would then have a year and a half to find another position.[27]

From the point of view of the candidate, the most unnerving component of the fourth year review was that the department opened up the position to an international search, and the candidate would be considered in terms of the world's finest scholars in that particular field. Harvard expected to hire the best. Even candidates who won the support of the department still had hurdles to clear. To prevent departments from becoming networks of friends and protégés, the Dean of the Faculty of Arts and Sciences formed an ad hoc committee of outside experts in the field and Harvard faculty in related disciplines. The committee consulted other outside scholars to evaluate the field, assess the work of the possible appointees, and make recommendations to the university appointments committee. If it was decided that if a superior scholar was available, the inside candidate was denied promotion and the associate professor position would be offered to the outsider.

After the war Conant also accelerated his campaign to establish research as the prime qualification for advancement at Harvard. The faculty's task was not simply the dissemination of knowledge, but the creation of it. This emphasis on research, based on Conant's conviction that good teaching was product of distinction in research, became the defining characteristic of faculty appointments at Harvard and in the history department.[28]

During the post-war period, Harvard made several critical promotions to associate professor, especially those of Arthur Schlesinger, Jr. and Oscar Handlin, with its decisions based mostly upon scholarship. In 1946 Schlesinger was twenty-nine years old, the author of a Pulitzer Prize winning study, *The Age of Jackson*, with the prospect of greatness before him. Since his father was a senior member of the department, a committee consisting of historians from outside Harvard was appointed to evaluate his record. The committee concluded that the young Schlesinger was the best historian in the country under fifty.

Oscar Handlin's record was almost as impressive. At age thirty-five he had published three major books, including *The Uprooted*, a Pulitzer Prize winning study of the immigrant experience in America. "Once I thought to study the role of immigrants in American history," Handlin wrote, "then I realized they were American history." But Handlin, himself the child of immigrants, lacked the pedigree and polish of Schlesinger, and he was Jewish. The department was eager to promote him, but Conant, of all people, expressed doubts. Should Handlin be promoted immediately? Perhaps the department should prefer Richard Hofstadter, then teaching at Columbia and the author of the recent critical success, *The American Political Tradition*. In the end the committee appointed to consider Handlin's professorship voted unanimously to support him. Handlin's promotion was a clear testament to Conant's vision of meritocracy. In the thirties, anti-Semitism might have derailed his career path; now he could sail through. Even his principal rival was Jewish. In 1954 both Schlesinger and Handlin were promoted to full professor. In the words of Dean Paul Buck the promotions should "guarantee Harvard distinction for many years."[29]

Appointments in non-western areas are another characteristic of modernizing departments. In the late forties and early fifties, Harvard made two promotions of significance in this area. The first of these was John Fairbank in Chinese history, and the second was Richard Frye in Middle Eastern history. On the surface, these decisions testified to the department's growing awareness, especially after World War II, of the importance of areas outside of the United States and Europe. Fairbank was to become the greatest Asianist of his time, and Frye was a pioneering scholar in the Middle East.[30]

But, despite these appointments, the department's emphasis remained in Europe and United States. Even the department's Latin Americanist, Clarence Haring, was listed as a professor of American history. While the histories and languages of other parts of the world were taught at Harvard, Fairbank and Frye were the only non-western specialists who were full-time members of the history department. Edwin Reischauer, a historian through and through, who taught Asian history courses with Fairbank (popularly known as "the rice paddy classes,") was housed for many years in the department of East Asian languages and was never a member of the history department. Benjamin Schwartz, a gifted pupil of Fairbank, took up a Harvard appointment in 1950, but it was held jointly with the government department.

Along with his teaching and writing, Fairbank devoted much of his Harvard career to crusading on behalf of East Asian history. And that crusade was waged on several fronts. On one hand, Fairbank continued the battle, first joined in the 1930s, with the Sinologists of the East Asian languages, who resisted the study of Asia after 1800. They also considered Fairbank an interloper into their turf and an opportunist using recent crises in Asia to shake money out of foundations. Nor could Fairbank interest the history department in creating positions for Asian history for periods before 1800. Benjamin Schwartz, the Fairbank student who held a joint appointment in history and government, was also a modernist.[31]

In the view of some, the department's inability to expand its offerings further in non-western areas could be attributed to the reluctance of its American historians to sacrifice a tenured slot in American history to replace it with one in a non-western area. Thus, non-western areas at Harvard developed through hybrid departments of area studies, which were usually funded partly by outside agencies, such as the Ford and Rockefeller Foundations. Thus, faculty in area studies were often paid through several sources, including grant money, private donations, and money from one or more departments. During the late fifties and sixties, the history department began to address more fully the need for faculty in such areas, with the appointments of Albert Craig in Asian history, and John Womack in Latin America.[32]

By the late fifties undergraduate teaching in the Harvard history department had changed in that several of the legendary teachers from the thirties and forties had retired. Harvard undergraduates no longer experienced the thrill of Merk leading students across the Great Divide, McIlwain explicating the Magna Carta, or Merriman, the great actor performing his greatest role.

The department still took teaching very seriously. In the late forties, when the department hired the Oxford medievalist Helen Maude Cam to a chair designed specifically for women, its first choice was C.V. Wedgwood, the author of several beautifully written books on aspects of the English Civil War. The department turned to Cam, however, when it learned that Wedgwood disliked undergraduate teaching.[33]

Undergraduate education at Harvard in the fifties and early sixties continued to have its own delights. Almost all of the history faculty, whether they had been educated at Harvard or not, spoke in pronounced Harvard accents. More importantly, the quality of teaching remained high. Charles Maier, a Harvard undergraduate in the late fifties, thought that he received a superb education. Arthur Schlesinger, Jr. was a spellbinder in the great Harvard tradition who taught the largest course in the department. David Owen and Frank Freidel had dedicated followings among the undergraduate population. But Harvard's real strength remained in the intellectual power and resources that it could provide. Edward Keenan, a Harvard undergraduate from 1953 to 1957, and later a department member, recalled that between Karpovich, Robert Lee Wolff, Richard Pipes, and Martin Malia, Harvard offered a greater range of courses in Russian history and culture than were available a few years later when he went to study at the University of Leningrad.[34]

By the sixties, some of the best undergraduate teaching came in tutorials. For James Wilkinson, a Harvard undergraduate from 1961 to 1965 and later a faculty member in History and Literature, the most challenging intellectual experience of his undergraduate career was a tutorial with Patrice Higonnet, a specialist in French history then beginning his Harvard career. The tutorial was conducted in the Oxford tradition of assigning a weekly essay for Wilkinson to write and read aloud as part of the tutorial. And it was also conducted in the classic Oxford slash and burn style. Wilkinson would read his essay, and Higonnet would tear it apart. Wilkinson quickly learned that safe, conventional ideas wouldn't work; Higonnet expected him to think outside the box. At first it seemed overwhelming, too much to expect from an undergraduate. But, battered if unbowed, Wilkinson eventually learned how to do it.[35]

In the decades after World War II, there were also some indications that the quality of graduate study, generally regarded as stale and even demoralizing by many graduate students in the thirties, was improving. David Landes, a graduate student at Harvard shortly after the end of World War II, found his experience there to be rewarding. Landes had remarkably broad interests, including economic history and change over wide geographical and chronological boundaries. To pursue these interests, Landes needed interdisciplinary study, which was an alien concept at most American graduate schools, only a few of which even had an economic historian. It was possible at Harvard, where Landes found an economic historian, Abbott Payson Usher, in the history department, as well as Arthur Cole and several others in the economics department, interested in his work. He received another boost, when Donald McKay, a department chair in the early fifties, nominated him for membership in the Society of Fellows, which gave him the immense advantage of contact with other fellows as well as time and money for research.[36]

Bernard Bailyn, beginning graduate study at about the same time, also found it stimulating. Bailyn was not a Harvard undergraduate, but, like the Harvard students of the thirties, Bailyn was enchanted by Perry Miller, who he once described striding across the Harvard yard in a trench coat, trying to look like Humphrey Bogart.

Bailyn also studied with the medievalist Charles Taylor. Taylor was not one of the department's brightest stars and in fact published little, but his broad interdisciplinary interests offered insights that could be applied to other historical subfields.[37] His reluctance to publish was attributed by some to his perfectionism and by others to his experience as a graduate student at Harvard with his mentor, Charles Homer Haskins, who expected total dedication from his students. Years before, when Taylor finished writing his dissertation on Christmas Eve, he went to the Widener Library to find Haskins in his study. Haskins took a quick look at the dissertation and said, "Very good, Taylor, why don't you take tomorrow off."[38]

It was, however, Oscar Handlin who exerted the greatest influence on Bailyn. Using some of the techniques that Handlin had developed in *Boston's Immigrants* and in *Commonwealth*, his landmark study of the political economy of Massachusetts, Bailyn wrote his own dissertation, *The New England Merchants in the Seventeenth Century*, very much under Handlin's direction and influence.

It was not long before Bailyn realized his extraordinary promise. In 1967 he published *The Ideological Origins of the American Revolution*, probably his greatest and most influential book. It also came to serve as a model for the kind of scholarship that the department would expect its faculty to produce, the kind that would completely alter the direction of research in its particular subfield.

Ironically, Bailyn came to write *Origins* almost by accident. A few years before, he had accepted an invitation from the Harvard University Press to edit a collection of the pamphlet literature of the American Revolution. Like most specialists in colonial history, he knew about a dozen of the pamphlets quite well and reckoned that there were maybe a dozen more worth serious scrutiny. But as he worked through the collection, he discovered that there were over 400 pamphlets, including political treatises, historical essays, letters, sermons, songs, and poems. Bailyn decided that there were seventy-two items worthy of publication, and in 1965 he published them, along with an introduction, as *Pamphlets of the American Revolution*.[39]

But, during the course of his research, Bailyn realized that there were some recurring themes in the pamphlets that required a more comprehensive treatment. In particular, he decided that the ideas expressed in them were not simply ideological camouflage for economic grievances. Instead, the writings of the pamphleteers reflected deeply held convictions and principles that were the true inspiration for the revolution. Bailyn decided to write *Ideological Origins* to explain their significance.

In addition to emphasizing the profound intellectual roots of the revolution, Bailyn, in *Ideological Origins* also contended that those ideological roots were not entirely derived from the usual sources cited by scholars, such as John Locke or the writings of the Enlightenment *philosophes*. For Bailyn, more important were the ideas emanating from a group of English eighteenth century writers and thinkers, sometimes called "Commonwealthmen," who had criticized the expansion of government and ministerial power in the early 1700s. Their writings, Bailyn contended, provided Americans with considerable ideological ammunition with which to attack British policy in the colonies and the agents of its enforcement.

Moreover, Bailyn, far in advance of most historians, made language an agent of change. With each new element in British policy toward the colonies, pamphleteers committed themselves to more and more radical positions on such issues as taxation, representation, sovereignty. Many of them agreed that there was a conspiracy on the part of the British government to take away their liberties. In the process of elucidating this conspiracy, they moved well beyond criticisms of British policy. In what Bailyn called the "contagion of liberty," the pamphleteers even challenged fundamental assumptions about the legitimacy of slavery, the right of the state to maintain religious establishment, and, most important, questioning the need to require a just measure of deference to one's social superiors.

Ideological Origins of the American Revolution won both the Bancroft and Pulitzer Prizes for 1968, and was one of these rare books, like *The Age of Jackson* or *The Uprooted* which not only redirected study in the subfield of American colonial history, but which had profound implications for the study of revolutionary ideology in other areas. Bailyn seemed to have explained brilliantly how the colonists' mounting political fears about the threats to their liberties led up to the Revolution. But he also showed how that process was only part of the story. The pamphleteers' concerns about their liberties also led them to the construction of an ideological system that had serious implications for the future on a far greater range of issues than just independence.

While graduate education at Harvard in the sixties represented an improvement over the thirties, it was still described by a visiting committee as a Darwinian struggle for survival. When Caroline Bynum began graduate study at Harvard in 1962, the department chair, Robert Lee ("Bobby Lee") Wolff told the assembled graduate students to look to their right and to their left. By the next year, he informed them, only one of the three of them would still be there. But, rather than hostility, graduate students more often encountered indifference. When Charles Maier submitted a proposed reading list for his oral examination in modern European history to Crane Brinton, known to be demanding, Brinton's only comment was to point out a misspelled name.[40]

Bailyn himself developed into memorable instructor of graduate students, directing nearly eighty dissertations, and his seminar soon acquired a legendary quality. Students in his seminars learned little of the mechanics of scholarship, but they were challenged to learn how to think critically, by identifying a book's main argument, evaluating its sources, and analyzing its strengths and weaknesses. Bailyn frequently assigned readings that had little to do with colonial history or even history for that matter. He liked novels, statistical studies, and works only a few had ever heard of, but which offered some unique perspective. In one of his seminars students were assigned E.H. Carr's *Romantic Exiles*, an account of Alexander Herzen and his circle of romantic liberals. Another read John Fowles' bestselling novel, *The French Lieutenant's Woman*. Students sometimes found the experience to be somewhat Kafkaesque, as they wondered, "where is he going with this?"[41]

There were risks inherent in such an approach. While it is imperative that students learn how to read and think critically, such skills can only be learned through practice, and Bailyn could be an intimidating presence. While some students found his seminars a thrilling intellectual exercise which afforded them the opportunity to watch a world-class mind in action, others found it a little unnerving. Some were even unable to sleep the night before one of his seminars. Pauline Maier, who took her doctorate with Bailyn and admired him greatly, remembered watching, years later, one of his best students, by then himself a star in colonial history, tangle with the master over a relatively minor issue and refusing to give an inch. Maier wondered whether the student was exorcising the demons of seminars past or had just learned Bailyn's lessons too well. Another student had a t-shirt made that said "so what?" across the front, which was Bailyn's favored and often somewhat playful response to a student who thought they had discovered something interesting.[42]

But most graduate instruction at Harvard, like that at other elite universities at the time, was auto-didactic. There was little handholding or encouragement. The faculty seemed to believe that if you were good enough to be admitted to graduate study in history at Harvard, you must be a bright, highly motivated and self-directed individual, so you were on your own. It was your job to figure out what to do; if you couldn't, too bad.

In many ways the faculty's approach to graduate education mirrored their own experiences. When Oscar Handlin was a graduate student at Harvard, no one told him much about what to do, nor was he told what to do as a junior faculty member, where he often taught in areas, such as Greek history, in which he had no background. As a supervisor of graduate students, he took pains not to direct students to his answers. He refused to recommend dissertation topics to students, and in his seminars long periods of silence could pass as he waited, seemingly with nerves of steel, for students to respond to a question. To amuse themselves, students occasionally timed these periods of silence, and kept data on them. One legend has the record for consecutive minutes of Handlin silence in a seminar as twenty-three.[43]

While his methods were exasperating to some, other students testified to their effectiveness. In the Handlin seminar that Richard Bushman took, the class was assigned to read on a particular theme and one student was designated to raise questions for discussion. Near the end of the class, Handlin, after being silent for most of the period, summarized the drift of the discussion and raised new questions, which the students were to sort out for themselves. In retrospect, Bushman recalled, the point was less to find answers but to make the journey and learn to frame good questions. Handlin preferred specific rather than general questions. The classic Handlin question, his students thought, concerned why more railroads went east and west when north-south lines were more profitable.[44]

Handlin was not shy about encouraging students. Women whose work was interrupted by marriage and family were not immune. After Anne Scott reported the news of her first child, Handlin replied, "Glad to hear the baby arrived safely. Are you back at work?" At the same time, Handlin was always ready with advice about jobs, fellowships, and career building to his students long after they had left Harvard.

The auto-didactic quality of graduate education in history can also be seen in the experience of John Womack. In 1961, Womack, after an undergraduate career at Harvard in which he aspired to be a journalist, decided to go to graduate school at Harvard in Latin American history, undeterred by the fact that Harvard no longer had a Latin Americanist. Clarence Haring retired in 1954 and had not been replaced. In fact, in the early sixties, McGeorge Bundy, the former Harvard Dean of the Faculty of Arts and Sciences, then working in the Kennedy administration, scolded his successor as dean for not making an appointment in the Latin American field. Latin America was an urgent foreign policy issue in the early sixties, Bundy explained, and how could he expected to make decisions in that area without a Harvard man to advise him?[45]

Lacking a specialist in Latin America, Womack managed to cobble together a team of able people, including Ernest May, the department's foreign policy specialist, who was knowledgeable about Latin American affairs, as well as several faculty from other disciplines. When Womack produced a successful and largely self-directed dissertation, the department decided to hire him as its Latin American specialist.

Yet, by the early sixties, despite the self-directed nature of its graduate programs and limited commitment to hiring specialists in non-western areas, the Harvard history department enjoyed an enviable position. In the manner of Conant, it was perhaps the first history department to make appointments and promotions based on research potential and achievement rather than pedigree and position. And, in the forties and fifties, it was able to replace its star faculty, such as Arthur Schlesinger, Sr., Samuel Eliot Morison, and Frederick Merk with equally estimable figures, such as Arthur Schlesinger, Jr., Bernard Bailyn, and Oscar Handlin. At the same time, while research moved to center stage in evaluating faculty members, Harvard maintained its commitment to undergraduate teaching, providing memorable experiences for their students. It was in many ways a golden age for the department.

---

[1] Arthur Schlesinger, Jr., *A Life in the Twentieth Century* (New York and Boston, 2000), p. 37.

[2] James Harvey Robinson, *The New History: Essays Illustrating the Modern Historical Outlook* (New York, 1912).

[3] William Langer, *In and Out of the Ivory Tower* (New York, 1977), p. 101.

[4] The former or future A.H.A. presidents at Harvard in the 1930s included Morison, Langer, Schlesinger, Ferguson, Merk, McIlwain, and Crane Brinton.

[5] Oscar Handlin, "A Career at Harvard," *American Scholar* (Winter, 1996), pp. 47-8.

[6] Edwin O. Reischauer, *My Life Between Japan and America* (New York, 1986), p. 40.

[7] Morton Keller and Phyllis Keller, *Making Harvard Modern: The Rise of America's University* (Oxford, 2001), p. 14.

[8] Ibid., p. 16.

[9] Ibid., p. 23.

[10] John King Fairbank, *Chinabound: A Fifty-Year Memoir* (New York, 1982), p. 144; Langer, *In and Out of the Ivory Tower*, p. 165.

[11] Schlesinger, Sr., *In Retrospect: The History of a Historian*, (New York, 1963), p. 99.

[12] Elliott Perkins to Wallace Notestein, March 22, 1940; Wallace Notestein Papers, Yale University, Department of Manuscripts and Archives.

[13] John Morton Blum, *A Life with History* (Lawrence: University of Kansas Press, 2004), pp. 62-3. It should be noted that Oscar Handlin remembers Perkins as a man without prejudice, see p. 20.

[14] Ibid., p. 28.

[15] Ibid., p. 28.

[16] Barbara Tuchman, *Practicing History: Selected Essays by Barbara Tuchman* (New York: Alfred Knopf, 1981), p. 14.

[17] Theodore H. White, *In Search of History: A Personal Adventure* (New York, 1978), pp. 44-5.

[18] Carl Schorske, *A Life in Learning: The Charles Homer Haskins Lecture* (Washington, D.C., 1987), pp. 2-5.

[19] Blum, *Life with History*, pp. 24-5, 29-30.

[20] White, *Search for History*, pp. 49-51.

[21] William Palmer, *Engagement with the Past: The Lives and Works of the World War II Generation of Historians* (Lexington, Ken., 2001), pp. 32-3.

[22] David Courtwright, "Fifty Years of American History: An Interview with Edmund S. Morgan," *William and Mary Quarterly*, 3rd Series, 44, 2(April, 1987), pp. 338-41; See also Kenneth S. Lynn, "Perry Miller," *American Scholar* (Spring, 1983), pp. 221-27; and *Idem.*, "F.O. Matthiessen," American Scholar (Winter, 1976-7), pp. 86-93.

[23] J.H. Hexter, "Call me Ishmael; or, a Rose by Any Other Name," *American Scholar* (Summer, 1983), p. 342; H. Stuart Hughes, *Gentleman Rebel: The Memoirs of H. Stuart Hughes* (New York, 1990), p. 109; John Hope Franklin, *A Life in Learning: The Charles Homer Haskins Lecture* (New York, 1988), pp. 5-6.

[24] George Mosse, *Confronting History: A Memoir* (Madison, Wis., 2000), pp. 122-6.

[25] Handlin, "Career at Harvard," pp. 47-8.

[26] Richard Bushman, et al, eds., *Uprooted Americans: Essays to Honor Oscar Handlin* (Boston, 1979), p. 4; Handlin, "Career at Harvard," p. 49.

[27] Richard Pipes, *Vixi: Memoirs of a Non-Belonger* (New Haven, 2004), pp. 78-9.

28 Kellers, *Making Harvard Modern*, pp. 23-4.

29 Kellers, *Making Harvard Modern*, p. 86, 223.

30 Fairbank, *Chinabound*, pp. 355-65; Richard Frye, *Greater Iran: A 20th-Century Odyssey* (Costa Mesa, Cal., 2004), pp. 99-103; Palmer, "Interview with Richard Frye," February 16, 2005.

31 White, *In Search of History*, p. 50; Palmer, "Interview with Philip Kuhn," May 3, 2005.

32 Palmer, "Interview with Richard Frye," February 16, 2005.

33 W.K. Jordan to Wallace Notestein, September 5, 1947; Wallace Notestein Papers; Yale University, Department of Manuscripts and Archives.

34 Palmer, Interviews with Charles Maier, March 21, 2005; Pauline Maier, March 22, 2005; and Edward Keenan, March 22, 2005.

35 Palmer, "Interview with James Wilkinson," April 28, 2005

36 Palmer, "Interview with David Landes," March 1, 2005.

37 Jack N. Rakove, "Bernard Bailyn," in Robert Allan Rutland, ed., *Clio's Favorites: Leading Historians of the United States, 1945-2000* (Columbia, Missouri, 2000), pp. 6-7; Palmer, "Interview with Bernard Bailyn," December 15, 2004.

38 Palmer, "Interview with Hannah Holborn Gray," December 8, 2005.

39 Bernard Bailyn, *The Ideological Origins of the American Revolution* (Cambridge, Mass., 1967), pp. v-xii.

40 Palmer, "Interview with Charles Maier," March 21, 2005; Palmer, "Interview with Caroline Bynum, May 27, 2005;" Kellers, *Making Harvard Modern*, p. 409.

41 Rakove, "Bernard Bailyn," p. 11.

42 Palmer, "Interview with Pauline Maier," March 22, 2005; Palmer, "Interview with James Wilkinson," April 28, 2005.

43 Palmer, *Engagement with the Past*, pp. 154-5; Palmer, "Interview with Pauline Maier," March 22, 2005.

44 Bushman, ed., *Uprooted Americans*, p. xi.

45 Palmer, "Interview with John Womack," March 25, 2005.

Chapter Two

The Crisis of the Harvard History Department

The department's golden age, however, did not last forever. History departments evolve primarily through their appointments, and in the early fifties the first signs of an impending crisis began to lurk. Despite its success in replacing its stars from an earlier generation, evidence appeared that other universities intended to compete with Harvard for quality faculty. In the early fifties, Oscar Handlin received an offer from the University of Chicago that amounted to approximately four times his Harvard salary. Handlin took the offer to McGeorge Bundy, the Dean of the Faculty of Arts and Sciences. Bundy offered little comfort and no additional money, but pleaded with Handlin to stay at Harvard on the basis of loyalty to the department and university, which Handlin agreed to do.[1]

Other problems began to surface. As another example of outside competition, the size of the history departments against which Harvard was completing was increasing. But, while the Harvard department replaced its retiring faculty, its total number of members did not increase at the rates of competing departments. For example, the University of California at Berkeley had 25 faculty members in 1950 and 65 in 1970; during the same period, Harvard went from about 25 to 42.[2]

The Harvard history department also continued its tendency to make most of its appointments from those who had been students or junior faculty at Harvard. This was not necessarily bad, since many of these truly were the best faculty available, although occasionally it was hard to decide which Harvard man was the best. When Morison retired in 1958, the three leading candidates to replace him were Edmund Morgan, then teaching at Yale, Carl Bridenbaugh, then teaching at Berkeley, and Bernard Bailyn, a junior faculty member at Harvard. All held Harvard degrees. When the department became divided over Morgan and Bridenbaugh, Bailyn was offered the job, and three years later, he was promoted to full professor.[3]

The Bailyn appointment was important first of all because he was an extraordinarily promising and innovative scholar, the kind every department aspires to recruit. But the appointment was also important in a symbolic sense because Bailyn was a Jew, and a Jew replacing Samuel Eliot Morison, the member of the department who possessed the most impeccable New England pedigree and who was teaching the subject closest to the heart of Puritan New England. Moreover, by the fifties, after a slow start, the department was moving with considerable dispatch to appoint Jews. In addition to Bailyn and Handlin, Benjamin Schwartz, Richard Pipes, and, later, John Clive and David Landes all joined the department.

How Harvard made its choices, however, became increasingly mysterious. The experience of Richard Pipes provides an interesting example of the ways in which careers were made in the history department in the fifties. Pipes received a doctorate in Russian history from Harvard in 1950 and was initially offered an appointment as an instructor in History and Literature, renewable annually for up to three years, with no possibility of tenure. In 1954 he was offered a position as a lecturer for one year. At this point, his future at Harvard did not appear to be particularly promising, since only people appointed at the assistant professor level were eligible for the highly sought associate professor appointment. Pipes' prospects fell even farther when the department offered another Russian historian, Martin Malia, an assistant professorship in Russian history. Malia had already served a period as an instructor and had even been allowed the rare privilege of teaching his own graduate seminar. In addition to Malia, Harvard also had Karpovich and Robert Lee Wolff offering courses in Russian history.[4]

Russian history at Harvard therefore seemed distinctly overpopulated. The bleakness of the situation was actually a blessing in disguise for Pipes. Recognizing the hopelessness of his position, he wasted no time worrying about it. In 1955 he received an invitation from the University of California at Berkeley to come for a term as a visiting lecturer, which he accepted. Robert Kerner, the Russian historian at Berkeley, was about to retire, and the department was considering three possible successors, Malia, Pipes, and Nicholas Riasanovsky. At the same time, Karpovich was ready to retire at Harvard and Malia was in his fourth and pivotal year as an assistant professor. In December 1957 Pipes was unexpectedly summoned to the office of department chair Myron Gilmore and informed him that the department, "after long and careful scrutiny," had voted to recommend him for an associate professorship at Harvard in Russian history, the rank that conferred tenure.

Another curious appointment was made in American history after the retirement of Paul Buck in 1954. The department's Americanists defined the position in such a way that brilliance in undergraduate teaching, especially in teaching the American survey, would be the critical consideration. The emphasis on undergraduate teaching virtually eliminated the two most distinguished Americanists outside of Harvard, Richard Hofstadter and C. Vann Woodward. Both were exemplary, innovative historians, but neither had a Harvard connection or excelled at undergraduate teaching. The department turned instead to Frank Freidel, a Wisconsin Ph.D. then teaching at Stanford, who was an excellent undergraduate teacher, though not quite at the Hofstadter-Woodward level in scholarly terms. Indeed, one of the justifications offered by Oscar Handlin for his appointment was that Freidel went to a lot of historical meetings and was well-liked. The Freidel appointment was also surprising given his specialty. Freidel was an authority on Franklin Roosevelt, and the department already had Arthur Schlesinger, Jr., who was in the early stages of his Roosevelt biography.⁵

The appointment had mixed results. On one hand, Freidel delivered exactly what the department wanted. He was an excellent undergraduate teacher and a productive scholar. On the other hand, over the years, Freidel would find himself doing far more undergraduate teaching than his colleagues in American history, and, as a Wisconsin Ph.D., he came to feel that the Americanist wing of the history department, consisting mostly of Harvard Ph.D.s, was a club in which he was decidedly not a member.⁶

Before World War II the history department's reputation had been built in part by appointing a mixture of Harvard Ph.Ds, such as Langer, Merk, and Morison, and people from outside Harvard, such as Charles Homer Haskins, Frederick Jackson Turner, and Arthur Schlesinger, Sr. Even Perry Miller, the inspiration of many Harvard history undergraduates in the thirties, was not a Harvard man. But between about 1940 and 1960, Harvard history department changed direction and begin overwhelmingly appointing people from its own department. Up to 1960, this tendency was enormously successful, as several of the university's most distinguished faculty, including Handlin, Schlesinger, Jr., Fairbank, Bailyn, and Pipes joined the department.⁷

But there were also some curious decisions, such as in 1954 when the department chose Franklin Ford over Carl Schorske, both Harvard Ph.D.s. In some ways, the decision came back to haunt the department. While Ford soon produced an excellent book, *The Robe and the Sword*, about the Old Regime French aristocracy, at the time of the appointment, Schorske was more advanced as a scholar, having published *German Social Democracy*, a book on the Weimar Republic, and he enjoyed a reputation as a superb teacher. In the sixties, when Schorske's articles began appearing on late nineteenth century Viennese culture, his immense depth and vision as a scholar was revealed. But when Harvard turned to him in the sixties, he turned them down, accepting instead an appointment at Princeton, which received the harvest of his scholarship when he published the collected essays in *Fin de Siecle Vienna* and won a MacArthur Foundation "genius" grant.[8]

The Ford decision was not the only strange appointment made by the department during this time. H. Stuart Hughes was a Harvard Ph.D. who by his own admission had served an undistinguished period in the early fifties as a Harvard assistant professor. While he was a popular lecturer, his publications were slight, and the department declined to promote him, in effect terminating his appointment. He managed to land a job at Stanford, which had many things to recommend it. The sun shone; people smiled; there were few personal rivalries; and he had a house with a swimming pool.[9]

But, despite its charms, Stanford was not Harvard. In early 1956 Hughes received a call from McGeorge Bundy, the Dean of Harvard's Faculty of Arts and Sciences, inviting him back to Harvard as a full professor at the princely salary of $12,000. Hughes was initially skeptical, but when John Fairbank told him that the department needed him badly, he decided to accept. What was curious about the appointment was that he had not published any more than he had in 1952, the time at which the department had chosen not to promote him. At the time of Harvard's offer in 1956, he had not written a line of what would turn out to be his finest book, *Consciousness and Society: The Reorientation of French Social Thought, 1890-1930*. Harvard took him entirely on faith, even allowing him to spend a year at Stanford's Center for Advanced Study in the Behavioral Sciences before taking up the appointment, although why they suddenly decided to have faith in him in 1956 was not clear.

Hughes' appointment also reflected another tendency in the department's appointments which would recur over the years, the Harvard Ph.D. who might or might not receive a junior appointment at Harvard, but, who, in any case, would have to go somewhere else to make their reputation before returning to Harvard. Others who fit this profile included Robert Lee Wolff,

John Clive, Donald Fleming, Wallace MacCaffrey, Stephan Thernstrom, and, somewhat later, Philip Kuhn, William Kirby, and Charles Maier.

At the same time, a kind of hubris may have afflicted the department.[10] Its post-war success in recruiting its own Ph.D.s seems to have led it to believe that it need not look beyond Harvard to seek the best faculty. Given that success, this conviction was understandable, but it did lead to an inbred department, still something of a gentleman's club, albeit not quite as waspy as in the thirties. But it was a club laden with Harvard Ph.D.s who had been taught by other Harvard Ph.D.s, thereby depriving the department to a large extent of the necessary stimulus of new ideas and fresh perspectives.

Moreover, by the 1960s, the conditions of American academic life were changing. Other departments, such as those at Yale, Princeton, and Berkeley, were striving to build quality faculties. In the early 1960s Brandeis stunned the world of elite history departments when it lured Stephan Thernstrom away from Harvard. Also, the expansion of the American economy meant that, for the first time, state universities, especially those at Berkeley and Ann Arbor, could offer higher salaries and lesser teaching loads than Ivy League schools.[11]

Faced with stiff competition for promising faculty, many universities learned to be more flexible about working conditions, such as teaching loads, research and travel support, housing, tuition for faculty children, and positions for spouses, in order to lure talented faculty into their ranks. The department, and Harvard generally, fearing that concessions made to new faculty would create tensions and bad feeling among the older faculty, was late to adapt to changing times.

Other problems loomed. During the sixties the Boston area, primarily due to skyrocketing housing costs, became one of the most expensive areas of the country in which to live. Even a handsome Harvard salary could be eaten up quickly. Cost of living issues became far more pressing later on, but the first signs were visible even in the late fifties. Upon his return to Harvard in 1957, Stuart Hughes discovered that what at a distance looked like a fine salary was on closer inspection not nearly as much as it seemed.[12] Moreover, the search for affordable housing eventually compelled younger faculty to live farther and farther away from the campus, which in turn forced them to make long commutes to campus on Boston's traffic-clogged freeways. In the twenties and thirties, many history faculty lived on Brattle and Trowbridge Streets, in easy walking distance of the fabled Yard. By the sixties that luxury was becoming prohibitively expensive. At the same time Harvard offered only minimal perks to its faculty. Richard Pipes, one of the department's most luminous stars, never received money from Harvard to travel to meetings, and, when he sent his son to Harvard, he received no tuition break.[13]

The creation of the Charles Warren Center for the Study of American History was in theory designed to address some of these problems at least from the perspective of American history. In the mid-sixties, Annielouise Bliss Warren, the widow of former assistant attorney general and constitutional scholar Charles Warren, left $7.5 million in her husband's memory to further the study of American history at Harvard. Some of the money went to endow chairs in areas outside the history department, including law, education, and divinity, where the study of American history was also important. But the rest of the money went to establish the Charles Warren Center, whose structure and plan of operation were designed by the department's senior Americanists. Their expressed goals were to use the center to strengthen the reputation of American history at Harvard, enhance undergraduate instruction in American history, and increase the number and distinction of Harvard's Ph.D.'s in American history. The designers also planned to bring in promising Ph.D.s from elsewhere who might benefit from a postdoctoral year at Harvard and to provide Harvard faculty with money for research and release from teaching without them having to seek outside aid.

In practice the reality did not match the dream. Undergraduate teaching in particular may have suffered at its hands. The faculty in American history, supported by funds from the Warren Center, did less and less teaching. As the Warren Center money went increasingly to Harvard's Americanists, the anticipated influx and stimulation of outsiders did not materialize.[14]

In 1967 Judge Henry Friendly, heading a Board of Overseers' visiting committee to evaluate the department, was alarmed to find that seven of the twenty-one permanent slots in the department were vacant, as well as ten of the thirteen assistant professorships. Friendly suggested that the department make a more determined effort to identify the best candidates and offer them tenured positions or non-tenured positions with reasonable assurance of promotion. And he also urged them to consider more strongly appointing people from other universities.[15]

As if these problems were not enough, Harvard and the history department were also swept up by the student unrest of the late sixties.[16] Before 1969 Harvard faced a few minor anti-draft demonstrations and prided itself on being above the chaos afflicting other universities. The episodes that did occur were few and sporadic. In 1966 Secretary of Defense Robert McNamara, facing a hostile crowd after emerging from a talk with students, had to escape through one of Harvard's steam tunnels. In 1967 the Students for a Democratic Society (SDS) barricaded a Dow Chemical recruiter in the Mallinckrodt Laboratory and made repeated demonstrations against the racism and militarism which it believed was corrupting the true purpose of what the United States should be.

After the eruption of violent student uprisings at Columbia in 1968, Harvard administrators and faculty could again take pride in the fact that the most serious disturbances had occurred elsewhere. But, ominously, certain dividing lines were emerging at Harvard, particularly among the faculty. Several perceived the student protests not only as threats to liberal democracy but to their conception of the university as an ivory tower, above the pettiness and self-interest of partisan politics. And they urged Harvard President Nathan Pusey and Dean of the Faculty of Arts and Sciences Franklin Ford to take a harder line against student protestors. Others expressed sympathy with the students' goals, though not necessarily with their methods.

In the fall of 1968 the atmosphere on campus became more highly charged. SDS launched an attack on Harvard's Reserve Officer Training Corps (ROTC), which they considered the most visible symbol of Harvard's complicity with the military-industrial complex. After a meeting in Paine Hall, the university's music building, SDS resolved to confront physically university administrators and faculty if they did not immediately disband ROTC at Harvard. Harvard's Administrative Board, consisting of administrators and faculty, voted to reject SDS's demand, but at the same time to deny college credit for ROTC courses and to deprive ROTC instructors of faculty status, virtually emasculating the program. Later that month another committee recommended terminating all ROTC programs in two years.

By the spring of 1969, despite the fact that the administration had made significant concessions to the protestors, rumors abounded that SDS would try to take over University Hall, which housed the offices of the dean of the Faculty of Arts and Sciences, on the grounds that ROTC should be disbanded immediately. On April 9th, a group of about three-hundred students and assorted outsiders entered the building and forcibly, in some cases, evicted its occupants.

Once in control of the building, the students reiterated their demands that ROTC be eliminated, and broke into the file cabinets in the dean's office, uncovering evidence of what they believed was the university's connection with the C.I.A. and of its heavy investment in companies profiting from the war. They also extracted confidential personnel files and inflicted some physical damage to the building.

Faced with the occupation, the rifling of files and what appeared to be the fundamental disregard for law and order inherent in the seizure, Pusey and Ford decided that they could not allow the students to remain in the building. This conviction was reinforced by the advice of Archibald Cox, a Harvard law professor, who had led an inquiry into the Columbia disturbances and concluded that if the police were to be used, they had to be sent in early or not at all.

Early in the morning of April 11^(th), with little warning, Pusey sent into about 200 local police officers to remove the occupiers. Despite taunts of "fascist pigs" made by the students, the police, wielding battering rams on the doors and tear gas and nightsticks on the students, cleared the building quickly. The reoccupation of the building, however, may have played into the demonstrators' hands, since police had to use force in many instances to remove the students and several of them were injured in the process. In an image that recalled the attacks made by Birmingham police on civil rights protestors earlier in the decade, the public saw defenseless students being clubbed and gassed by helmeted officers.

The episode ignited an intense debate on campus. Both sides charged the other with totalitarianism and portrayed themselves as real defenders of American freedom and the true mission of the university. Further divisions arose between those faculty members sympathetic to the students and those who were appalled by their behavior. The history department contained a large number of faculty, including Oscar Handlin, Donald Fleming, Robert Lee Wolff, and Richard Pipes, who were outspoken critics of student radicalism. Moreover, the Dean of the Faculty of Arts and Sciences, Franklin L. Ford, a favorite target of the radicals, was a former department member.

After the events of the spring of 1969, Harvard administrators and faculty gloomily confronted the prospect of an unceasing procession of student protest with no obvious ground for compromise. The events of the spring seemed to represent the academic equivalent of the Tennis Court Oath, a defining moment at which an old, unresponsive, authoritarian regime began to collapse. But, to the surprise of almost everyone, the battle over University Hall represented the height of student protest at Harvard. Periodic demonstrations and clashes still erupted, but nothing like the events of the spring of 1969 occurred. Even the student fury touched off by President Richard Nixon's decision to expand the war in Viet Nam into Cambodia did not result in the violence that accompanied the takeover of University Hall.

One of the reasons why the Cambodian incursion did not trigger the anger of earlier events was that university officials and faculty learned from their experience. When student protests against the Cambodian incursion began to erupt, the Harvard faculty passed a resolution introduced by the historian of Japan and former ambassador to Japan Edwin O. Reischauer deploring the expansion of the war into Cambodia. An even more radical proposal by the historian of science Everett Mendelsohn calling for the immediate withdrawal of troops from Southeast Asia also passed with broad support.

The faculty also learned to be more accommodating on academic matters. The Cambodian incursion occurred when classes were over but examinations were in progress, so a critical issue to be decided was how to respect students' desire for political involvement without their grades suffering. With hardly any objection, Pusey sanctioned alternative ways of determining final grades, including pass-fall options and the possibility of taking examinations in the fall.

Yet while the student protests did not have the cataclysmic effect that some feared and others hoped for, Harvard did change, particularly in the regulation of student behavior. Many signs of traditional authority at Harvard, such as parietals, and coats and ties at dinner, soon vanished. Drug use and sexual promiscuity were rampant. In 1971, in a scene that would have been unthinkable a few years before, both sexes swam naked in the Adams House swimming pool. There were also many attempts at curricular change, including pass-fail options, reduced requirements, and student representation on academic committees.

But perhaps the most profound change came in attitude, where Harvard's conception of itself as America's university for elite students taught by elite faculty was called into question. Many thought that, after the period of unrest, Harvard should endeavor to become an agent of social change, rather than the educator of tomorrow's political and social elites. To them, elitism, even intellectual elitism, became almost disreputable. Selection of students and faculty were increasingly based on sexual and racial diversity. While many believed that the inclusion of women and minorities was a necessary extension of the Harvard meritocracy, others contended that making choices on the basis of diversity simply amounted to social engineering.[17]

Oscar Handlin was one of those who deplored the concessions made to the students and the rise of so-called interest group politics on the grounds that these changes compromised academic integrity. In his view the first sign that interest group politics superseded scholarly concerns came when he was asked to recommend teachers not according to ability but in terms of race and political orientation. At the same time, the erosion of basic skills among the students, the need to teach with an eye fixed on class enrollment, the harsh reality of grade inflation, and lightened reading assignments to achieve popularity all incurred his displeasure. Moreover, Handlin detected a malaise among the graduate students, beginning in the mid-sixties. Many of them came to Harvard supremely gifted and qualified, with impressive test scores and golden recommendations. But to Handlin they seemed to believe they already knew it all and did not have to work. "Take it easy," was the standard departing remark of one of his students, who all too often followed his own advice.[18]

But, student issues aside, the inability to make appointments was still the department's thorniest problem. In 1970 it had twenty-five senior professors, while Yale had thirty-six and Columbia had thirty-four. In 1972 the number of assistant professors was down to fourteen from twenty-seven the year before. In *Chinabound: A Fifty-Year Memoir*, John Fairbank attributes the inability to make appointments to "Harvarditis," an affliction which manifested itself when department members became so impressed with Harvard's magnificence that a certain arrogance was unavoidable. Even if they themselves felt unworthy, they were nevertheless arrayed, like Horatius at the bridge, as the last line of defense against creeping mediocrity.[19]

The most obvious consequence of the inability to make appointments was the lack of course offerings, especially in American history. In 1971 Columbia offered fourteen lecture courses in American history; Harvard offered three. The lack of offerings in American history inspired a popular t-shirt with history in brackets ("[History]"), which was the designation in the schedule for a course announced but not offered.[20]

The department also struggled to meet demands for expanding its offerings in non-western areas. In his autobiography, John Fairbank diplomatically expressed his frustrations on this issue. While he conceded that the departments had to honor its obligation to offer courses in traditional areas, Fairbank charitably concluded that the history "faculty was not organized to accommodate an increase of tenured professors in East Asian history." Perhaps his greatest frustration was the constant struggle for funding. With the reluctance of the history department to create full-time positions, it was necessary to lobby for funds from other department and granting agencies. Depending on who put up the funds, it was even possible to become a faculty member in East Asian history without coming under the purview of the history department. Moreover, Fairbank suggested, department members tended to evaluate Asian candidates by the same standards that they evaluated candidates in traditional fields, that is, by the publication of a major book relatively early in one's career. As if promotion at Harvard was not hard enough in any event, this attitude made advancement even more difficult for Asianists since acquiring the languages necessary to write a major book would take considerably longer in Asian fields than in traditional ones.[21]

Fairbank was also aggrieved about the department's treatment of Alexander Woodside, hired as a junior faculty member to teach Vietnamese history. Fairbank had expended a great deal of energy to recruit Woodside at a time when the war in Viet Nam dominated American foreign policy and discourse about the country's direction. But, despite the publication of a major book,

Woodside was not promoted and it was a long time before the department found a replacement for him.

The shortage of courses was compounded when department members were summoned frequently to continue Harvard's venerable tradition of advising world leaders. In 1961 Arthur Schlesinger, Jr., took a leave of absence to serve in the Kennedy administration. Edwin Reischauer was ambassador to Japan from 1961 to 1967. Others, especially those who specialized in non-western areas, such as Fairbank and Reischauer, were often abroad for long periods of time. Harvard took pride in the fact that its faculty served the nation and advised the world's leaders, but when faculty assumed this role, it also meant that they were not teaching.

In 1971-2, journalist and Harvard undergraduate in the thirties, Theodore H. White, headed a visiting committee to evaluate the history department. White declared that the department's biggest problem was the fear of its senior members that administrative pressure to expand would lead to the dilution of quality in the department's scholarship, which in turn led to the application of standards that virtually no one could live up to when it came to promoting junior faculty. The difficulty of getting promoted to a rank carrying tenure at Harvard was most conspicuous in American history, where no junior faculty member since Ernest May in 1959 had received tenure in the department. Promotion in non-American areas was somewhat easier. Between 1970 and 1971, Patrice Higonnet in French history, Edward Keenan in Russian history, and John Womack in Latin American history, were junior faculty who were promoted.[22]

Over the years, many attributed the department's resistance to promoting junior candidates, particularly those in American history, to a cabal of mandarin Americanists, including Oscar Handlin, Bernard Bailyn, and Donald Fleming, who guarded the gates to Olympus like French *poilus* at Verdun, proclaiming with equal determination "they shall not pass." The three were a curious trinity. Bailyn and Fleming were Handlin's students. But, while Handlin and Bailyn were prodigious scholars and Pulitzer

Prize winners, the most conspicuous examples of the department's highest aspirations, Fleming had not published a book on his own since 1954.[23]

The extraordinary tenacity of the gatekeepers produced a largely demoralized junior faculty. Junior faculty entertained little hope of promotion while carrying most of the teaching burden, including tutorials and a good part of graduate teaching. At the same time, they were clearly second-class citizens. Their offices were apart from the senior faculty, and they had very limited role in department decisions. They were also excluded from most of the department's social events, and senior faculty normally remained aloof, knowing that most junior appointees had no chance of surviving, although most would labor mightily to be the one who would break through.

Junior faculty found solace in graveyard humor. They joked that the Dunwalke Chair, held by a junior faculty member in American history, was aptly named. When their time at Harvard was done, they walked. They met for regular potluck dinners, which they called the "Dinners of the Ephemeral Faculty," and they held an annual ritual to commemorate the publication of the last book published by Donald Fleming, Darth Vader in the eyes of the junior faculty.[24]

In the early seventies, the department took steps to address its problems in American history by appointing David Donald and Stephan Thernstrom to senior positions. Both appointments were critical. Donald was an acclaimed scholar of the American Civil War and a rare Harvard senior appointment who had no prior connection with the institution. Donald was teaching at Johns Hopkins when he received a phone from Bernard Bailyn asking if he would be interested in coming to Harvard. Donald stated frankly that Harvard could not afford him. Bailyn replied that at Harvard salaries are negotiated directly between the faculty member and the dean of the Faculty of Arts and Sciences and Donald could receive whatever he was able to negotiate. In Donald's case negotiation also meant a position for his wife, who also held a Ph.D. in history, and who later became managing editor of the Harvard University Press.[25]

The Thernstrom appointment was also designed to strengthen the American wing. Thernstrom was a classic example of the Harvard Ph.D. and junior faculty member who had to go away before he could come back. During his period as a junior faculty member at Harvard, Thernstrom received tenured offers from Brandeis, Brown, and Michigan, and decided to ask the department to make an early decision on his promotion. The department declined, even though, as a junior faculty member, Thernstrom had published *Poverty and Progress*, a complex, groundbreaking study of the rate of social mobility in Newburyport, Massachusetts during the nineteenth-century. Not only was the book well-received, but it addressed issues of class and social mobility, important to scholarship in the late sixties and seventies, but not much engaged by other Harvard faculty. Disappointed by the department's decision not to promote him, Thernstrom accepted the offer from Brandeis and, later, moved to U.C.L.A., before returning to Harvard with a senior appointment in 1973.[26]

The department also made several strong senior appointments in European history, including David Landes in economic history, William Bouwsma in the Renaissance, and David Herlihy in Medieval history. Landes and Bouwsma were Harvard Ph.D.s who had established excellent reputations while teaching at Berkeley. Landes in particular had acquired prominence for his book on the Industrial Revolution, *The Unbound Prometheus*.[27]

But, as impressive as these appointments were, they also testified to the department's weakness. Landes and Bouwsma came to Harvard as part of the so-called Berkeley exodus, as several Berkeley history faculty fled a department that experienced considerable upheaval with the Free Speech Movement and student troubles generally. Thus, Harvard's ability to lure them away from the warm climes of the Bay Area to the cold and dreariness of Cambridge winters was misleading. Eventually, all would leave the department. Bouwsma returned to Berkeley after a brief period in Cambridge, stunned by the department's hierarchy and treatment of younger faculty. Disappointed with the department's approach to appointments, Landes moved bitterly to the Harvard economics department; and in 1980 Herlihy left Harvard for Brown when his wife, a trained historian in Russian history, was offered a position there.[28]

By the early seventies, however, several of the components of the old gentleman's club had vanished. There were fewer people who owed their appointments to social position, and there were many more serious scholars. There were also more Jews and more people teaching in non-western areas. An African, Nathan Huggins, held a joint appointment in history and African-American studies.

But several aspects of the club remained. The junior faculty were largely a class of "untouchables," and even among the senior faculty, there were clubs within the clubs. The senior Americanists provided as one example of a super-elite club to which not everyone was welcome. Moreover, another aspect of a gentlemen's club remained; the department was all-male. And, by the seventies, the Harvard department, like others, had to confront the prospect of appointing women to faculty positions.

Before the early seventies, the issues involving women had been relatively rare. Because of the presence of Radcliffe College, Harvard had been dealing, if reluctantly, for some time with issues involving the education of women. From 1948 to 1954, the department had a female faculty member when the medievalist Helen Maud Cam held an endowed chair designed for women. And it had been admitting small, but increasing numbers of women as graduate students since after World War II, and the program had produced some outstanding graduates, such as Hannah Holborn Gray, Pauline Maier, Marybeth Norton, and Caroline Bynum.

The case of Judith Hughes, however, was probably the first time that gender issues became the subject of serious debate. She was a graduate student at Harvard in the early sixties who married Stuart Hughes, the department's modern Europeanist. She eventually received a Ph.D. under his direction and began teaching in a recently created honors program in social studies as a junior faculty member. There was no hope for promotion from this position, so, when her term was about to expire, Hughes asked the history department to consider promoting her to the next non-tenured step. An acrimonious debate erupted. To some, even though Stuart Hughes absented himself from the proceedings, it was a power play on his behalf to get his wife a job. To Hughes, it was simply about a junior candidate getting a chance to be judged on her own merits. The episode was also the department's first encounter with a phenomenon that would be become commonplace in academic life later, the spousal hire. In the end the department declined to promote her, and the Hughes' spread the word that they would be interested in leaving Harvard as a couple. In 1973 they accepted an offer to move to the new University of California in San Diego.[29]

At the senior level, the department had little success in the seventies appointing women. They were prepared to offer a senior appointment to the southern historian Willie Lee Rose before she suffered a stroke. They also offered a senior appointment to Jean Baker, teaching at Goucher College in Baltimore and author of several books on the Civil War and Reconstruction subjects, but she decided against accepting Harvard's offer because her husband taught at the Johns Hopkins medical school. Later, another senior appointment was offered to a historian of Japan teaching at Columbia who decided she did not want to come to Cambridge. It was not until 1982, when the Byzantinist Angelike Laiou decided to accept Harvard's offer, that a woman, the first since Helen Cam, held a senior appointment in the Harvard history department.[30]

But there were increasing numbers of qualified junior women willing to accept junior positions at Harvard. One of them was Caroline Bynum, a medievalist and future president of the American Historical Association, who received a Ph.D. from Harvard in 1969 on the very day the students took over University Hall. Like other graduate students with outstanding records, she was offered an instructorship in the department. Not long after, the university abolished the rank of instructor, leaving the department with little choice but to fire her or promote her to assistant professor.[31]

Fortunately, the department chose to promote her, and she became one of the few women on the Harvard faculty. In 1972, out of approximately six-hundred faculty members at Harvard, only eleven were women, and all were at untenured ranks. Bynum was the only woman on the Harvard history faculty. Despite throwing herself into teaching and into service by heading Harvard's Committee on the Status of Women, she was denied promotion by the department in 1973.

Bynum's experience testified to the difficulties faced by junior faculty women at Harvard and not simply the history department in the early seventies. Despite landing a position at Harvard's Divinity School where she might have gotten tenure, Bynum left Harvard for the University of Washington in 1976. On one hand, it was hard for her to leave. She had been at Harvard since 1962 and many of her formative experiences had occurred at there. The story of her early adulthood seemed to be etched into the very bricks of Harvard's buildings. On the other hand, she had been denied promotion by the history department, and she had been sexually harassed by other faculty at the Divinity School. It was time to leave.

The department's difficulties can be seen in two other searches. In the late sixties, the department had the chance to appoint Robert Darnton, one of its own undergraduates, a Rhodes Scholar, and a member of Harvard's Society of Fellows. If this was not enough to mark him as a scholar of distinction, Darnton had already published a remarkable and widely praised book, *Mesmerism and the End of Enlightenment* in 1968. His potential seemed to be unlimited. But the department clashed over his appointment, and, while it was making up its mind, Darnton accepted an offer from Princeton. Years later, when Harvard approached Darnton after he had fully realized the potential so evident before, he chose to stay at Princeton.[32]

In 1980 John King Fairbank, the father of East Asian studies in the United States, retired. The reputed frontrunner to replace him was Jonathan Spence, who was teaching at Yale, a prolific scholar and a future president of the American Historical Association. Two versions of the department's failure to lure Spence to Harvard emerged. In the first, several senior members decided that Spence's work, popular and sometimes experimental, was too soft for the high-powered scholarship the department desired. In the second, several other senior faculty were dispatched to New Haven to ascertain Spence's level of interest in coming to Cambridge, and they found him decidedly uninterested. In the end, the department hired Philip Kuhn, a Harvard Ph.D. teaching at Chicago, who, become another prodigal son of Harvard to return home. But whether the department decided Spence's work did not meet Harvard's standards or that Spence displayed little interest in coming to Harvard, the episode seemed to reflect its most recurring problems. Attractive candidates were not good enough for them or were not interested in coming.[33]

The story of the Harvard history department has several distinct phases. In the first, beginning in the 1920s and ending around 1940, the department emerged as an outstanding body partly because it was willing to recruit a mixture of exceptional faculty from outside Harvard along with Harvard Ph.Ds. During a second phase, from about 1940 to 1980, the department began making most of its appointments from a pool of its own Ph.D.s. Some of these, like John Fairbank, Bernard Bailyn, Richard Frye, and Richard Pipes, were Harvard Ph.D.s and junior faculty members, who received their senior appointments directly after their service as junior faculty. Others, such as Donald Fleming, Robert Lee Wolff, and Stephan Thernstrom, were Harvard Ph.D.s who had to prove their mettle elsewhere before they could return to Harvard as professors.

In either case, the pattern of hiring its own proved successful as the department acquired a number of extraordinary scholars. But, by the sixties several problems were beginning to surface. Faced with intense competition from other universities, several of them trying to emulate Harvard, Harvard administrators were reluctant to offend senior faculty by offering more attractive packages to younger people, and the department itself closed its ranks. Whether it was a reluctance to change previously successful hiring patterns or the inevitable pride in being part of America's greatest university, the department repeatedly hired its own and often simply refused to promote, especially after 1971, junior faculty, especially in American history and often could not make up its mind on senior appointments.

By the early eighties, the department's problems stood out in bold relief. Statistically, the most obvious ones were its dwindling size in comparison with other elite departments and inbreeding. In 1982-3 the Harvard history department had 38 full-time faculty members; 26 held Harvard Ph.D.s. At the same time the Yale history department had 71 full-time faculty of whom 17 held Yale Ph.D.s. The University of California at Berkeley reported 53 full-time faculty of whom 4 held Berkeley Ph.D.s.[34]

Most contentious, however, were the issues of promoting junior faculty and making senior appointments. The patterns established in the sixties and seventies regarding promotion were repeated in the eighties. In the mid-1980s the department, controversially, declined to promote several junior Americanists. When Alan Brinkley was a junior faculty member at Harvard, he seemed to be the one destined to enter the hallowed ground of the faculty who hold tenure in the Harvard history department. He was a Harvard Ph.D., and a dynamic teacher with the polish and social grace expected of a Harvard professor as well as the author of a Bancroft-prize winning book, *Voices of Protest*. He even turned down outside offers reportedly in the belief that his promotion was secure. But, at a key department meeting, several senior Americanists reportedly expressed the opinion that his scholarship was too shallow, and his tenure was rejected. The news of his rejection was significant enough to be reported on National Public Radio.[35]

The senior faculty also voted against Patricia Nelson Limerick, a scholar of the American West. Limerick would later be awarded a MacArthur Foundation "genius" grant and write the kind of book, *The Legacy of Conquest*, that the department claimed it coveted, one that would completely redirect the thinking of scholars in the field. She found out about her rejection when she wandered into the chair's office and saw written on a yellow pad, "no tenure for Limerick."[36] There were occasional moments when the department seemed poised on the brink of reform. In the early eighties, Donald Fleming, one of the hardest of the hardliners, stormed out of a department meeting, when the other senior members overrode his objections and voted to offer a senior appointment to a Harvard Ph.D. and former junior faculty member who had been exiled to another university.

Change, however, has come recently to the Harvard history department. Harvard has promoted a junior Americanist, Sven Beckert, the first so honored since Ernest May in 1959. Three junior faculty in European history, James Hankins, Susan Pederson and MacArthur Prize winner, Ann Blair, were all promoted, though Pederson later left for Columbia. The promotions of Pederson and Blair, along with the outside appointments of Laurel Thatcher Ulrich, Lizabeth Cohen, Jill Lepore, and others suggest that the climate for women has improved. Finally, the promotion of the Europeanist Peter Gordon, who won a Phi Beta Kappa teaching award, an achievement that might have been held against him in decades past, seems to be another sign of changing times.

---

[1] Handlin, "A Career at Harvard," p. 50.

[2] Morton and Phyllis Keller, *Making Harvard Modern*, p. 409; Gene Brucker, Henry F. May, and David Hollinger, *History at Berkeley: A Dialog in Three Parts* (Berkeley, 1998), pp. 6, 26.

[3] Palmer, "Interview with Morton and Phyllis Keller," January 15, 2005; Rakove, "Bernard Bailyn," p. 9n; Palmer, "Interview with Bernard Bailyn," December 15, 2004. Rakove notes the widespread suspicion that Bridenbaugh, a Harvard Ph.D. who dreamed of the day that he would be asked to return in glory to fair Harvard, was crushed by Harvard's decision. Not only was Bailyn a younger man, but he was Jewish. Bridenbaugh's disappointment might have been what lay behind his notorious presidential address to the American Historical Association in 1963, where he deplored the entrance of "urban-bred" persons of "lower middle-class and foreign origins" into the profession. Such persons, he

contended, frequently let their emotions get in the way of historical understanding. It was widely thought that Bridenbaugh was referring to Jews. See Bridenbaugh, "The Great Mutation," *American Historical Review*, 68, 1 (January, 1963): 315-31.

[4] Pipes, *Memoirs of a Non-Belonger*, p. 78.

[5] Keller and Keller, *Making Harvard Modern*, p. 224.

[6] Palmer, "Interview with Richard Pipes," February 3, 2005.

[7] This is also the principal contention of the Kellers in *Making Harvard Modern*.

[8] Kellers, *Making Harvard Modern*, p. 223.

[9] Hughes, *Gentleman Rebel*, pp. 229-31.

[10] I owe the use of the term "hubris" to Morton Keller in Palmer, "Interview with Morton and Phyllis Keller," January 15, 2005.

[11] Kellers, *Making Harvard Modern*, p. 224; Palmer, "Interview with Bernard Bailyn," December 14, 2004.

[12] Hughes, *Gentleman Rebel*, pp. 238-9.

[13] Palmer, "Interview with Richard Pipes," February 3, 2005.

[14] Kellers, *Making Harvard Modern*, pp. 224-5.

[15] Kellers, *Making Harvard Modern*, p. 225.

[16] My discussion of "the troubles" at Harvard is based on the account in the Kellers, *Making Harvard Modern*, pp. 307-29.

[17] Pipes, *Memoirs of a Non-Belonger*, p. 110.

[18] Oscar Handlin, *Truth in History* (Cambridge, Mass., 1979), p. 6; Idem., "A Career at Harvard,"; Boston Globe, "Tenure System Comes Under Fire," June 2, 1998, Metro, p. A1.

[19] Kellers, *Making Harvard Modern*, pp. 389-90; Fairbank, *Chinabound*, p. 394.

[20] Kellers, *Making Harvard Modern*, p. 410.

[21] Fairbank, *Chinabound*, pp. 392, 395.

[22] Kellers, *Making Harvard Modern*, p. 409; Palmer, "Interview with John Womack," March 25, 2005.

[23] *Boston Globe*, "Tenure System Comes Under Fire," June 2, 1998, p. A1.

[24] Ibid..

25 Palmer, "Interview with David Donald," December, 9, 2004.

26 Palmer, "Interview with Stephan Thernstrom," April 8, 2005.

27 Kellers, *Making Harvard Modern*, p. 410.

28 Palmer, "Interview with David Landes," March 1, 2005.

29 Hughes, *Gentleman Rebel*, pp. 296-8.

30 Palmer, "Interview with Stephan Thernstrom," April 8, 2005.

31 Caroline Walker Bynum, "Curriculum Vitae: An Authorial Aside," *Common Knowledge* 9, 1 (Winter, 2003), pp. 9-11.

32 Kellers, *Making Harvard Modern*, p. 410.

33 Palmer, "Interview with Morton and Phyllis Keller," January 15, 2005; and Palmer, "Interview with Richard Frye," February 16, 2005.

34 I arrived at these figures by counting the institutions from individuals received their Ph.D.s according to the rosters provided in the *Guide to Departments of History, 1982-3* (Washington, D.C.: American Historical Association, 1983). It is worth noting that by 2003 the situation in the Harvard department had greatly improved. According to the A.H.A.'s *Directory of History Departments, Historical Organizations, and Historians, 2002-3*, the Harvard history department listed forty-two full-time faculty, of which only sixteen held a Harvard Ph.D.

35 *Boston Globe*, June 2, 1998, p. A1

36 Ibid., p. A1.

Chapter Three

On or About 1955 the Yale HistoryDepartment Decided to Keep Up with Harvard

In April, 1957, John Morton Blum, at the time a Harvard Ph.D. teaching at M.I.T., came to the office of George Wilson Pierson, '26, Ph.D.'33, the chair of the Yale history department. Pierson was the epitome of Yale, a New England patrician, tall, imposing, aloof, and expensively dressed. A few weeks before, he offered Blum, then thirty-six and a Jew, a professorship at Yale over the telephone. Now Blum had come to New Haven to work out the details of the appointment.[1]

The man known as "father Yale" eyed Blum suspiciously. "What business have you at your age looking at a Yale professorship?" Pierson asked. Momentarily shaken, Blum reminded Pierson that he had not pursued the job; Pierson had offered it to him. Undeterred, Pierson continued with his examination, asking Blum why a Harvard man would want to come to Yale. (Pierson always referred to Blum as "a Harvard man;" M.I.T. did not rate in his universe.) When Blum replied that the excellence of the Yale department was a compelling factor, citing Pierson's own work on Alexis de Tocqueville, Pierson snapped, "Present company excepted."

Blum was rescued from further interrogation when Edmund Morgan, who had been teaching at Yale since 1955, knocked on Pierson's door and offered a more gracious welcome. The three went to lunch at Mory's, the classic Yale club where oars hung from the rafters and Yale memorabilia covered the walls, and where only persons, like Pierson, who were graduates of Yale College, could sign for lunch. After lunch, Blum returned to Pierson's office, where Pierson offered him a salary that was less than what he was making at M.I.T., although Blum did not agree to come until Pierson matched his M.I.T. salary.

Blum's appointment, however, was not complete. Pierson still had to convince the assembled full professors of Yale College to approve the appointment, and he told Blum that the full professors would require recommendations from distinguished Yale graduates; did he know any? Blum asked if McGeorge Bundy and Kingman Brewster would do. "Very nicely," Pierson replied.

Despite this unpromising beginning, Blum enjoyed a long and productive career at Yale, writing or editing nearly a dozen books, teaching one of Yale's most popular classes, and remaining there until his retirement in 1991. More importantly, he was a critical step in the process, initiated primarily by George Pierson, of advancing the Yale history department to a much higher status than it previously enjoyed.

For the first half of the twentieth century the Yale history department was excellent, graced with the presence of such distinguished scholars as Ullrich B. Phillips, Wallace Notestein, Charles McLean Andrews, Hajo Holborn, Samuel Flagg Bemis, and David M. Potter. But, it contained an abundance of historians of Great Britain, at one point over one-third of the department. And, with a few exceptions, such as Holborn and Robert Lopez, the department was deeply inbred, consisting in large measure of faculty who held Yale degrees.[2]

The importance of a Yale pedigree can be seen in the reaction of the Yale administration to the coming of World War II. In 1940 university officials, fearing a decline in enrollment and revenue if the United States entered the war and large numbers of students were summoned for military service, fired the junior faculty in the history department who did not have a Yale connection. The group that was terminated included such promising young scholars as Gordon Craig, Douglas Adair, and Theodore Mommsen. "It was a stupid thing to do," Craig, a future president of the American Historical Association, recalled, "I would have stayed at Yale, but money talks."[3]

Department chairs before World War II exercised virtually dictatorial powers, and the department itself was as stratified as the institution of which it was a part. At departmental lunches, the chair sat at the center of a long table, flanked by the full professors, who were in turn flanked by associate professors. The junior faculty were relegated to the far ends of the table and were not permitted to address the senior faculty by their first names.[4]

But the most salient characteristic of the department in the fifties was its reliance on Yale graduates for its faculty. At the time of Edmund Morgan's arrival at Yale in 1955, there were only a few members of the history department who did not hold a degree from Yale College or the Graduate School, or both. Hiring its own was not necessarily bad. Yale's Ph.D. program in history produced many outstanding faculty, such as David Potter, who became one of the department's most distinguished members, and, later, Howard Lamar and Gaddis Smith, who was also a Yale undergraduate.

But inbreeding did have dangers. Reliance on Yale graduates meant that the department hired people with similar backgrounds and attitudes. This made for homogeneity and conviviality within the department, but compromised its overall quality. The Yale department, like any department in a major university that aspired to distinction, needed an *élan vital*, an injection of new blood, people who would bring energy, new ideas, and innovative approaches to both teaching and research.

The man who did the most to inject new life into the Yale history department was Pierson, who became department chair in 1956. On one hand, Pierson was an unlikely reformer. He was a collateral descendant of one of the original founders and, as a thorough Old Blue, the exact opposite of the kind of faculty member he wished to hire. But he was steadfastly loyal to Yale. In 1957, when John Shy turned down Yale's offer of a handsome graduate stipend in favor of one from Princeton, he received a testy note from Pierson demanding to know why.[5]

A product of patrician New England, Pierson also retained many of the social convictions and prejudices of his class and upbringing. He opposed the admission of women to Yale and, J. H. Hexter, who became a member of the Yale history faculty in 1964, thought that Pierson remained "faintly suspicious of Jews." Even after John Blum had been in the department for several years, he still heard Pierson make anti-Semitic remarks. Pierson once opposed the appointment of Leonard Krieger, who was Jewish, in the history department by telling Blum that "we don't want to go the way of the law school," which, in Pierson's view, had too many Jews.

Pierson could also display an almost comic insensitivity to the problems of those who had less money than he. In 1980, when he heard that John Merriman, by then a tenured member of the department, had been turned down for a modest mortgage, Pierson offered to contact a friend who had some land outside New Haven on which Merriman might be able to put up a trailer.[6] At the same time, he could be exceedingly generous. In 1957 he helped David Cronin, a junior faculty member in American history, find the money he needed to go the meeting of the Mississippi Valley Historical Association so he could look for a job. Cronon was never sure whether the funds came from department sources or from Pierson himself.[7]

Yet, in the fifties, Pierson was able to cast off his prejudices to try to make the Yale history department the best in the world. After declaring that a woman would only teach at Yale "over his dead body," he was instrumental in the hiring of Mary Wright, the first woman to be appointed to a faculty position in the Yale history department. And, despite his anti-Semitism, championed the hiring of Blum and became one of his closest friends.[8]

At Yale in the 1950s the phrase "modernizing the history department" meant several things: hiring people without a Yale pedigree, appointing faculty to teach in areas outside American, European, and English history, and hiring Jews when they were the most qualified, although one, the medievalist Robert Lopez, was already a member of the department. It also meant balancing the department's traditional emphasis on undergraduate teaching with graduate education, and between teaching and research generally. And, at Yale, it meant trying to create a history department that would rival Harvard's.

Other departments at Yale were experiencing some of the same tensions. The Old Yale died hard. "The Yale English Department is now getting its instructors off the New York subway," remarked Benjamin C. Nangle, a member of the English Department and a product of the Old Yale, as he observed with suspicion the entry of Jews and faculty from outside Yale into the English department's formerly waspy corridors.[9]

The first step in upgrading the history department actually began the year before Pierson assumed his duties as chair when his predecessor, Harry Rudin, at Pierson's urging, lured Edmund Morgan away from Brown. After becoming chair, Pierson was instrumental in the critical appointment of C. Vann Woodward to replace David Potter in 1961. Morgan and Woodward were the prototypes for the kind of faculty Pierson wished to recruit. Neither had a Yale connection, but they were already two of the profession's foremost Americanists. Pierson also hired Jews, such as Blum, and was disappointed when he failed to tempt another, Richard Hofstadter, away from Columbia.

The Woodward appointment reveals a great deal about how Pierson operated. When Potter decided to leave, Morgan and Blum went to Pierson to tell him that the only person who could replace him was Woodward, then teaching at Johns Hopkins and who was the leading historian of the American South. Pierson deliberated for only a moment before telephoning Woodward and offering him a Sterling Professorship, the wealthiest and most prestigious chair Yale had to offer. There was no consultation outside Pierson,

Morgan, and Blum. Appointments were supposed to be approved by the department's full professors, which they usually were, but not in this case.[10]

The appointment of Woodward led to the hiring of Hans Gatzke, a historian of modern Germany. Gatzke was also teaching at Johns Hopkins, and Woodward alerted Pierson to the possibility that Gatzke would be interested in coming to Yale, too. Pierson also recruited Gaddis Smith, a former of student of Samuel Bemis, to succeed Bemis in American foreign policy.

Moreover, Pierson played a key role in the decision to hire historians in fields outside of Europe, Great Britain, and the United States. Such appointments at Yale included John W. Hall in Japanese history and Arthur and Mary Wright in Chinese history. The appointment of the Wrights was particularly important. Not only were they specialists in East Asian history, but they were among the first academic couples, if not the first, hired at an American university. They were working at Stanford at the time of their appointments. Arthur Wright was a professor in the history department; Mary Wright was a curator at the Hoover Institution. Oddly, the Stanford history department declined to offer her a faculty position, but the Wrights went to New Haven because all-male Yale did.

The hiring of the Wrights paid unexpected benefits. In the early 1960s, Jonathan Spence, an undergraduate at Clare College, Cambridge, came to Yale as part of an exchange program financed by the Mellon Foundation. Spence originally thought that Yale would be an excellent place to study American history. But, at the urging of John Blum, he decided to take some of the courses offered by the Wrights. Their teaching inspired him to make Chinese history his field of study and to take a Ph.D. at Yale under their direction. In 1967 they helped him get a junior appointment at Yale, and Spence would eventually become one of the university's most celebrated faculty members.[11]

The Wrights also helped persuade Yale President A. Whitney Griswold to accept their plan for developing Yale's offerings in non-western areas, financed by the Ford Foundation. Like

Harvard, Yale recognized the need for coverage of areas outside the west, but was reluctant to surrender its regular tenured slots to support them. The Wrights were instrumental in raising money for positions in non-western areas, and they also insisted that the department appoint people who were real specialists in non-western areas rather than Europeanists who had colonial interests. Before the sixties, for example, Harry Rudin taught African history at Yale, but he was really a German historian, who taught Africa from a colonial perspective. With the help of the Ford grant, the department was able not only to add positions in non-western fields such as Africa and Latin America, but to appoint real specialists in those fields. A few years later, the department agreed to try to balance its composition by trying to make one-third of its appointments in American history, one-third in Europe, and one-third in non-western areas.[12]

Yale's salaries at that time were usually lower than those at many of the institutions against which it traditionally competed. As we have seen, John Blum was initially asked to take a pay cut to come to Yale from M.I.T., and Pierson regularly informed new faculty that they would be expected to "suffer for Yale." Yet there were several cards that Pierson could play in the recruiting process, one of which was the Yale name. When Morgan was considering Yale's offer, he asked his chair at Brown, James B. Hedges, for advice. "Brown is Brown, but Yale is Yale," Hedges replied, "you should go." One of the attractions of Yale for J.H. Hexter, who came to Yale in 1964, was that when he told people he was going there, nobody ever said, "Yale? Where's that?"[13]

Pierson was also able to offer teaching loads that allowed the history faculty plenty of time for their research. Hexter and Woodward taught mainly graduate students. Morgan taught five hours a week. To clinch the deal when he came to Yale, Woodward was given a year's paid leave before he had even taught his first class. Later, in the 1960s, Morgan and Blum convinced Yale President Kingman Brewster to give productive faculty a semester off every three years.[14]

Pierson stepped down as chair in 1962, but his work was continued by several successors, most importantly, Howard Lamar. Lamar was a Yale Ph.D. and an accomplished historian of the American West, who would later serve a brief term as Yale's president. Playing a role almost as important as that of Pierson, Lamar was able to make several critical hires, including J. H. Hexter in early modern history, David Brion Davis in American history, Donald Kagan in ancient history, Leonard Thompson in African history, Robert R. Palmer in French history, and Peter Gay in European intellectual history, the final steps in the transformation of what was once a gentleman's club into a highly professional department.[15]

Lamar's job was not always easy, especially in the case of Hexter, where Lamar had to tolerate truly Olympian procrastination. At the time of the offer, Hexter was teaching at Washington University in St. Louis and had become deeply attached to the institution. Normally a decisive person who made up his mind about most issues quickly, Hexter waffled for nearly a year before accepting Yale's offer.[16]

The experience of John Blum reveals much about the Yale of the sixties. Outsiders sometimes find the transition to Yale uncertain, since Yale's customs and hierarchy can be mysterious. Blum was no exception. Anti-Semitism still existed at Yale, and the department clung to a number of stuffy social rituals. Attendance at some of these functions was required, but not at others; in the early years of his Yale career Blum was not always certain. He was also resented by some of the assistant professors in American history, since his appointment took the last tenured slot in that area. But his friendship with Edmund Morgan made life at Yale much easier. They knew each other from Morgan's time at Brown and often met at professional meetings. Blum admired Morgan's work, and, since Morgan had already been at Yale for two years, he was able to guide Blum through many of Yale's mysteries.[17]

Blum also valued the friendship of David Potter, although Potter left for Stanford in 1961. But, to his surprise, he discovered that George Pierson, despite his initially forbidding demeanor, had a witty and fun-loving side. In later years, Blum and his wife enjoyed regular dinner parties and family gatherings with Morgan, Pierson, Vann Woodward, several others, and their wives.[18]

Teaching at Yale proved to be immensely satisfying. Blum's class in twentieth century United States was one of the most popular undergraduate courses at Yale, and he also enjoyed teaching the graduate course in the literature of American history, which he taught with Morgan and Potter, and to which he introduced a section on African American history. The graduate students he taught were enormously gifted. One of them, David Kennedy, later won a Pulitzer Prize for *Freedom from Fear*, a study of the Great Depression. Another, Cynthia Russett, eventually joined the Yale history department.

As an instructor, Blum ran a tight ship. Winter or summer, he always wore a jacket and tie. He allowed no smoking, talking, sleeping or reading of newspapers. After Yale became co-educational, necking and knitting were added to the list of forbidden behaviors. Students who violated the rules were asked to leave, and Blum would not resume his lecture until they did. But he had a softer side, reserving a table in the dining hall of Branford College to have lunch with interested students every Thursday from 12 to 2.

Blum did not realize that he had made the transformation from a Harvard man to a Yale man until he attended the 1959 Harvard-Yale game. Before the game, his wife, knowing the strength of his ties to Harvard, asked him who he was rooting for. Blum replied that he didn't know yet. He found out, however, when a Yale player fumbled the opening kickoff, and Blum instinctively shouted, "God damn it!" A few years later, when Princeton approached him with an offer that would have paid more than Yale, Blum elected to stay at Yale.

During the 1960s the department also sought to impose stronger requirements for tenure on younger faculty. European and American historians were expected to have published two books, favorably reviewed. Such younger faculty as Howard Lamar, Henry Turner, Robin Winks, and Gaddis Smith were among the first to meet this standard. Occasionally, exceptions had to be considered. Jonathan Spence was one of the ablest of Yale's young faculty in the sixties. He learned Mandarin Chinese rapidly and his dissertation was published by the Yale University Press. But when it came time for promotion, he had two books, but only one based on Chinese sources. Arthur Wright, however, came to his defense by arguing that scholars in fields requiring difficult languages needed more time to publish their books than did American and European historians. The tenured professors agreed, and Spence was granted tenure.[19]

The department also benefited from the university's decision in the mid-sixties to reckon its budget differently. Before the sixties, Yale proceeded with the utmost caution in financial matters, spending only a portion of the interest on its investments along with a small part of its gifts and donations. But, in the sixties, based on a recommendation from the Ford Foundation (then run by McGeorge Bundy, a Yale man), the Yale Corporation, the university's governing board, decided to switch to a policy of "total return." Total return, which had already become a standard practice in the business world, offered a formula by which the Corporation could justify spending a much larger portion of the university's endowment, including projected gains. There was of course a large element of risk in this practice, for which in time Yale would pay dearly, but at the time it allowed Yale to pay much higher salaries to its faculty and to afford to hire many new ones, including those whom Howard Lamar was able to attract to Yale during his chairmanship.[20]

But, as the salaries and status of the department improved, there were some casualties. In the early sixties, Norman Pollack, the author of an important book challenging Richard Hofstadter's view of the Progressive Movement, ran into trouble for his highly dramatic teaching. For his last lecture in the first half of the American survey course, Pollack reenacted the assassination of Abraham Lincoln by having his graduate assistant, Jesse Lemisch, fire a shot at him with a toy pistol. Pollack then slapped a packet of ketchup to his chest and keeled over. Today, such performances are the stuff of which teaching awards are won. But at Yale in 1963 it was ungentlemanly. The chair at the time called Pollack and Lemisch in, and, after hearing their side of the story, said, "My God, it's worse than I thought." Pollack was not retained, and Lemisch believes that he lost whatever chance he had for a junior position at Yale.[21]

Pollack's work on the Progressive Movement was a leftist answer to Hofstadter's charge that most of the Progressive leaders were ignorant bigots. And, as the sixties progressed, the political views and activities of junior faculty often overshadowed their academic qualifications. While the older faculty were often in sympathy with the causes espoused by the younger ones, they were also sometimes dismayed by the violence of their rhetoric and methods of protest. In several instances, their response to radical historians revealed a conservative strain in the department.

The most conspicuous example of the tension between radical historians and the established members of the history department appeared in the case of the colonial historian Staughton Lynd. Lynd was the son of Robert and Helen Lynd, who were the authors of the acclaimed *Middletown*, an innovative sociological study of the community of Muncie, Indiana. As an undergraduate, Lynd was a leader of Students for a Democratic Society and had worked hard for civil rights. A combination of Quaker, Marxist, and pacifist influences, Lynd gained national prominence when denounced the Warren Commission's report on the Kennedy assasination. "We lied about the U-2," he told one audience, "we lied about the Bay of Pigs, and in my judgment we are lying about the Kennedy assassination." It was not long before he decided that United States was lying about Viet Nam, and he became a fiery and unrelenting opponent of American involvement in Southeast Asia.[22]

He was also a gifted historian, tackling complex and controversial topics, such as class conflict in the American Revolution and the intellectual origins of American radicalism. His work attracted national attention, and no less an authority than Edmund Morgan praised his first book, *Anti-Federalism in*

Dutchess County, NY: A Study in Democracy and Class Conflict. When Lynd's *Intellectual Origins of American Radicalism* was published in 1968, it received a full-page review in *Time* magazine, and David Donald wrote that "of all the New Left historians, only Staughton Lynd appears able to combine the techniques of historical scholarship with commitment to social reform."[23]

Lynd was hired at Yale by Morgan in 1964. During his time in the department, Lynd received praise not only for his impressive record of publication, but for his seminars. Some questions about his priorities, however, were raised when he traveled to Hanoi with fellow historian Herbert Aptheker and radical leader Tom Hayden in December, 1965, and scheduled his classes on two successive days so that he would have more time for his political commitments. In early 1967 Lynd delivered an anti-war speech in Ottawa, Canada, which included a blistering attack on the United States government and which was reported in a local newspaper. The American ambassador to Canada was a Yale man, and he sent Yale President Kingman Brewster a copy of the article.[24]

Brewster decided that it was important to find out exactly what Lynd said, although it is not clear what he intended to do after he acquired the information. He asked John Blum, then the chair, to arrange a meeting with Lynd. Blum duly summoned Lynd to his office and asked him to make any corrections in the newspaper's version of his remarks, which he did. An air of tension prevailed on both sides. Lynd believed that the meeting was the first step toward censoring him, although Blum had not threatened any penalty over his remarks.[25]

But, in the meantime, the issue of the Ottawa speech was overtaken by other events. Yale's Provost, Charles Taylor, asked all department chairs to submit detailed projections of their budgets for the next five years. After consulting with a departmental committee and the tenured professors, Blum submitted a recommendation to the provost that stated the department's needs were most urgent in modern Europe, Latin America, ancient Greece, and modern Russia. Since American history was very strong at Yale, the department projected the need for no more than one tenured position in that area. The department's budgetary projections had an ominous ring for junior faculty in American history like Lynd. Lynd believed that the recommendation had been designed specifically to block his promotion, which, deliberately or not, was what happened.[26]

News that Lynd had been denied promotion sparked enough national attention that Morgan and Woodward went to *The New York Times* to defend the department's decision. They contended that it was based entirely upon academic considerations, not Lynd's politics. After Yale's rejection, Lynd had difficulty finding another position. He was recommended for faculty appointments by history departments at several universities in the Chicago area, but, in each case, the recommendation was rejected by the university administration.[27]

A few years later, the Yale department, largely at the urging of Woodward, declined to allow Herbert Aptheker to teach a course at Yale, even though Aptheker, another political radical, was a pioneering scholar in the history of slavery. The denial prompted Jesse Lemisch to write an op-ed piece, "If Howard Cosell can teach at Yale, why can't Herbert Aptheker?" A resolution calling upon the Organization of American Historians to investigate the Aptheker case passed in a mail ballot, but died when Yale cited its policy of refusing to divulge the reasons behind appointments.[28]

To a large extent, the episodes with Lynd and Aptheker reflected changing times. By the mid-1960s there were signs that student unrest, already in view at Berkeley, could be spreading to Yale. In 1965 the Johnson administration widened the war in Viet Nam by approving bombing raids into North Viet Nam. Yale students and faculty responded by forming an ad hoc committee to protest the air strikes and organize a march for peace in downtown New Haven. Other signs of student activism appeared, such as involvement in civil rights activities and protesting the denial of tenure to popular teachers.

Kingman Brewster, who had succeeded the historian A. Whitney Griswold as Yale's president in 1964, found himself under attack on several fronts. Brewster was committed to building the "New Yale," along the lines of the merit-based model, with scholarship as the principal consideration for faculty appointments, and for which the history department believed it stood as a shining example. Brewster also believed that the meritocracy should extend to student admissions. Yale had traditionally given preference to students who had attended elite preparatory schools, those with prominent family backgrounds and, those who were descendants of Yale graduates. Academic distinction traditionally played a partial role in admissions decisions, but Brewster now decided to make it the university's highest priority. His decision meant the admission of fewer of the types Yale had traditionally admitted and more public school students and Jews.[29]

Many alumni were outraged, and they saw the appearance of campus demonstrations as the natural consequence of new admissions policies. "Does Yale wish to produce and foster the kind of educational and moral climate that spawned riots at the University of California?" questioned one alumnus. "By placing all emphasis," he continued, "on scholarship and little on character, discipline, and moral stability this result seems inevitable." Contesting the same policies, a member of the Yale Corporation remarked, "you're talking about Jews and public school graduates as leaders. Look around this table," he said, pointing to the men of wealth and privilege seated there, "these are America's leaders. There are no Jews here. There are no public school graduates here."[30]

The coming of coeducation to traditionally all-male institutions also cast a long shadow over American higher education in the sixties. Yale had traditionally considered its all-male student body an essential part of its mission. In the eyes of most of its powerful alumni and trustees, Yale men were the future leaders of the country, and the university's primary goal should be to cultivate the male intellect and capacity for leadership as well as facilitate friendships and kinship networks between the young gentlemen who would soon be running the world. The presence of women, insisted those who opposed their admission, would distract those young men from fulfilling this purpose. Moreover, they contended, since women would get married and raise children, they would not be as likely as male students to assume positions of responsibility and uphold their duties in public service. The admission of women, then, would arguably take spots away from men, thereby potentially depriving the nation of future leaders. Lurking still deeper beneath the surface, was the fear on the part of many alums, already alarmed by the new admissions policies, that the admission of women would further reduce the number of openings for their sons and grandsons.[31]

Such arguments of course revealed a basic hypocrisy behind all-male institutions. Single-sex universities like Yale believed it was their duty to train tomorrow's leaders, and justified denying admission to women on the grounds that there weren't many women in leadership positions. But such an attitude posed an obvious conundrum. How were women to prove that they belonged in leadership positions when those in power, almost invariably men, would not accept them unless they had graduated from all-male enclaves like Yale? At the same time, coeducation also emerged as an issue in the recruitment of the highest quality male students. By the mid-sixties, a Yale admissions official reported that nearly every student who rejected Yale went to a coeducational school; Yale's monastic atmosphere was not conducive to recruiting.

In the late sixties, after several false starts, including a proposal to admit women by merging Yale with Vassar College, Yale began serious consideration of admitting women directly into Yale College on an equal basis with men. One of the motivations behind Yale's action was its fear that it might be upstaged by Princeton. In September, 1968 a committee at Princeton recommended complete coeducation and the admission of one thousand women. If coeducation was the wave of the future, Yale did not want to be beaten to the punch by Princeton. In November, 1968 the Yale Corporation voted to accept women to Yale College on a full coeducational basis beginning in the fall of 1969.

By the fall of 1969, however, co-education was a secondary issue compared with other weighty matters that were seizing national attention. The earliest protests at Yale were sporadic, and

Yale, like Harvard, prided itself on the fact that the most violent demonstrations had taken place elsewhere. Radical students sometimes appeared to be searching for the right cause, and, in the spring of 1970 they found it in the trial of Bobby Seale. Seale was a drug lord and leader of the Black Panther Party, who was on trial in New Haven for the torture and murder of one of his local followers who he suspected of being a police informant. While many people believed that Seale was probably guilty, others wondered if it was possible for him to receive a fair trial.[32]

The trial became a lightning rod for many disaffected people, and, even though it had nothing directly to do with Yale, the campus soon became a nerve center for radical activity. Indirectly, however, since Yale was an investor in large, presumably racist corporations, and the owner or landlord of many local apartments and businesses, it was perceived by the radicals as complicit in the conspiracy against Seale. Several extremists threatened to shut down the university if Seale was not freed. Their ideas were not the only sign that the times were out of joint. Still others proposed that until Seale was freed one student a day should commit suicide, that Brewster be killed and his children kidnapped, that the library's copies of the Gutenburg Bible be sold, or that New Haven's water supply be sabotaged.

The radical dialogue, however poisonous, did expose the need for more black faculty at Yale and more money for programs dealing with African-American issues. Students also began challenge several aspects of the curriculum, including the long-standing requirement that students take two years of a foreign language. There was even a proposal to eliminate grades. The Yale faculty yielded on several of the proposals, but decided not to eliminate grades entirely, since students would need them to get jobs and admission into graduate and professional schools. In the end it was decided that only failing grades would be eliminated.[33]

Armageddon arrived at Yale in the May Day observance of 1970. May Day was conceived by radical leaders as a pulpit for the expression of all of the various forms of discontent swirling around campus. Numerous radicals, many coming from long distances, prepared to descend on campus. Many of Yale's administrators believed that the situation was so ominous that Yale should simply send the students home, shut down the campus, and enlist as many faculty and staff as possible to protect the buildings and grounds.

Brewster rejected the idea of shutting down the campus, although he did ask the faculty to approve a suspension of ordinary academic expectations in order to give students the option of going home if they chose or to postpone the taking of their final examinations until the fall. The university community then braced for what gave every indication of being a tragedy on an immense scale. Rumors of all kinds circulated through the community. One had the Hell's Angels motorcycle gang gathering outside New Haven, with the intention of using the ensuing chaos to pillage the town. Another rumor being spread had the university renting a fleet of trucks to remove the anticipated corpses.

Fearing the worst, Brewster set up a secret "war room" on the edge of campus where May Day activities could be closely observed. He had summoned many of his friends, including Cyrus Vance, a member of the Yale Corporation, who had been Lyndon Johnson's trouble shooter in emergencies as diverse as the Detroit riots and Viet Nam peace talks, to help him monitor events. Brewster had also asked the New Haven police to be on alert; they in turn called upon the National Guard. The best thing that could happen, most agreed, was rain.

But May Day dawned bright and clear. Like the "Sitzkrieg" in France in 1940, two armies stared across New Haven Green at each other. On the Green and on various college courtyards were thousands of young people, some Yale students, some not, in various states of undress and mind alteration. Lined up around the Green, were the New Haven police, the National Guard, ominous and forbidding, along with several dozen Yale faculty, including John Blum, who had volunteered to be on campus that day to preserve order and protect their buildings, but not exactly sure how they were to do so.

May Day proved anti-climatic. Despite enormous potential for violence and provocation on many levels, the day passed without major incident. Marijuana smoke, obscene language, loud music, and even traces of tear gas regularly wafted through the air, but no serious eruptions of violence occurred, although there were a few minor tragedies. One occurred when George Pierson, by then in his mid-sixties, came to campus, determined to do his part to protect Yale from the forces of unreason. But he unwittingly wandered into a pocket of tear gas without a wet handkerchief to protect his mouth and eyes, and ended up being gassed. But, as the day came to a close, faculty and administrators convened at the president's house and congratulated each other on dodging a bullet.[34]

The History Department was affected in several ways by the difficulties of the late sixties. While there were clear differences of opinion on how the radicals should be handled, the department did not split as bitterly in ideological terms as some other departments did. In retrospect most faculty claimed to have had little trouble with students. Morgan recalled that the students "were a tame group, contemptuous of the value of early American history, but they challenged the sociologists." Jack Hexter considered the students' demands to be nonsense and thought that he survived because he made no concessions to them. On the other hand, Vann Woodward thought the students of sixties were of extremely high intellectual quality, comparable to the post-World War II veterans. Three of his graduate students from that time won Pulitzer Prizes, and he encountered few problems with radicals. "I considered myself a leftist," he recalled, "I could sympathize."[35]

Donald Kagan even offered a course in which the students would write a history of the event. Kagan, a classicist, studied the work of the Greek historian Thucydides, who wrote a famous history of the Peloponnesian War, an event as contentious in its time as the student rebellions were in theirs. Thucydides also established several principles which formed the basis of the modern study of history. Among other things, Thucydides advocated the importance of gathering source materials, carefully evaluating their reliability, constructing a narrative of what actually happened, and using detachment from the event as a basic tool of analysis. The point for Thucydides was to determine fairly what happened before trying to interpret it.

Kagan realized that the students in his seminar trying to understand May Day and the events leading up to it, faced the same problems as Thucycides. The historical record needed to be assembled, and the student historians needed to be able to step back from the events and passions aroused by them, something that would not be easily done. In the end, the students produced a book, *Mayday at Yale*, recounting their findings.[36]

John Blum had a more challenging experience. On the day of a proposed student strike, he found the entrance to his classroom blocked by several large black men. He suggested that they let him in and allow him to begin his lecture. If he said something offensive, they could raise their hands to signal disagreement. He would consider the class disrupted and dismiss it. The black students considered his offer for a moment and decided to let him in. Blum began by telling everyone in the class that they could stop the lecture by raising a hand. He then spoke on the various styles in recent American politics. No one left the lecture hall or raised their hand. His wife, who had attended without his knowledge in order to offer protection if that became necessary, slipped away quietly.[37]

The department's reputation survived the student troubles unchallenged. When Donald Kagan arrived in New Haven as one of the Class of '69, the group of faculty brought to Yale in Howard Lamar's great recruiting triumph, he went to the first meeting of the full professors in the history department and was awed by the constellation of stars seated around him. There were thirty-five full professors, several of them at the top of the entire profession. Looking back, Jack Hexter believed that the department was the best one in which he or anyone else had ever been a part.[38] Others were less impressed. The department still had several alleged "dollar-a-year men," and several others, who, whether they were "dollar-a-year men" or not, simply did not have the scholarly credentials to be in a major history department.

Nevertheless, during the meeting Kagan witnessed an example of how the department had improved itself. The senior faculty were considering candidates for an opening in modern European history, and Hexter rose to discuss the possibilities. For Kagan, what followed was a report, so complete, so fair, so nuanced, that Kagan, even though he had been a faculty member at Penn State and Cornell, had never heard anything like it. Hexter had read the candidates' books, their articles, and reviews of their works, and made shrewd assessments of the strengths and weaknesses of each and what they could bring to the department. It was, in Kagan's eyes, a stunning *tour de force*, and it occurred to him that this was the reason that the department was so distinguished; its members put in the work to make it happen. As Hexter later said, "we look for people who are smarter than we are. If they are, we hire them."[39]

There were, however, some problems. In the fall of 1969, the department had one African American, John Blassingame, and it had one woman, Mary Wright. Moreover, the free spending ways of the Brewster administration were coming to an end. Yale was entering an extended period of financial problems. The physical plant was crumbling after years of neglect; the university's support staff was abysmally underpaid; and a new health care plan would prove to be excessively generous. Budget austerity became a regular feature of life at Yale, and the administration resorted to taking ever larger chunks of the endowment to make ends meet. By the end of his presidency, Brewster had to face the realization that in his zeal to build a rival to Harvard, he had allowed serious financial problems to fester. A few years later, his successor, A. Bartlett Giamatti, ruined his presidency by refusing to give big raises he felt that the university could not afford to the support staff.[40]

One effect of the sixties at Yale was the emergence of women's history as a discipline. Now that there were female students on campus, they wanted courses in women's history. In 1969 a group of female undergraduate students approached Ramsay MacMullen, then the chair, to ask why Yale had no courses in women's history and why one couldn't be offered. MacMullen did not know if any of the regular faculty at that time were willing to teach women's history, so he asked Cynthia Russett, a recent Yale Ph.D., if she would teach a one-semester course in the subject at the undergraduate level. Russett was willing, but soon discovered that one semester on women's history was not nearly enough time to do justice to the subject, and was pleased when she was allowed to expand the course into a year-long survey. Occasionally, she heard whisperings, though never to her face, that women's history was not a real subject; it was only being taught for political reasons.[41]

In 1975 Nancy Cott was hired at Yale with a joint appointment in history and American Studies. Not long after her arrival, she was approached by female graduate students wanting to know if she would be willing to teach a graduate course in American women's history, which she was. Cott later received a grant from the National Endowment for the Humanities to aid the department in incorporating women's history into its courses and curriculum.[42]

At the same time, junior faculty in the department generally faced a dispiriting experience. Like virtually all junior faculty in the history departments of major universities of this time, they existed in an academic twilight zone, trying desperately to meet high standards in research and teach brilliantly, while endlessly worrying about their futures and terrified of making the fatal error that would consign them to the nether world of the unworthy. Strangers in a strange land, junior faculty were judged by mysterious and sometimes shifting standards as well as by people who seemed to inhabit a world other than their own. In the words of one, "in my previous life, I was always one of the brightest people in whatever group I was in. I believed that by hard work I could achieve whatever I wanted, even tenure at Yale. But it was not possible there. When I got to Yale, everyone was just as smart, just as hard working as I was. But we were scrambling for something that was just not there. Yale left me very tired."

The department did have a paternal side. Jonathan Schneer, a junior faculty member at Yale in the late seventies, remembers talking a walk with Henry Turner, the department's specialist in modern Germany. Turner told Schneer frankly that he had absolutely no chance of being tenured, but also told him that when the time came, the department would do everything in its power to help him get a job elsewhere.

One study indicated that between 1970 and 1975, out of 124 assistant professors across the university, only six received tenure. Even though the senior faculty made it clear to the junior ones that their chances of survival were very slim, many, if not most, of the junior faculty persisted in the belief that they were the ones destined to enter the promised land of tenure at Yale.[43]

Junior faculty members were also subjected to stress from several other angles. They were allowed to attend department meetings as long as the subjects were bureaucratic and mundane. But when important matters pertaining to the direction of the department came up, they were asked to leave. When John Merriman came to Yale in 1972 from the University of Michigan, the only moving expense he was allowed was $21 for gas for his drive from Ann Arbor. He received no help in finding a place to live, and spent his first year at Yale living in an unheated beach cottage so poorly constructed that during the winter snow drifted in through cracks in the doorway.[44]

There were occasionally small triumphs for the junior faculty. Not only were the senior faculty much better paid, but they had much lighter teaching loads. In the mid-seventies the junior faculty rebelled, and persuaded the department to equalize teaching loads. And, in the early eighties salaries for the junior faculty began to improve.[45]

As if the academic expectations were not high enough, junior faculty had to navigate through a labyrinth of social minefields. Yale expected its faculty to possess a veneer of social polish befitting a faculty member at an Ivy League university. The "sherry hour," preceding lunch was a test of that polish and a notorious rocky coast against which even the most promising junior faculty ship occasionally foundered. One junior faculty member attended one shortly after John Paul II had been chosen pope. When he appeared for the sherry hour, he was asked what he thought of the choice. Before he could answer, Robert Lopez declared that he planned to pray everyday for the death of the new pope. The junior faculty member was then placed between Scylla and Charybdis. He could agree with Lopez and look like a complete sycophant, or he could argue with him and put his future at Yale at risk. He chose to say nothing.[46]

John Merriman also noticed a clear difference in the way he was treated as a junior faculty member by the senior faculty. With a few exceptions, the department's most illustrious members, including Morgan, Gay, Hexter, Blum, and several others, went out of their way to be cordial. It was, however, the department's lesser lights who were more likely to be aloof.[47]

The difficulty of being a junior faculty member at Yale was particularly pronounced for women. One woman in the early seventies was invited to a dinner for junior faculty. Much against her will, she decided to go. After she got there, no one talked to her. Following a long period of standing alone by herself, a senior faculty member came up to her and said, "to whom do you belong?"[48]

Intellectually, the radicalism of the sixties was perhaps the first indication that time's winged chariot had also begun to catch up to the Yale department. Several of its stars, including Morgan, Woodward, Blum, Hexter, and Robert R. Palmer, belonged to the formidable generation of historians born between 1908 and 1922, sometimes known as the World War II Generation of Historians, whose generational identity was forged primarily through their experiences in the Great Depression and World War II.[49]

At Yale, the members of this generation produced such acclaimed books as Morgan's *The Stamp Act Crisis: Prologue to Revolution*, Woodward's *The Strange Career of Jim Crow*, and, later, Blum's *V was for Victory*. Morgan, Woodward, and Blum also were collaborators on a popular textbook, *The National Experience*, which brought their ideas to a wider public and helped shape the views of at least a generation of college students.[50]

But times and fashion change, the urgency departs. If it was to retain its preeminent position, the Yale history department by the mid-1970s was again in need of change. In this case, however, it was not necessarily change involving simply the hiring of persons who published. The profession itself was changing and change now involved the kinds of history they published. The fiercest winds of change in the historical profession concerned social history. The greatest books of the World War II Generation had usually rewritten traditional narratives of political, intellectual, and diplomatic history by placing them in the context of social and economic change. In the 1950s this approach was regarded as the cutting edge of the discipline. The assumption was that narrative history, and especially political history, remained the touchstone of the historian's art, but that it could not be understood without reference to underlying social and economic changes.

By the 1960s, however, this comfortable paradigm was under assault, as a new generation of historians wished to invert the order. Traditional political and diplomatic history became *passé*, and the social and economic forces shaping these histories took pride of place. At the same time, under the influence of E.P. Thompson's powerful *The Making of the English Working Class*, historians increasingly rejected the study of political and intellectual elites and turned to the study of the industrial working class, and other disadvantaged groups, such as Africans and women.[51]

The historian who perhaps best reflected these changes was Herbert Gutman, who taught at the University of Rochester and later at City University of New York. Highly influenced by Thompson, Gutman studied both the working classes and slaves. In 1971 he published "Work, Labor, and Society in Industrializing America," in which he described workers shaping their own destinies and creating their own cultures, by political engagement and protest, and by utilizing native religious ideas and cultural institutions to resist the tidal forces industrialization. Later, in *The Black Family in Slavery and Freedom, 1750-1925*, Gutman challenged the idea that because the slave family was fragmented it was impossible for slaves to transmit and share a common culture.[52]

The impact of Gutman's work, along with that of several others, such as Eugene Genovese and Christopher Lasch, was immense. First, it continued the shift away from the history of political elites to that of disadvantaged groups. Second, this shift had a distinct political connotation in that it appealed to the new generation of students which had, through the Viet Nam War, become suspicious of elites, and through the civil rights movement, become interested in disadvantaged groups. Third, since the new "history from the bottom up" concerned disadvantaged groups who left few records of their own, it borrowed heavily from other disciplines such as sociology and anthropology and was extremely theoretical in its approach.

Ironically, several of Yale's senior historians had a history of political and social activism. In the 1930s Morgan had been a pacifist, and he considered applying for conscientious objector status at the beginning of World War II; almost all of them had been strong supporters of the civil rights movement, and Vann Woodward's *The Strange Career of Jim Crow* had been proclaimed by Martin Luther King as the movement's bible. Moreover, by the 1980s the department had hired a labor historian with clear working class sympathies in David Montgomery, and had also hired John Blassingame in African American history and Nancy Cott in women's history.

Yet it was not enough. A quiet clash of cultures and generations ensued. A new generation appeared who wished to push the social history envelope much further, both historically and politically. Social history was no longer simply the context for the political and intellectual change; social history was the history that mattered. History could no longer be understood by constructing a narrative combining political events with a social background; it now required theory and interdisciplinary consideration. Symbols, myths, rituals, and linguistic strategies became as important as parliamentary debates. Interest in culture combined with social history to dethrone political history from its place of prominence within the profession. The extent to which the profession had changed may be seen in the comment of the cultural historian

Warren Susman who declared that historians who studied the 1930s would find that the cartoon character "Mickey Mouse might in fact be more important than Franklin Roosevelt."[53]

Yale's senior historians still commanded respect, and, to their credit, most of them realized that the department needed to evolve, to change with the discipline. In fact, several of them were themselves at the frontiers of change. Peter Gay was in the process of transforming himself from the fairly conventional intellectual historian who wrote the prize-winning *The Enlightenment: An Interpretation* to the historian who published suggestive works on Freud and the cultural history of the nineteenth century bourgeoisie. Howard Lamar was in many ways the father of the "new" western history which placed less emphasis on the heroic nature of the westward movement than on its entrepreneurial aspects.[54]

One place in which changing times could be seen was in the increasing student interest in American Studies. Yale's American Studies department had faculty interested in new approaches, such as Allan Trachtenburg, who had written a book on the importance of the Brooklyn Bridge in the mythology of New York City. But several of Yale's senior historians regarded American Studies as a soft department, which lacked the intellectual rigor at the core of the history department. At the same time, while opinions varied, students sometimes found some of the senior professors of the Yale History Department to be aloof and inaccessible. Everyone respected the great Vann Woodward, who had by this time assumed iconic status, but, as a teacher, some students found him inscrutable and almost inert. He said little in his seminars and provided minimal guidance for his dissertation students.[55]

The historian who perhaps best bridged the gap between the old and the new history was David Brion Davis. Davis had arrived at Yale in 1970 after the publication of his first book on slavery, the remarkable *The Problem of Slavery in Western Culture* in which he traced ideas about slavery from ancient times to around 1770. He seemed to have tracked down virtually every significant comment about slavery made by European observers and to have succeeded in imposing coherence on a seemingly intractable mass of material. Davis followed the story through centuries of defenses and rationalizations about slavery to the point where a small, but significant number of Euro-Americans began to denounce slavery as an intolerable evil.[56]

In the sequel, *The Problem of Slavery in the Age of Revolution*, Davis picked up the story of attitudes toward slavery around 1770 and took it through the turbulent period of initial opposition to the slave trade to the beginning of its abolition. As stunning as Davis' first book on slavery was, the second was even more remarkable. The time period covered in *The Problem of Slavery in the Age of Revolution* was considerably smaller, a little more than fifty years as opposed to the two millennia covered in the first book. But it was densely packed with activity related to slavery. First, there was the expansion of the intense humanitarian crusade after 1770 where the morality of slavery was fiercely debated and contested. Second, it was also the age of the great Atlantic Revolutions, such as those in the American colonies, France, and Latin America, whose supporters often claimed to be fighting for the rights of all human beings. Finally, the period from 1770 to 1823 was the time during which the Industrial Revolution created a mass of factory workers who sometimes labored under conditions more oppressive than those of the slaves.

Thus, examining ideas about slavery during the period from 1770 and 1823 required a much more complex and sophisticated book. There was much more to explain, including some seemingly contradictory impulses. Why, for example, could many of the revolutionary leaders who claimed the embrace the doctrine of the universal rights of man, be slave owners themselves? Why also did many of the passionate opponents of slavery care hardly at all for the plight of the industrial poor? And why did factory owners join the campaign against slavery when they often treated their own workers even more wretchedly than slave owners treated their slaves? Davis revealed over and over how the big structures of ideological change were connected to the bigger structures of the state and economic change.

While *The Problem of Slavery in the Age of Revolution* explored many aspects of the emerging abolitionist ethos, the section that proved to be the most controversial was where Davis explored the issue of class interest on the part of the abolitionists. Pursuing this issue was a risky enterprise, since conventional historical methods had long since revealed that the abolitionists came from a vast range of socioeconomic backgrounds.[57]

To find a way to incorporate class interest into his argument, Davis turned to theory, partly as the result of a chance encounter with Eugene Genovese. In 1972-3 Davis took a year's leave at the Stanford Center for the Behavioral Sciences to finish the manuscript for *The Problem of Slavery in the Age of Revolution*. Genovese was also a fellow the Stanford Center that year, and was finishing *Roll, Jordan, Roll*. The result was a mutually beneficial convergence. They read each other's drafts and exchanged ideas, quickly discovering that while they were working on different aspects of slavery, they were working along parallel lines toward Gramscian interpretations. Genovese was exploring the relationship between the masters and the slaves; Davis was studying the motives behind why some people supported abolitionism.[58]

Abolitionism, Davis suggested, in part reflected the hegemonic needs of capitalism and the factory owners, who wished to legitimize factory labor. One way they could accomplish this was to portray it as a system of free labor in contrast with the coercion inherent in slavery and the slave trade. Supporters of industrial labor concluded that whatever the defects of factory labor, factory workers had the freedom to choose where they worked; slaves did not.

The Problem of Slavery in the Age of Revolution was one of the most celebrated books of the decade, winning a National Book Award, the Beveridge Prize of the American Historical Association, and the Bancroft Prize. Perhaps because he was equally comfortable with conventional historical methods and with theory, Davis was also probably the closest thing to a bridge between the older generation of historians and the students who arrived at Yale in the seventies. Books like *Roll, Jordan, Roll*, and *The Problem of*

Slavery in the Age of Revolution, more theoretically grounded, were the wave of the future, and Davis' book was perhaps the first sign that theory had invaded Yale's hallowed halls.

A remarkable group of students grew up around Davis. Coming to Yale in 1975, Edward Ayers noted that the graduate students he admired the most seemed to be advisees of Davis.⁵⁹ People as diverse as Jackson Lears working on late nineteenth century anti-modernism, Sean Wilentz on class formation in New York City in the early 1800s, Christine Stansell on working women in New York City in a similar period, Edward Ayers on criminal punishment in the nineteenth century South, and Elliott Gorn on bare-knuckle prize fighting, all found Davis to be a guiding light.

In some ways Davis' influence was surprising in that he was not a historian of labor or the American South; he was really an intellectual historian. Ayers thought Davis knew everything. Richard Fox thought that Davis was a true intellectual who just happened to be a historian. Lears was impressed by the sensitivity and intelligence that Davis brought to students' written work. For Gorn, Davis encouraged him to take chances, to push a little further. Davis also possessed broad interdisciplinary interests, having published his first book on homicide in American fiction.⁶⁰

Several of Davis' students in the late seventies were in American Studies program rather than history, which was perhaps another sign of changing times. American Studies continued to attract students with historical interests. The things that interested the students of the seventies, race, gender, religion, literature, and working-class and consumer culture begged for interdisciplinary approaches that were seemingly more readily available in American Studies than in history.

The importance of changing times was not lost on the department, and its senior faculty took steps to hire several new faculty who would introduce much of the new social history and theories into the department. In European history, the department hired John Merriman, a student of Charles Tilly at the University of Michigan, who incorporated social history and sociology, and, at about the same time, Robert Harding, a Yale Ph.D. and student of Jack Hexter, who studied the ruling elites of provincial France from an Annales School point of view. The department also hired two junior faculty, Jonathan Schneer in modern Britain and Elizabeth Blackmar in American urban history, who were not only at the cutting edge of their subfields, but who were also members of MARHO, an organization of left-wing historians.

In American history, largely at Davis' urging, there were several exciting appointments. In 1975 Paul Johnson arrived from U.C.L.A., with an exciting dissertation on the impact of the Second Great Awakening in Rochester, New York, which he would revise into *A Shopkeeper's Millennium*. In the same year Richard Wightman Fox was hired from Stanford to teach Yale's first course in social history, and the joint appointment of Jean-Christophe Agnew, another member of MARHO, in history and American Studies provided the department with a scholar deeply versed in the new theoretical approaches to history.[61]

While, among the new appointees, only Agnew would get tenure, the new faculty brought needed energy and direction to the department. Thirty students signed up for Fox's course in social history. Edward Ayers and Elliott Gorn found themselves in an independent reading course with Paul Johnson. Assigned to read Peter Berger's *The Homeless Mind*, Ayers found that Berger's distinction between dignity and honor could serve as the basis for his research on honor and vengeance in the nineteenth-century South. Gorn, who also found Berger's division valuable, remembers the class as the one at Yale where the material was the newest and most stimulating as well as the one where he learned the most.[62]

Other moments signaled changing times. One afternoon Fox and Robert Westbrook, another Yale instructor, were walking past the Sterling Library when they noticed that librarians were discarding old issues of *Life Magazine*. Recognizing that *Life* was a critical source for exploring American culture, they quickly snatched them up.[63]

Students and younger faculty also mentored themselves through reading groups. As graduate students, Christine Stansell and Carol Karlsen organized one for those interested in women's history. Those interested in consumer culture, such as Jackson Lears, Richard Fox, Robert Westbrook, Michael Smith, and Jean Agnew, had their group, which produced a volume of essays, *The Culture of Consumption*, in 1983.[64]

The reading groups sometimes produced interesting mixes. Steven Hahn, studying southern populism with Woodward, found his greatest stimulation from a group of Latin Americanists centered around Emilia da Costa. Hahn was attracted to the Latin Americanists because they discussed in a broad, theoretical sense the things that were of interest to him as a historian of the nineteenth century South: political economy, theories of modernization, and comparative revolution.[65]

By the early 1980s the Yale graduate students of the 1970s in American history began to publish their work, and it overwhelmingly reflected changing times. Sean Wilentz and Christine Stansell produced, respectively, studies of the working class and women in early nineteenth century New York City partly inspired the new labor history of Thompson and Gutman. Jackson Lears published an article on the importance of Gramsci for historians and a book on antimodernist thought. Steven Hahn wrote a book on populism and modernization of the Georgia upcountry. And Elliot Gorn published a groundbreaking article on the significance of backcountry fighting in early America.[66]

The works of these students had several common components. First, they were usually about pre-twentieth century American history. Only a few students at Yale seem to have been studying recent America. And their work was also usually about modernization in some sense, examining those critical points where industrialization or settlement threatened an existing culture. But the subject was usually not the modernizers, but those, workers, women, and the poor, who were feeling the effects of modernization.

They also suggest the emergence of two cultures of history at Yale in the 1970s and early 1980s. The traditional political and diplomatic history that had dominated the profession since the 1950s and was practiced by older members of the history department remained, with many students still choosing to write dissertations on fairly conventional topics. But it was being challenged by a new history, the history of Gutman and Genovese, and of cultures and American Studies.

Thus, the Yale history department appears to have had three distinct phases in the period from about 1940 to 1980. Up to about 1950, it was a very good, but inbred department. In the mid-fifties, largely at the initiative of George Pierson, it undertook a sustained period of reform, including the hiring of Jews, people without a Yale pedigree, and more people to teach in fields outside of Europe and the United States. With the additional endeavors of Howard Lamar, the department had been transformed into a highly professional body with an outstanding national reputation, especially in American history. The department also seems to have survived the tumults of student and radical protest. But by the mid-seventies, the profession was again changing, and the department adapted again, this time to the demands of the new social and cultural history.

---

[1] John Morton Blum, *A Life with History* (Lawrence, Kan., 2004), pp. 136-40.

[2] Palmer, "Interview with Edmund Morgan," December 22, 2003.

[3] Palmer, "Interview with Gordon Craig," January 4, 1996; Norman Cantor, *Inventing the Middle Ages: The Lives, Works, and Ideas of the Great Medievalists of the Twentieth Century* (New York, 1991), p. 402.

[4] Ibid.

[5] Palmer, "Interview with Gaddis Smith," December 16, 2003; Email communication with John Shy, July 3, 2004.

[6] Blum, *Life with History*, pp. 155-6; Palmer, "Interview with J. H. Hexter," December 19, 1995; Palmer, "Interview with John Merriman," June 29, 2005.

[7] Palmer, "Interview with David Cronon," January 27, 2005.

[8] Blum, *Life with History*, pp. 156-7.

[9] Alvin Kernan, *In Plato's Cave* (New Haven and London, 1999), p. 86.

[10] Blum, *Life with History*, p. 157.

[11] Palmer, Interview with Jonathan Spence," July 6, 2005.

[12] Palmer, "Interview with Spence," July 6, 2005.

[13] Courtwright, "Fifty Years of American Colonial History: An Interview with Edmund S. Morgan," *William and Mary Quarterly*, 3rd Ser., 44(1987): 336-69; J.H. Hexter, "Call Me Ishmael; Or, a Rose by Any Other Name," *American Scholar* (Summer, 1983): 191-216.

[14] William Palmer, *Engagement with the Past: The Lives and Works of the World War II Generation of Historians* (Lexington, 2001), p. 125.

[15] Blum, *Life with History*, p. 185; Palmer, "Interview with Howard Lamar," January 8, 2004.

[16] Hexter, "Call Me Ishmael," p. 192; Palmer, "Interview with Lamar," January 8, 2004.

[17] Blum, *Life with History*, p. 139.

[18] For the information about Blum's early career at Yale in the next few paragraphs, see Blum, *Life with History*, pp. 140-50.

[19] Ibid., pp. 180-1; Palmer, "Interview with Spence." In his memoirs, Blum writes that Spence had one book at the time his tenure came up, but in my interview with him, Spence recalled that he had two. The problem was that only the first one was based on Chinese sources.

[20] Ibid., pp. 185-6.

[21] Palmer, "Interview with Jesse Lemisch," December 15, 2004; On the problems faced by radical historians across the profession, see Lemisch, *On Active Service in War and Peace: Politics and Ideology in the American Historical Profession* (Toronto, 1975).

[22] Geoffrey Kabbaservice, *The Guardians: Kingman Brewster, His Circle, and the Rise of the Liberal Establishment* (New York, 2004), p. 235.

[23] Jon Wiener, "Radical Historians and the Crisis in American History, 1959-1980," *Journal of American History* 72, 2 (September, 1989), p. 417; Blum, *Life with History*, p. 183.

[24] Blum, *Life with History*, p. 183.

[25] Ibid.

[26] Ibid.

27 Palmer, *Engagement with the Past*, p. 128; Wiener, "Radical Historians and the Crisis," p. 418; *New York Times*, June 7, 1968.

28 Jesse Lemisch, "If Howard Cosell Can Teach at Yale, Why Can't Herbert Aptheker," *Radical History Review*, 3(Spring, 1976), pp. 46-8; Palmer, *Engagement with the Past*, p. 126; Kenneth Stampp, who was president of OAH when this issue emerged, has stated that the reason why Woodward opposed allowing Aptheker to teach at Yale was that Woodward was disappointed in the way that Aptheker was editing the papers of W.E.B. DuBois. See Ann Lage, "Historian of Slavery, the Civil War, and Reconstruction: An Interview with Kenneth Stampp," (Bancroft Library, University of California at Berkeley, Oral History Collection, 1996), p. 252.

29 Kabbaservice, *The Guardians*, pp. 259-71.

30 Ibid., p. 259.

31 Ibid., pp. 365-69.

32 Basic narratives of May Day and the events leading up to it may be found in Kabbaservice, *The Guardians*, pp. 402-12; and Kernan, *In Plato's Cave*, pp. 158-78.

33 Kernan, *In Plato's Cave*, p. 173.

34 Blum, *Life With History*, p. 224.

35 Palmer, *Engagement with the Past*, pp. 162-3.

36 Palmer, "Interview with Donald Kagan," June 16, 2005; John Taft, *Mayday at Yale: A Case Study in Student Radicalism* (Boulder, 1976).

37 Blum, *Life With History*, p. 222.

38 Palmer, "Interview with Kagan;" Palmer, "Interview with Hexter."

39 Palmer, "Interview with Kagan."

40 Kernan, *In Plato's Cave*, p. 270.

41 Palmer, "Interview with Cynthia Russett, June 23, 2005"

42 Palmer, "Interview with Nancy Cott," July 4, 2005.

43 Palmer, "Interview with Hexter"; Palmer, "Interview with Merriman," June 27, 2005; Palmer, "Interview with Jonathan Schneer," July, 6, 2005. It should also be noted that not everyone found their experience as a junior faculty member at Yale to be depressing. Richard Fox, a junior member of the department in the late seventies, had a wonderful time at Yale. The students were excellent, the department was intellectually

stimulating, and the senior faculty went out of their way to be friendly to him. Palmer, "Interview with Richard Fox," July 18, 2005.

44 Palmer, "Interview with Merriman."

45 Palmer, "Interview with Merriman;" Palmer, "Interview with Cott."

46 Ibid.

47 Ibid.

48 Ibid.

49 See Palmer, *Engagement with the Past*, esp. pp. 298-305, for a discussion of the intellectual outlook and achievements of this group.

50 Edmund S. Morgan and Helen M. Morgan, *The Stamp Act Crisis: Prologue to Revolution* (Chapel Hill, N.C., 1953); C. Vann Woodward, *The Strange Career of Jim Crow*; John Morton Blum, *V was for Victory* (New York, 1976).

51 E.P. Thompson, *The Making of the English Working Class* (New York, 1963).

52 Herbert Gutman, *The Black Family in Slavery and Freedom, 1725-1925* (New York, 1976); Idem., "Work, Labor and Industrial Culture," in his *Work, Culture, and Society: Essays in American Working-Class and Social History* (New York, 1971).

53 Warren Susman, *Culture as History* (New York, 1973), p. 103; for a broader discussion of how cultural history evolved, see Lynn Hunt, ed., *The New Cultural History* (Berkeley, 1989), esp., pp. 1-22.

54 Peter Gay, *The Bourgeois Experience: The Education of the Senses* (Oxford, 1985). The influence of Lamar is acknowledged by Patricia Nelson Limerick, the most famous of the "new" western historians and one of Lamar's students, in her classic work, *The Legacy of Conquest: The Unbroken Past* (New York, 1987), p. 10. Limerick also acknowledged the importance of C. Vann Woodward in her work, though, interestingly, in contrast to her emphasis on the continuity of western history, Woodward usually stressed the "discontinuity" of southern history.

It is also worth noting that John Blassingame's *The Slave Community: Life in the Antebellum South* (New Haven, 1972) is a work written in the spirit of the works of Gutman and Genovese.

55 Palmer, "Interview with Steven Hahn," December 15, 2003.

56 David Brion Davis, *The Problem of Slavery in the Age of Revolution* (New York, 1975).

⁵⁷ For an engaging discussion of some of the issues raised in *The Problem of Slavery in the Age of Revolution*, see Thomas Bender, ed., *The Anti-Slavery Debate: Capitalism and Abolitionism as a Problem in Historical Interpretation* (Berkeley, 1992).

⁵⁸ Palmer, "Interview with David Davis," February 13, 2004;

⁵⁹ Edward Ayers, *What Caused the Civil War? Reflections on the South and Southern History* (New York, 2005), p. 28.

⁶⁰ Palmer, "Interview with Edward Ayers," February 21, 2002; Idem., "Interview with Elliott Gorn," March 23, 2002; Idem., "Interview with Richard Fox," March 20, 2002.

⁶¹ Paul Johnson, *A Shopkeeper's Millenium: Society and Revivals in Rochester, New York, 1815–1837* (New York, 1978); Palmer, "Interview with Richard Fox;" Jean-Christophe Agnew, *Worlds Apart: The Market and the Theatre in Anglo-American Thought, 1550–1750* (Cambridge, 1986).

⁶² Palmer, "Interview with Edward Ayers."

⁶³ Palmer, "Interview with Robert Westbrook," March 13, 2002.

⁶⁴ Jackson Lears and Richard Wightman Fox, eds., *The Culture of Consumption: Critical Essays in American History, 1880–1980* (New York, 1983).

⁶⁵ Palmer, "Interview with Steven Hahn," December 15, 2003.

⁶⁶ Sean Wilentz, *Chants Democratic: New York City and the Rise of the American Working Class, 1788–1850* (New York, 1984); Christine Stansell, *City of Women: Sex and Class in New York, 1789–1850* (Urbana, Ill., 1983); T.J. Jackson Lears, *No Place of Grace: Anti-Modernism and the Transformation of American Culture, 1880-1920* (New York, 1983); Idem., "The Concept of Cultural Hegemony: Problems and Possibilities," *American Historical Review* 90. 3(June, 1985): 567-93; Elliott Gorn, "Gouge and Bite, Pull Hair and Scratch: The Social Significance of Fighting in the Southern Backcountry," *American Historical Review* 90, 1(February, 1985): 18–43; Steven Hahn, *The Roots of Southern Populism: Yeoman Farmers and the Transformation of the Georgia Upcountry, 1850–1890* (New York, 1983).

Chapter Four

Princeton: Teaching the Young Gentlemen

Before World War II, Princeton was mainly a gentleman's college, Presbyterian and southern in outlook, known for its selective dining clubs, enthusiasm for sports, and the epicurean lifestyles of its young gentlemen. Most of its academic departments were staffed with faculty who embodied the ideal of the gentleman teacher, devoted to undergraduate teaching and students, but, with a few striking exceptions, professed little scholarly vocation or interest in graduate education.

Undergraduate teaching was the heart and soul of Princeton and the history department in the thirties, centering on what was known as the "preceptorial" system. An attempt to promote critical thinking and closer interaction between faculty and students, the preceptorial system was introduced by Woodrow Wilson, president of Princeton from 1902 to 1910. Dissatisfied with the conventional system of lecture and recitation, Wilson proposed that students would meet in small groups with one faculty member, called a "preceptor," who would assign readings and lead discussions based on them.

Wilson quickly hired a number of extraordinary teachers, including Christian Gauss in literature and C.H. McIlwain in history, to serve as preceptors. Wilson's original concept called for the preceptor to supervise the reading and discussion for his group of students for all their courses. This concept soon proved to be impractical, since it compelled preceptors to undertake a staggering amount of reading. Thus, preceptorial instruction eventually became closely attached to specific courses.

In the history department most courses were large lecture courses, consisting of two lectures a week, delivered by the senior faculty member responsible for the course. To supplement the lectures, once a week the students were divided into small groups for preceptorials. The preceptorials were usually taught individually by the senior faculty member teaching the course and by the junior faculty members assigned to him. Senior faculty sometimes taught them, too, in areas where they had an interest or in heavily enrolled courses in which more preceptors were needed. By the thirties, preceptorials had also emerged as the testing ground for the junior faculty to demonstrate their mettle as undergraduate teachers. Junior faculty could be assigned to any course for which the department needed them, so that they often had to scramble to stay ahead of the students if they were assigned to areas in which they had little preparation. Only after several successful terms, even years, as a preceptor would junior faculty members be allowed to teach their own courses. The uncertainty and length of time spent precepting occasionally led to some tensions between junior and senior faculty. "You'll have to die before I get my own course," a frustrated instructor once shouted at a senior faculty member.[1]

But, during the same period, amidst its traditions and enthusiasm for sports, Princeton was also taking steps to improve its academic standing, and a more rigorous institution was emerging. The history department was one of many, including physics, mathematics, and art history, which were on the verge of establishing national reputations.

At the beginning of the thirties, however, the history department retained both an amateurish and professional dimension. The professional wing of the department included such scholars as T.J. Wertenbaker, the author of several important works on colonial Virginia, and the eminent medievalist Dana C. Munro, an authority on the Crusades. More representative of the Princeton history faculty, however, was Walter "Buzzer" Hall, a teacher of legendary dramatic gifts, but no scholar. One member of the department, the medieval historian Lynn White, remarked that the Princeton history faculty of the 1930s were the most intellectually conservative group he had ever encountered, with no use for novelties like anthropology or cultural geography.[2]

Wertenbaker, Dana G. Munro, (son of the distinguished medievalist), and Raymond Sontag, department chairs in the thirties and early forties, took several important steps to raise the level of professionalism in the department. They succeeded in recruiting an impressive group of young faculty who formed the department's core for several decades. These faculty included Harris "Jinks" Harbison, Robert R. Palmer, Cyril Black, Eric Goldman, and Joseph Strayer.

The new faculty were a mixture of outsiders and those who held Princeton degrees. While Strayer and Harbison were Princeton undergraduates, the others were not. Palmer's degrees were from Chicago and Cornell; Black's were from Duke and Harvard, and Goldman's were from Johns Hopkins. More importantly, in addition to embracing the ideal of being gentleman teachers, most of the faculty hired in the thirties aspired to be serious scholars.

The key figure in this group was Joseph Strayer, whose experience at Princeton eventually spanned the better part of five decades. After finishing his undergraduate degree at Princeton in 1925, Strayer went to Harvard to study medieval history with Charles Homer Haskins, at the time the premier American medievalist. Under Haskins, Strayer learned the rudiments of studying the administrative records of the early Norman rulers of England and France, and to share Haskins' admiration for the order and rationality behind the construction of the medieval state. During the twelfth and thirteenth centuries, governments in England and France emerged from their beginnings in loose and transitory confederations of Germanic tribes operating largely on the basis of arbitrary authority to highly evolved and efficient institutions. Under the leadership of able kings, leading churchmen, and others educated at the newly created universities, governments established rule of law as the basis for their authority. Government itself asserted its role as protector of peace and stability rather than acting simply as a body that seized their subjects' property in the form of taxation and compelled them to risk their lives in wars in which they had little at stake.[3]

Early in his career, Strayer followed Haskins' lead in developing his research interests. His dissertation, *The Administration of Normandy under Saint Louis*, published by the Medieval Academy of America, demonstrated his mastery of the administrative records of medieval French kingship. Most of his later work, including his famous synthesis, *The Origins of the Modern State*, was an extension of his work in these records.

Strayer received his Ph.D. in 1930. After a year of teaching at the Stevens Institute of Technology in Hoboken, New Jersey, he returned to Princeton as an instructor. For a while, he worked in the shadow of Lynn White, who was beginning his innovative studies on such matters as the importance of the invention of the stirrup. White, however, departed for Stanford in 1937, leaving Strayer as the senior medievalist. Strayer soon emerged as a dedicated teacher and one of the department's most productive scholars. In 1971 his achievements were recognized when he was elected president of the American Historical Association, sharing the honor with David M. Potter.

But Strayer's greatest contribution to the department was administrative, and he emerged as a figure comparable to George Pierson at Yale. By the skillful recruitment of new faculty, Strayer advanced the department beyond one that was simply improving its level of professionalism to one that commanded much more respect, especially in European history. Like Pierson, he usually consulted with the senior faculty, but, for the most part, he was the driving force behind most appointments.

With a few exceptions, such as the hiring of Frank Craven in American Colonial History in the early fifties, Strayer preferred to make most of the department's appointments at the junior level. This was in part because at Princeton, the appointment of an instructor or an assistant professor was within the chair's authority and need not receive the approval of the Dean of the Faculty or pass through a university appointments committee as it did for appointments at the higher ranks. For Strayer, the criteria for appointment included the promise of excellence in both teaching and research.

Under the rules of the time, when faculty joined the department at the instructor level, they were given a four-year contract. After three years, they were either promoted to assistant professor or given a terminal year. At the assistant professor level, the faculty member was normally given two three-year appointments at the end of which the faculty member was either promoted to tenure as an associate professor or given a terminal year. This system had advantages and disadvantages. On one hand, it allowed Princeton, like most other universities at the time, to delay having to make tenure commitments to younger faculty, since it could postpone a final decision for nine years. On the other hand, it gave faculty nine years to prove their worth. In the 1960s, when the instructor rank became reserved those who had not finished their Ph.D.s, it had a discernible effect on those who held the Ph.D. and were appointed as assistant professors. The change in effect reduced the period of time before a tenure decision had to be reached to six years, forcing a quicker commitment, but greatly increasing the pressure on junior faculty.

In making appointments, Strayer usually consulted the various "old boy" networks through which most elite universities operated at the time. Strayer had received his Ph.D. from Harvard, and he regularly solicited advice about promising faculty from the students and faculty he had known there, particularly Harvard's distinguished modern Europeanist William Langer. Langer was intimately connected to several of the key academic pipelines of the post-war era. First, he could easily direct Harvard's best students to Princeton as well as consulting Harvard Ph.D.s teaching at other institutions about who their best colleagues and students were.

And, second, during World War II, Langer had been asked by the State Department to recruit people for service as intelligence officers in the Office of Strategic Services, the forerunner of the C.I.A. He hired many historians, usually with Ivy League Ph.D.s for the O.S.S., including Gordon Craig, H. Stuart Hughes, and Carl Schorske, so that in the years immediately after the end of the war, no one knew more than Langer about whom the rising stars in European history were.

Strayer's later career has some parallels with Langer's. Like Langer, Strayer was committed to the ideal of government service and, in addition to his Princeton duties, he often served the C.I.A. as a consultant. During the fifties he was frequently summoned to Washington during times of international crisis. At first glance, medievalists might seem an odd choice to offer advice on contemporary crises, but Allen Dulles, director of the C.I.A. in the fifties and a Princeton undergraduate, believed that medievalists, like intelligence officers, were trained to make judgments on the basis of the thinnest evidence. When Norman Cantor, one of Strayer's graduate students, received a late night phone call asking him to take Strayer's lectures and preceptorials for the next day, he could be almost certain that somewhere in the world at that moment there was a serious crisis.[4]

In the years immediately after World War II, Strayer was instrumental in recruiting a second wave of gifted faculty who elevated the department's reputation. These faculty included Gordon Craig, Jerome Blum, Frank Craven, Theodor Mommsen, Stanley Stein, and Charles Gillispie. In the manner of Palmer, Harbison, and the group recruited shortly before World War II, they were expected to excel in the classroom. But they were also something different. With a few exceptions, they were part of the World War II generation, the generation that entered college during the Great Depression and had their education or early academic careers interrupted by World War II. Again, with exceptions, most of them had served in the war in some capacity, and they were serious professionals, some with families, eager to make up for lost time.

Gordon Craig's experience at Princeton is instructive. Craig was a Princeton undergraduate and Rhodes Scholar in the early 1930s, who, largely inspired by the teaching of Raymond Sontag, also received a Ph.D. from Princeton in 1941. Two years earlier, he began teaching at Yale, where he found the department stratified and the chair dictatorial. He was one of the faculty fired in 1940 when Yale officials, believing that American involvement in World War II was imminent, feared that enrollment would decline. Strayer invited Craig back to Princeton in 1941, but the war quickly intervened.

After service in the O.S.S. and in the Pacific, Craig returned to Princeton as an instructor in 1946. From his point of view, Princeton was the promised land. There was less hierarchy and stuffiness, and Strayer treated Craig with more respect than he had been accustomed to receiving as a junior faculty member at Yale. Under Strayer's direction Craig began to develop a reputation as an outstanding teacher and to lay the groundwork for his research on the development of the Prussian Army.[5]

Charles Gillispie was another young faculty member and war veteran who prospered under Strayer's leadership. As a teacher, he found the preceptorial system to be intellectually demanding, but ultimately rewarding. Since junior faculty at that time could find themselves teaching anything, Gillispie learned a lot of history on the run. Perhaps the most formative intellectual experience of his early years at Princeton was serving as R.R. Palmer's preceptor in Palmer's French Revolution course. Palmer was not one of Princeton's legendary classroom spellbinders, and in fact disliked undergraduate teaching. But his course struck Gillispie as the best undergraduate course, including any of his own, in which he ever participated, because it engaged the study of history at its deepest level.

The experience in Palmer's course also helped persuade Gillispie to change his area of research. He had been trained in English history, but while precepting for Palmer, acquired an interest in the relationship between science and political revolution in France. Was it coincidental that French scientists were challenging traditional approaches to science at the same time that others were challenging long established features of French government and society? These kinds of questions engaged Gillispie for the rest of his scholarly career, especially in his *Science and Polity in France: The End of the Old Regime*.[6]

As his interest in the history of science developed, Gillispie experienced freedom at Princeton that he might not have found elsewhere. Gillispie, who was an undergraduate chemistry major at Wesleyan, was able to change the emphasis of his teaching and research to the history of science and build up a program at Princeton in that area. In 1963 Gillispie brought Thomas Kuhn, the author of *The Structure of Scientific Revolutions*, one of the most influential historical works ever written, to Princeton. Unlike many programs in the history of science, the one started by Gillispie remained part of the history department. Today, it consists of five full-time faculty, and has conferred over fifty Ph.D.s in the history of science.

The teaching of non-western areas was another mark of a progressive department, and here the record of Princeton history department at this time was generally good. On one hand, in the fifties, history at Princeton meant for the most part the history of Europe from the Middle Ages to the present and the history of the United States. The department's coverage of these areas was superb, with the presence of formidable scholars such as Palmer and Strayer as well as dazzling lecturers like Craig and Goldman.

At the same time, the department was also making some progress in developing areas outside of the western tradition. By the early fifties the department had faculty offering courses in both Chinese and Japanese history. In Latin America, Dana G. Munro, after serving as department chair from 1936 to 1939, also served as director of the Woodrow Wilson School of Public and International Affairs from 1939 to 1958, and offered courses in Latin American history. Munro's work was continued by Stanley Stein, as a full-time faculty member in the history department, after Stein's arrival at Princeton in 1953.

For fields outside the western canon since the Middle Ages, the department utilized other resources. Ancient history was taught by the Classics Department. The existence of the Department of Oriental Studies, which included faculty with specializations in East Asia and the Middle East, meant that courses in these areas were already offered at Princeton. The History Department eventually benefited from a series of joint appointments, with Marius Jansen in Japanese history as one example, by which the history department taught the modern aspects of East Asia and the Near East, while faculty in Oriental Studies covered earlier periods. Eventually, feuds between the faculty in Oriental Studies, led to its division into two departments, East Asian Studies and Near Eastern Studies.

Moreover, during the 1960s, Cyril Black, the department's Russian specialist, played a key role in developing Princeton's curriculum in non-western areas. Black began his career at Princeton in 1939, and offered the department's first course in Russian history in 1946, which was, at least in part, a non-western offering. During a career at Princeton that spanned nearly fifty years, Black supervised thirty-five Ph.D. dissertations. In 1958 he served as a member of the United States delegation sent to observe elections in the Soviet Union, and his expertise was frequently sought by such groups as the United Nations, the C.I.A., and the Council on Foreign Relations. At Princeton he served as chair of Princeton's Committee on Foreign and International Relations from 1961 to 1968, and was instrumental in raising money and recruiting faculty for programs in Russian, East Asian, Near Eastern, and Latin American studies. This was by no means an easy task. Dealing with the frequently contentious faculty in these areas required diplomacy and good humor, gifts which Black possessed in abundance.[7]

Outside the academic sphere, many of the faculty of the fifties found the history department socially as well as professionally congenial. There were frequent family get-togethers and dinner parties, often enlivened by spirited charades games. And, several faculty, including Craig, Strayer, Craven, Jerome Blum, and Julian

Boyd, the editor of Thomas Jefferson's papers, were members of a Thursday night poker club that met at Elmer Beller's house.[8]

In many respects the 1950s was a golden age for the Princeton history department. Strayer had enjoyed extraordinary success in raising the reputation and level of professionalism in the department. The post-war students, especially World War II veterans returning to college after military service, were excellent, and the department was graced with many exceptional teachers, such as Craig, Goldman, Craven, and Harbison, several of whom lectured to standing room audiences. History was an increasingly attractive major. By the late fifties, history had more majors than any other Princeton department. Even the artist Frank Stella was a history major.

The department's reputation was also enhanced by the presence of two major collections of papers at Princeton. The first of these was the papers of Thomas Jefferson, whose editing commenced in 1943 as part of the observance of Jefferson's 200th birthday. Locating the project in Princeton occurred mainly through the efforts of Julian P. Boyd, University Librarian and later Professor of History, who was a member of the Jefferson Bicentennial Commission and the first editor of the papers. The archive included approximately 18,000 letters written by Jefferson and 25,000 written to him. The first volume of Jefferson papers appeared in 1950, and, by 1974 nineteen volumes had been published to wide critical acclaim.

Princeton also housed the papers of Woodrow Wilson, the twenty-eighth president of the United States and thirteenth president of Princeton. The decision to begin editing the Wilson Papers and to house them at Princeton was part of the commemoration of Wilson's one-hundredth birthday in 1956. Arthur Link, the author of an excellent, multi-volume biography of Wilson, and a former member of the Princeton history faculty then teaching at Northwestern, was appointed editor of the papers in 1958 and Professor of History in 1959. Under Link's direction, the Wilson Papers set exacting and extraordinary standards for editing. No detail was too small to be overlooked or cross-checked. "Our tolerance for error is zero," Link declared.

Link's achievement with the Wilson Papers was staggering by any standard. Between 1966 and 1994, under Link's editorship, sixty-nine volumes of *The Papers of Woodrow Wilson* were published. This achievement is even more remarkable when it is remembered that for all but the first few years of his editorship, Link suffered from several serious health problems, especially debilitating back pain. As Robert R. Palmer remarked, Link "wasn't human. He must have had God on his side."[9]

By the standards of the time, then, Princeton was highly evolved in professional terms and in some respects ahead of other elite schools. If the criteria for modernization include hiring faculty without a Princeton connection, a shift toward research and graduate education, and coverage of fields beyond Western Europe, the department receives high marks in several of these areas.

As we have seen, the group hired in the thirties contained a mixture of persons with Princeton degrees and outsiders. Of the group recruited after World War II, most of them, including Blum, Mommsen, Gillispie, and Craven, had no prior connection with Princeton. In the sixties, the department hired and tenured several young faculty with Princeton Ph.Ds., including John Shy and Jerrold Seigel. But most of its significant appointments, such as Martin Duberman, David Donald, David Bien, Raymond Grew, Robert Tignor, James McPherson, James Banner, Sheldon Hackney, Theodore K. Rabb, and Lawrence Stone, were outsiders.

The department was also from an early stage open to the hiring of Jews, another important component of modernization. In the early 1950s there were three Jews on the Princeton history faculty, Blum, Goldman, and Beller. While that might not seem like a high percentage for a department of about twenty members, it must be seen in context. In the 1950s the Princeton English department did not have any Jews, and the Yale history department had only one, Robert S. Lopez, before John Morton Blum's appointment in 1957. Anti-Semitism was a recurring fact of American academic life, but it was possible for Jews to see the Princeton history department as a place of shelter. Before coming to Princeton, Eric Goldman had not been renewed as a faculty member at Johns Hopkins in 1941, even though he had an impressive record as a student there. His chair informed him that he had been terminated because the president of Hopkins did not want Jews on the faculty.[10]

At the same time Princeton managed the transition from a department dedicated to undergraduate teaching to one that balanced dedication to undergraduate teaching with commitment to research and graduate education more smoothly than most. Undergraduate teaching remained paramount in the department's value system, but by the 1960s only a few faculty were not engaged in research. Much of that research was quite distinguished. The first volume of Palmer's *The Age of Democratic Revolution*, published in 1959, received the Bancroft Prize.

To some, however, there was a dark side. Strayer embodied the paternalist values by which most American colleges and universities operated in the fifties. Such schools were run by men raised and indoctrinated in the conviction that there was an intellectual and social elite, to which they belonged by virtue of their education. This elite believed that it was entitled to make most decisions on academic matters by themselves or in consultation with a small group of others of similar experience and wisdom.[11]

Strayer embodied both the virtues and defects of this system. His record of service is remarkable. He was chair from 1942 to 1962, the longest serving chair in terms of consecutive service in the department's history at that point. Jerome Blum once lamented that Strayer's reputation as a medieval historian, while estimable, suffered because in the prime of his career he devoted so much of his time to building the department and government service. In addition to his time-consuming administrative duties and trips to Washington, he was also active in community affairs, for many years serving on the Princeton Borough Council. Strayer also enjoyed the trust of J. Douglas Brown, the Dean of Faculty at Princeton for many years and a man of similar temperament and conviction.[12]

On the other hand, Strayer generally ran the department in the style of a medieval fiefdom. Like the feudal lords who were the subject of his research, Strayer guarded his turf carefully, rarely taking leave, perhaps in the fear that a palace coup might take place. By the standards of the time, he was probably a fairly democratic chair, if by democracy one meant consulting with certain senior professors and, in some cases, favored younger faculty. Candidates for faculty positions were rarely interviewed; they were identified with phone calls to friends and to Princeton Ph.D.s teaching elsewhere and subject to careful background checks.

When Raymond Grew, a Harvard Ph.D. then teaching at Brandeis, received a letter from Strayer offering him a job in 1958, he was unaware that the job existed or that the department was interested in him. No job notice was ever posted; no interview at A.H.A. or on campus ever took place. One morning the letter from Strayer simply arrived, and Grew had a job at Princeton. The next fall, when he came to campus, Strayer welcomed him to the department and informed him that the department had really wanted to hire him the year before, another fact of which Grew was unaware.[13]

Moreover, some believed that Strayer and several of the faculty with whom he either rose through the ranks or hired himself, including Craven, Palmer, and Harbison, formed an Old Guard that exercised an inordinate amount of control over departmental business. Their power was maintained, at least for a brief period, after Strayer stepped down as chair, when Jerome Blum, his carefully groomed successor, assumed his position as chair. Strayer, however, could not control everything. Despite his support for his pupil, Norman Cantor, Cantor did not get tenure in the Princeton history department.

Junior faculty existed in another world. On one hand they were joining a department that enjoyed a reputation as a place where expectations for tenure and promotion were high, but not wildly unrealistic. On the other hand, the department was hierarchical and junior faculty were low in the pecking order. There were numerous reminders of status. Department mailboxes, for example, were not arranged in alphabetical order; they were arranged by rank and length of service, with the new instructors and assistant professors at the bottom. And there were not enough mailboxes for the all the faculty. Junior faculty who did not have their own mailboxes found their mail tossed on a side table. Even department telephone numbers were listed by seniority. Strayer also preferred that junior faculty say little at departmental meetings and expected them to accept whatever preceptorial assignments they were given without complaint, often assigning junior faculty to subjects in which they had little knowledge to test their dedication to teaching and departmental loyalty.[14] New faculty were also well-advised not to run afoul of Elizabeth Darcy, the formidable departmental secretary. A spinster whose life revolved around the history department, she knew Strayer and what he wanted extremely well.

Junior and senior faculty were also expected to spend considerable time in their offices to be available to students as well as to live in Princeton and participate in the life of the community. Martin Duberman sent a minor shock wave through the department when he announced that he intended to take an apartment in Manhattan and come into Princeton only to teach his courses.[15]

Junior faculty were also subjected to a variety of informal tests. If they were asked to give a lecture in a course for which they were precepting, many of the senior faculty often attended. While teaching and scholarship remained the principal criteria for advancement, some of the tests, by no means unique to Princeton, were more like admission tests for a country club than for tenure or promotion at a major university. If junior faculty were invited to a dinner party with the senior faculty and their wives, it was a test not only for them but for their wives, with the opinion of certain senior faculty wives mattering as much as that of some of the faculty. Invitation to the poker game could be another critical test. Norman Cantor believes that the first indication that he was not destined to enter the high church of the Princeton history department came when, after he was invited to the poker game, it was revealed that he didn't know how to play.[16]

While teaching and scholarship were the prime considerations in hiring, it is clear from the various social tests that sociability remained an important consideration. In the words of one faculty member from the time, "Princeton wished to invest in people." Often the candidate was more important than the field. In the early sixties, when the department was debating whether to make an appointment in African history or in another field, one senior member of the department suggested that the real question was whether or not they wished to hire Robert Tignor, an African historian who had been an instructor for several years, which, it turned out, they did. Expectations of sociability extended to wives, who, during this time, rarely worked outside the home, and who were expected to entertain and volunteer in various community activities.

To be a junior faculty member in the fifties and sixties at Princeton, as in almost any other elite department, was a stimulating, but unsettling experience. Beginning instructors knew they were members of one of the world's finest departments, but that they would be expected to dedicate themselves to teaching and students, find time for research, and would have only a brief period to prove themselves. They also knew that the odds were against their receiving tenure, though in the sixties, many, including John Shy, David Bien, James McPherson, Robert Tignor, Jerrold Seigel, and several others succeeded in capturing the golden fleece. But it was also unsettling that during the process the senior faculty, to avoid the taint of favoritism, would generally remain detached and that it would be considered bad form to cultivate them. Jerome Blum, in particular, was regarded as distant and aloof by several of the younger faculty in the sixties.

Some faculty found the department's hierarchical priorities and social scrutiny to be excessive and a bit unnerving. Martin Duberman recalls a black tie dinner party where afterward the men retired to the library for cigars and liqueurs, leaving the women to less serious matters.[17] Others, however, scarcely noticed the tensions that could arise, and some even found it a reassuring part of the department's paternalism that they were immediately welcomed into a regular cycle of social events.

Graduate education was another matter. From the time of its creation, Princeton's Graduate College held an ambiguous place in the university. Not only did the aims of graduate education clash with Princeton's traditional emphasis on undergraduate teaching, but the Graduate College was founded in the aftermath of a bitter fight over where the building to house the new college should be located. Woodrow Wilson, president of the university at the time, wanted it located in the center of campus where graduates and undergraduates could interact, while Andrew Fleming West, the first dean of the Graduate College, insisted that it be separate from the rest of the university, both physically and academically. West eventually won, and a handsome, Gothic building was eventually erected overlooking the university's golf course, far from the undergraduates.[18]

Graduate study in history during the fifties retained some of this ambivalence. Graduate teaching was not a high institutional priority and the department's graduate program was small and highly selective. In the 1950s Princeton faculty were not paid to teach graduate students; they did it in addition to their regular teaching load. Oddly, as carefully as Princeton monitored the progress of young faculty in the undergraduate courses and made them earn their right to teach their own courses, it was sometimes easy by comparison to get a graduate course. John Shy, a specialist in American colonial history, knew he would not get an undergraduate course in that subject as long as his mentor, Frank Craven, continued to teach. However, his research involved military history, and he quickly got a chance to teach American military history as a graduate course.[19]

Other policies testified to a certain level of ambivalence about graduate education. In the late fifties R.R. Palmer proposed that the department provide only three years of support for graduate students, two years of coursework leading up comprehensive exams, and a third year to write enough of a dissertation to justify conferring the degree.[20] Palmer, who did not publish his Cornell dissertation, hoped to prevent students from taking absurdly long periods of time to finish their degrees. To a certain extent, it worked. Lester Little, a student of Strayer's, finished his Ph.D. in two years. But, in attempting to expedite the process, Palmer's proposal pushed students, especially in non-American fields, to eschew work in foreign archives and, instead pick topics that could be done in the Firestone Library.

On a personal level graduate education in the department could also be harsh and intimidating. Senior faculty from the thirties to sixties referred to graduate students who were dismissed from the program as having been "terminated." Norman Cantor spent over $700, a huge sum for a graduate student in the fifties, on tweed jackets and blazers after he was informed by Jerome Blum that he was expected to look like an Ivy League graduate student. "You're not smart enough to do intellectual history," snapped one faculty member after discussion of a student paper. The same faculty member once declared to the students in his seminar that it was his "job to stand at the pearly gates and keep out the undeserving," a task he assumed with relish.[21]

The next change of consequence in the Princeton history department was the appointment of Lawrence Stone as Dodge Professor of History in 1963. Before Stone's appointment the department faced a period of transition and uncertainty in which several key faculty were either leaving for other institutions, suffering from serious illness, or nearing retirement, perhaps some early indications that the department constructed so carefully by Joseph Strayer could not endure forever. The department made an impressive appointment in bringing in Thomas Kuhn in 1963. But in 1961 Gordon Craig departed for Stanford, and in 1963 R.R. Palmer, the holder of the Dodge Chair of History and author of the widely acclaimed *The Age of Democratic Revolutions*, decided to accept a position as Dean of the Faculty at Washington University in St. Louis. The uncertainty was greatest in the field of early modern Europe. Elmer Beller was nearing retirement, and Harris Harbison, in the last stages of an illness that would soon take his life, could only teach part-time. Palmer's departure opened up a chance to make a senior appointment, and Stone was an early modernist whose star was on the rise.²²

In 1963 Lawrence Stone was Fellow and Tutor at Wadham College, Oxford, and was about to publish his masterpiece, *The Crisis of the Aristocracy, 1558–1641*. His early Oxford career had been somewhat unusual, and his blunt and sometimes combative personality was probably forged in the crucible of his Oxford experience. In 1938 he had won an undergraduate scholarship to Christ Church, the most aristocratic of Oxford colleges, though Stone himself lacked the pedigree and social standing of most Christ Church undergraduates. Hugh Trevor-Roper, one of his tutors at Christ Church, remembers him as a reserved, almost timid, undergraduate. During World War II, Stone served aboard a destroyer and, after the war, returned to Oxford to finish his undergraduate degree. He received a coveted "first" on his "schools" or final examinations, which enabled him to win a research fellowship at University College, Oxford. The research fellowship was prestigious but paid little, and the post-war job market was bleak. Under these circumstances, and lacking the social position so important in Oxford, Stone found it difficult to find a permanent position in the late forties. After three years of poverty at University College and numerous rejections on the job market, Stone landed the Wadham post in 1949.²³

Soon after he started teaching at Wadham, however, Stone became involved in a nasty academic dispute with Hugh Trevor-Roper. In 1948, as he was trying to improve his position in the job market, Stone published an article in the *Economic History Review*, widely regarded in Britain at the time as the cutting edge historical journal, intended to support the claim by R.H. Tawney that the English Revolution was primarily a class struggle.

Three years later, Trevor-Roper pounced, publishing an article, also in the *EcHR*, that subjected Stone's work to a savage critique in which Trevor-Roper challenged virtually every argument Stone offered. Trevor-Roper, moreover, left no doubts about his intentions in writing the piece. "I have decided to liquidate Lawrence Stone," he wrote Wallace Notestein just before his article appeared.²⁴

The intensity of his attack, however, came as a surprise to Stone and many others. Not only had Stone been Trevor-Roper's pupil at Christ Church, but the two had worked together at the Public Record Office in London on the Recognizances for Debt on Statute Staple, the body of documents that formed the main source for Stone's claim that the aristocracy was in decline. Moreover, Trevor-Roper's first book, *Archbishop Laud*, had been written sympathy with Tawney's framework of class struggle between the declining aristocracy and the rising gentry. Many also thought it was ungentlemanly for Trevor-Roper to unleash such a brutal attack when Stone was at such an early stage of his career.

But the attack put Stone's career in doubt. He had secured the Wadham post before Trevor-Roper's article appeared, but now he appeared in Oxford to be that most unflattering of British academic terms, "unsound." He decided to write *Crisis* in part to clear his name. During the course of research and writing, however, Stone had become increasingly dissatisfied with Oxford. After a decade of teaching at Wadham, he had wearied of Oxford's impenetrable curricular emphasis on English political and constitutional history and the relentless burden of tutorial teaching. While in Princeton as a visiting fellow at the Institute of Advanced Study in 1961, a short distance from the university, Stone discovered a new world of historical scholarship far beyond the narrow confines of the Oxford curriculum, as well as a new interdisciplinary world, promising new approaches and insights for historical study, which was also foreign to Oxford.

While at the Institute, Stone met most of the members of the Princeton history department, and the department, then chaired by Jerome Blum, decided to offer him a job. Because Palmer's decision to leave Princeton left the Dodge chair vacant, one member of the department suggested that, given the "fondness of Englishmen for titles," the special distinction suggested by the Dodge chair might help induce Stone to accept their offer.

From Stone's point of view, Princeton had many advantages over Oxford. He had more time to himself and more flexibility about what he had would teach. In contrast to the endless battles at Oxford over curriculum, Stone went to Blum with a proposal for a new course that would combine history, sociology, and anthropology. Blum told him to go ahead and try it, and not to worry if it didn't work. Princeton also offered a sabbatical leave every four years. The benefits of Princeton were enough to keep him there until his retirement in 1989, despite offers from Nottingham, Pittsburgh, Johns Hopkins, the University of California at Los Angeles, Yale (in 1969 and 1976), and the Massachusetts Institute in Technology.[25]

Like all new marriages, Stone's arrival in Princeton required a period of adjustment. While Princeton in Stone's mind was an immense improvement over Oxford, he arrived in Princeton ready to drag what he perceived as a somewhat parochial and old-fashioned department kicking and screaming into the brave new world of the sixties. He related well to the younger faculty, who were excited by his vision and boldness, but some of the older faculty were less pleased by the implication that they had fallen behind the times. In particular there was tension between Stone and Strayer, which even a skilled conciliator like Frank Craven could not smooth over.[26]

With his quick mind and legendary bluntness, Stone could also be intimidating, even to those who admired him. Faculty and students alike felt the sting of his candor. "I read your paper. So what?" he snapped at a graduate student at a departmental colloquium. Others remember Stone's habit of suddenly asking them a difficult historical question, usually on an incredibly broad topic. If they reacted quickly and came up with a thoughtful answer, they visibly rose in his estimation and received more respectful treatment from him. If they did not, they fell further in his judgment or were dismissed altogether.[27]

But there was some truth to Stone's assessment of the history department as behind the times. In the mid-sixties the department built by Strayer was at a crossroads. Strayer himself was near retirement, and while he had recruited a superb group of faculty, the discipline of history was now going in different directions from what that generation of historians had been trained to do.

Strayer and the generation that entered academic life before World War II had generally been trained in the fairly narrow study of political and diplomatic history. The generation of Stone, even though only a little bit younger, had been trained to study it in economic and social context. The debate among Tawney, Stone, Trevor-Roper and others about the English Revolution was the most explicit manifestation of this kind of history. All the principal figures in the debate agreed that political narrative alone was inadequate to explain the revolution; the debate was over which set of economic and social conditions were the most important. By the mid-sixties, however, economic and social context had been elevated to a yet higher status. A new generation, influenced by the French Annales School of historians, and dazzled by the work that appeared in the journal, *Annales, Economies, Societies, Civilizations*, believed that economic, social, and demographic variables did not simply comprise the background to political events; they were the real subjects of historical inquiry.

Stone was a historian with a rare sense of where the discipline was headed and, influenced by the Annales School, was eager to elevate the importance of economic, social, and demographic forces. Moreover, while his specialty was early modern English history, he never limited himself to that subfield. As much as any historian of his time, he had a truly Olympian sense of the discipline, reading and writing on a daunting variety of subjects. There were occasional train wrecks along the way. Stone's conviction, for example, that quantitative history was the wave of the future, conspicuously crashed and burned, although Stone himself devoted considerable effort in his own work trying to make it come true. Nor was he particularly interested in developing areas outside of Europe and the United States.

But he did succeed in expanding the department's horizons. In addition to advocating that the department move in the direction that history was going, Stone also championed archival research.

Stone's own work on English aristocracy was social history based on intensive archival research, but most Princeton historians in the sixties worked from printed sources readily available in most university libraries. "Not one historian, faculty member or graduate student, was doing archival research at the time I arrived in Princeton," he once remarked, albeit inaccurately.[28] Within a decade the department's research interests had shifted away from the traditional political and diplomatic history, and perhaps more than half of the department was engaged in serious archival research, particularly its stars of the seventies and eighties, Robert Darnton and Natalie Davis. Along the same line, he urged the department to extend the length of time that graduate students might receive financial aid and encouraged students to use the time to utilize archival materials, an important step toward improving the quality of their dissertations.

While Stone gloried in Princeton and its impressive new world of intellectual opportunity, there were occasional reminders of his Oxford past. At his first department meeting, unaware that Princeton was more advanced than Oxford in offering non-western fields of study, Stone looked across the room at Marius Jansen, the department's Japanese historian, and wondered why Jansen was present at a history department meeting.[29]

In addition to the force of his personality, Stone was able to change the culture of the history department by several other means, mainly through his tenure as chair of the department from 1967 to 1970, and his role in development the Davis Center. As chair, he helped lure Carl Schorske away from Berkeley in 1969 and to recruit Robert Darnton as an assistant professor. He also altered several department procedures used by Strayer to reinforce departmental hierarchy. In contrast to Strayer, Stone listed the mailboxes in alphabetical order and served as the principal author of a departmental constitution in which junior faculty and students acquired the right to be consulted on curriculum decisions and included on planning committees. Junior faculty also won the right to participate in the hiring of new assistant professors.[30]

But Stone's greatest contribution to historical study at Princeton was the development of the Shelby Cullom Davis Center for Historical Studies. He had barely arrived at Princeton when the department received an unprecedented windfall. Largely through the efforts of Joseph Strayer, a Princeton graduate named Shelby Cullom Davis donated 5.2 million dollars to the Princeton history department toward the goal of the making the department the best in the world. Davis had been a history undergraduate at Princeton who went on to make a fortune in insurance and felt indebted to the department for the education he received.[31]

At first, nothing was done with the money, allowing the university administration to use it to cover other expenses. Stone took the lead in demanding that it be spent for the purposes that Davis intended. In his view the money would be best used to advance the department closer to the new subfields that formed the cutting edge of history, and he proposed that the money be used to create a center for historical study and helped form a committee to design it.

After studying existing models for centers, such as the Charles Warren Center at Harvard, Stone decided upon an arrangement by which a committee selected a theme that would be the focus of study for two years. The center also offered fellowships to scholars from other institutions working on problems related to the theme. The primary medium for exchange was the Davis Seminar itself, which met most Friday mornings in the Firestone Library. At the seminar one of the visiting scholars, another invitee, or on occasion a member of the Princeton history department presents a paper, which usually summarizes work in progress and is subjected to the criticism of the audience.

Over the years, the seminar helped bring to Princeton many distinguished scholars, often French historians, such as Emmanuel Le Roy Ladurie, Maurice Agulhon, and Pierre Goubert, connected with the Annales School approach to history. The seminar also witnessed some remarkable performances and probably helped many of the participants refine their ideas. Carlo Ginzberg presented the ideas that made up the basis for *The Cheese and the Worms*, and Natalie Davis outlined the plot of *The Return of Martin Guerre*. Stone, who served as director of the Davis Center until his retirement in 1989, and regularly displayed a gift for delivering masterly summations, as the meeting came to a close, of the strengths and weaknesses of the paper under consideration and its place in historical thought.

But the seminar also acquired aura of mortal combat where many a scholar found him or herself transformed into a wounded and hunted animal, hounded remorsely by a pack of wild dogs. As director, Stone himself set the aggressive tone. Following a paper by the director of a lavishly funded social history project that had produced few tangible results, Stone inquired, "aren't you devouring all of the remaining provender that might otherwise sustain dozens of smaller but better conceived studies?"

The tables could occasionally be turned. After listening to the English social historian E.P. Thompson denounce the government of Sir Robert Walpole as little better than a banana republic, Stone launched a frontal attack, quoting a number of overheated phrases that Thompson had used against Walpole, and asked, "Is this history? Is this kind of language even helpful, much less objective?" Thompson smiled and replied, "Why, Lawrence, a new deity has recently been erected in the land, and it is called 'political stability.' When someone creates new gods, the only proper response is blasphemy."[32]

The sixties also saw other significant changes in the history department. The massive expansion of the American universities during that time made it that rarest of times, a period in which the demand for faculty sometimes exceeded supply. With intense competition among leading departments for the best faculty, top candidates were able, to a greater extent than before, to call their own shots. In the Princeton history department this development signaled the end of the preceptorial system as it had been practiced for several decades. Where Princeton had traditionally hired new faculty as instructors and sharpened their teaching skills by having them precept for several years, this practice was becoming increasingly unfeasible. Younger faculty were beginning to chafe at precepting in areas in which they had little preparation, and the practice was also making it difficult to recruit new faculty, who wanted to teach their own courses. The demands of preceptorial teaching were also factors in the decision of David Donald to leave Princeton in 1962, and John Morton Blum's rejection of Princeton's attempt to lure him away from Yale in 1961.[33]

The attitudes of some of the younger faculty toward preceptorial teaching clashed with the department's traditional values. Many of the older faculty believed deeply in the value of precepting in a wide variety of classes, and were fond of recalling how much they had gained from the practice while pointing to the fact that many senior faculty continued to precept in courses outside their fields. Frank Craven, a specialist in American colonial history, precepted in Strayer's medieval history courses; David Donald, a specialist in the Civil War era, precepted for Eric Goldman's courses in recent America; and Marius Jansen, a Japanese historian, precepted in European history courses.

Defenders of the status quo also believed that adding new courses would disrupt what they perceived as the organic unity of the history curriculum and its emphasis on western traditions. Until the mid-sixties, the department's course offerings were small, fewer than twenty actual courses, but they presented a coherent narrative of western progress through the origins of the modern state and representative government, the development of religious toleration and individual freedoms, the rise of the middle class, and the growth of scientific thinking. This narrative gave a meaning and coherence to the history of the West that was deeply relevant to the students in their courses who were its principal beneficiaries.

But, under pressure from the younger faculty and the need to compete with other elite schools for new faculty, the tradition of younger faculty precepting in a wide range of courses taught by senior faculty was largely abandoned. Graduate students took over much of the preceptorial teaching, and younger faculty began teaching their own courses. The result was end of not only the generalist tradition at Princeton, but the offering of many more courses than the department had previously offered and the coverage of many more areas.

The sixties brought other changes in the department's culture. Faculty members from the sixties have different recollections about how radical movements affected the history department. For some, the Princeton students of the era were generally conservative, and the university president at the time, Robert Goheen, proved remarkably skillful in handling the few angry students that existed, saying the right things and making shrewd tactical concessions at just the right moments. In their recollection few of the tensions that erupted in other campuses and history departments spilled over into either the campus or the history department.[34]

Many of the ingredients for trouble, however, existed. The tensions brought about by the war in large measure mirrored the generational clash that the entire nation experienced in the 1960s and which could be seen in the history department. Joseph Strayer and most of the Old Guard, including Blum, Black, and Goldman, were men of similar outlook and temperament. They were, for the most part, Cold War liberals, opposed to communism, and they had served and advised government agencies, including the clandestine ones now whose aims and methods were now being questioned. Eric Goldman had even been a member of the Johnson administration as "Special Consultant to the President of the United States." These men were probably not enthusiastic about the war in Viet Nam, but for the most part they believed at least early on that it should be supported.

While some remember general harmony within the department, others remember debates over such issues as whether the university was a proper forum for the expression of dissent and whether it was proper to give low grades to students that would cause them to lose their draft deferments.

One clear sign of tension occurred in 1965 when John Pomfret, a Princeton graduate and son of a former Princeton history professor, wrote a front-page story in the *New York Times* declaring that the level of opposition to the war by Princeton faculty had been exaggerated. Pomfret's piece was based on interviews with several Princeton faculty, including Strayer and Arthur Link of the History Department, and J. Douglas Brown. In response John Shy, one of the younger faculty, wrote a letter disputing Pomfret's assertion and distributed it in departmental mailboxes. Lawrence Stone convened a meeting of those in sympathy with the letter at Arno Mayer's house, where Shy's draft was improved and the letter received more signatures than the *Times* would print. Several older faculty, however, including Strayer, Link, Frank Craven, and Marius Jansen were among those who did not sign.[35]

By the late sixties the Princeton history department also confronted the entrance of women and minorities into its ranks. Again, faculty recollections on this issue vary. Some recall resistance particularly to the hiring of women on the part of some of the older faculty; others recall a relatively smooth transition from the era of white male domination to the new era of multiculturalism.

On the question of minority hiring, Joseph Strayer played an important role. In addition to his willingness to recruit Jews to the history department, Strayer was remarkably open to recruiting black graduate students, including William Chester Jordan and Bennett Hill. Strayer regarded Jordan as his finest student, and in 1972, strongly supported by the department, Jordan was the first black faculty member hired in the Princeton history department.

Women were another matter. Prior to becoming coeducational in 1969, Princeton was an all-male enclave and a strong sense of male traditions remained. While the first woman was admitted to graduate study at Princeton in the early sixties, it was only after an anguished debate in the Graduate Council. Administrators at Princeton were generally convinced that graduate education was so demanding that it could only be undertaken by men, preferably unmarried, who would be undistracted by marital and child-rearing obligations. In the history department women occupied only secondary roles.[36]

The first woman admitted to the history department's graduate program was probably Miriam Slater in the mid-sixties. Princeton occasionally admitted women in programs that did not attract large numbers of students, but resisted admitting them in fields, such as history, where the department usually attracted far more students than it could accept. Indeed, Slater was only admitted after a two-year battle with university authorities and because Lawrence Stone lobbied hard on her behalf. Even then, she was admitted as an "incidental student." One of her seminars met in a building where a sign read, "No women allowed in the building after 10 p.m.;" Slater thought the sign could have read, "before 10 p.m." just as easily.[37]

By the late sixties, the Princeton history department was not only responding to institutional changes regarding the admission of women, but to societal changes. When women once came to Princeton primarily as faculty wives, they now came to Princeton as faculty members themselves and as wives of faculty members who had careers of their own.

In the fall of 1968 Nancy Weiss (now Malkiel) was a teaching fellow at Harvard when Frank Friedel, her advisor, told her one day that Frank Craven, who was chairing the search at Princeton for a position in twentieth-century American history, had called him asking if he knew suitable candidates. Freidel said he recommended her. "You might not get it," Freidel admitted, "but it would be good for them to have to consider you." Malkiel had not finished her dissertation and was not looking for a job, but recognized the opportunity afforded her, even though the Princeton history department had no female faculty. She applied and was quickly invited to campus. The entire department turned out to meet her, which was unusual. Lawrence Stone, the chair at the time, explained the absence of female faculty in the department by saying that it wasn't that the department had a policy against it, they had just never thought of it.

The department offered her a job, and, finding the department and community attractive, she accepted. She was received graciously by her male colleagues, who were eager to find what she was about, and she was regularly invited to lunches and dinner parties, even beyond Princeton's normally high level of social engagement, all of which helped smooth her passage to Princeton.

Occasionally, however, there were signs that some of the men in the department were having difficulty coping with the presence of a woman. At the time of her arrival in Princeton, there were only three female faculty members, Suzanne Kelly, a senior appointment in sociology, a new assistant professor in Near Eastern Studies, and Malkiel, on the entire university faculty. It was during searches for new faculty that old prejudices were sometimes exposed. During her second year at Princeton, the department was considering a female candidate when a senior colleague remarked to Malkiel that "you're in an impossible position; if you're for her, it's because she's a women; if you're not, it's because you want to be the only woman." During another search where most of the initial candidates were women, another senior colleague asked, "where are the real candidates?" A few years later, when the applicant pool included a female candidate with children, a male faculty member remarked, "if we offer her the job, she'll have a fundamental decision to make."[38]

Other problems surfaced. Female graduate students believed that male students received preferential treatment. Among other things, they managed to obtain data that indicated that women failed their oral examinations more often than men, and they could cite anecdotal evidence that men were given favors to enable them to pass. One male student, for example, was allowed to pass even though he admitted that he only answered one of the three required questions.

Armed with their data, a group of women asked for a meeting with the department. While several senior faculty defended the department's practices with graduate students, Lawrence Stone argued that the department needed to face up to the fact that the data seemed to show a pattern of prejudice toward women. While conditions seemed to improve for female graduate students, and the department continued to appoint women to junior positions, it was also true that two of the ablest junior appointees, Estelle Freedman and Dorothy Ross, did not receive tenure in the department.[39]

One consequence of these changes was a gradual reduction in the social life of the department. Women faculty and the wives of new faculty who had their own careers were less interested in entertaining and dinner parties than were the faculty wives of an earlier generation. While the department's social life did not vanish, (Lawrence Stone and his wife, Jeanne, entertained frequently), it was no longer conducted on the scale that existed in the Strayer years.[40]

The differences over Viet Nam, the change in the preceptorial system, the expansion of the department's traditional curricular boundaries, and the arrival of new faculty, were all indications that the sun was beginning to set on the old Princeton history department as well as its world of generalist, gentleman scholar, and that a new generation was starting to take its place. The new generation had received more highly specialized graduate training than their predecessors, which led them to believe that it was unprofessional to be expected to teach in areas in which they had little or no preparation. They wished to place more emphasis on research, to incorporate more of the new history into the curriculum, and to make the department more democratic. The departmental constitution largely drafted by Lawrence Stone reflected changing times.

Princeton of course was not the only history department force to confront changing times. But, like Lawrence Stone's English aristocracy, the department recovered from the somewhat troubled times of the late sixties to again emerge as a cutting edge department in the 1970s.

Princeton's recovery can be attributed to several factors. The first of these was the presence of numerous built-in advantages. The main advantage was the Davis Center, which, as advertised, exposed members of the department to new approaches, to distinguished scholars from other institutions, and to high level discussion of some of the best work in progress. A second built-in advantage was the presence of the Institute for Advanced Study, formed in the 1930s to provide a haven for Jewish academicians fleeing the Nazis. Like the Davis Center, the Institute brought a steady stream of visiting scholars and also offered its own seminars.

One of the seminars offered at the Institute was taught by the anthropologist Clifford Geertz, who had already gained fame as the author of several studies of change in Indonesia and his work attracted the interest of many historians. Geertz's essay, "Deep Play: Notes on the Balinese Cockfight," was perhaps the most influential article among historians written in the last half-century. In this essay Geertz located a deeper meaning in a seemingly straightforward phenomenon, cockfighting in Bali. For other scholars, cockfighting was intense and it was somewhat surprising to discover it in an otherwise non-violent culture like Bali, but it could be best understood as a simply a healthy form of recreation and release.

For Geertz, however, it was an intense battle over status, whereby the Balinese fought for their place in society. The value of the essay was that Geertz opened up the possibility of deriving deep behavioral meaning from the study of seemingly minor episodes and rituals. It was what he called "local knowledge," a story that "the Balinese tell themselves about themselves." [41]

It would be hard to exaggerate the importance of Geertz' work to the historical profession as a whole or to the Princeton history department. Among other things, Geertz's seminar was the inspiration for the *Journal of Interdisciplinary History*, started by Theodore K. Rabb of the history department and Robert I. Rotberg of M.I.T., to publish work that expanded historical understanding through interdisciplinary inquiry.

More importantly, Geertz was a key figure in the marriage between history and anthropology and the development of cultural history as a historical subfield. As the Princeton history department rebuilt itself in the seventies, the leading figures in that reconstruction were cultural historians, though not always influenced by Geertz. As in the fifties, shrewd recruiting was critical.

In the late sixties Carl Schorske was teaching at Berkeley and had published a book on the Weimar Republic and a couple of articles on the political, literary, artistic, and musical culture of late nineteenth century Vienna. His output was relatively modest for a man who occupied a full professorship at what was perhaps the nation's most prestigious state university. But there was obvious brilliance in his articles, several of which had been published in the *American Historical Review*. At the time few scholars could match the level of interdisciplinary sophistication that Schorske revealed in those articles. While the department had been pursuing him for some time, it was Lawrence Stone who finally persuaded him to join the department in 1967. A few years later, he published *Fin-de-Siecle Vienna*, a collection of his essays on late nineteenth century Viennese culture, which won a Pulitzer Prize, and he was an early winner of one of the MacArthur Foundation's "genius" grants.[42]

Robert Darnton was another recruiting prize. A classic academic golden boy, Darnton was a Harvard undergraduate and Rhodes Scholar, a member of Harvard's Society of Fellows, an Oxford D.Phil., and, later on, another MacArthur Prize recipient. Darnton had already made a name for himself with a series of innovative studies of the journalistic underground of Paris on the eve of the French Revolution. This underground was comprised of a mass of hack journalists who swarmed like locusts into the Paris of the 1780s, hoping, like their predecessors of the High Enlightenment, to write their way to glory. Instead, they found their path to fame and fortune blocked by poverty and class prejudice, and, more tellingly, by the fact that the radical ideas of the Enlightenment had already been integrated into to society, leaving them with nothing new to say.

Darnton's work had powerful implications. Most historians believed that the ideas of the Enlightenment provided the ideological ammunition necessary to bring down the Old Regime in 1789. Now Darnton seemed to be saying these ideas were as commonplace in France as a bottle of Bordeaux. But he also suggested that the real revolutionary energy derived from the anger with which these impoverished hack journalists lashed out at a society that relegated them to poverty and insignificance.[43]

An earlier article by Darnton had signaled the advance of a new generation of intellectual historians. Darnton had been asked to review Peter Gay's prize-winning, two-volume history of the Enlightenment. Gay, born in 1923, had advertised his book as an example of "the social history of ideas," which meant in the best sense of his generation, a study of the ideas of Enlightenment placed in the context of the social and economic forces of the time.

Darnton criticized Gay's work on several grounds, the first of which was that it could have been done in almost any good university library. In fact, said Darnton, "pulling a little Voltaire off the shelf will not put one in contact with a representative slice of the eighteenth- century," nor will reading secondary works on economic and social trends be sufficient to provide real context. The real context and impact of the Enlightenment, argued Darnton, can only be found by "grubbing in archives," and through the study of the processes by which the books of the *philosophes* were produced.[44]

The department's dominance in cultural history and its traditional strength in European history were strongly reinforced when Natalie Davis was lured away from Berkeley. Davis was perhaps the best known of the Princeton historians, and arrived in Princeton in 1977 after a somewhat nomadic academic life. Like Schorske and Darnton, her most important early work was a collection of essays, *Society and Culture in Early Modern France*. While the essays had several themes and relied on a variety of interdisciplinary studies, their most significant contribution was to reveal how many popular sixteenth century rites and rituals were subtle means of social protest. Davis' appointment also clinched the future of women in the department.[45]

By the end of the decade the department was again riding high. The heady days of the fifties had returned, but in a different key. Not only were department members writing many of the "hot" books of the time, but there was an atmosphere of shared exchange and collective enterprise. Informal reading groups were scattered around the department. As one example, some forty students and faculty devoted several Sunday afternoons each semester to reading key texts in late antiquity with Peter Brown, who came from Berkeley in the early eighties. Graduate students went to lectures by faculty outside their fields hoping to gain insights that might be helpful to them. Carl Schorske's lectures in particular acquired a devoted following that cut across conventional disciplinary boundaries. Members of the department were also increasingly visible to a lay audience through contributions to such periodicals as *The New York Review of Books*, to which Stone, Schorske, Darnton, Brown, Davis, and the Americanist James McPherson were frequent contributors.

Despite the department's renown, American history remained an area of concern. While the department possessed several superb Americanists, including Daniel Rodgers and James McPherson, the members who generated the most attention were the department's glittering array of Europeanists. Some even referred to the presence of a "fame deficit" in the department in terms of American history. Joseph Strayer had once remarked, perhaps whimsically, that since Yale was superior in American history, Princeton should concentrate on maintaining its excellence in European history. In the 1960s the department had been unable to retain David Donald, John Shy, or Martin Duberman, or to lure John Morton Blum away from Yale. In the 1970s, it decided not pursue the hiring of Eric Foner, Winthrop Jordan, Eugene Genovese or Herbert Gutman.[46]

With its emphasis on undergraduate teaching and relatively small graduate program, Princeton occupies a unique position among elite history departments. But it also follows a pattern common to several. Between 1940 and 1980 the Princeton history department experienced several different phases and managed to successfully reinvent itself several times. During the first phase, from about 1941 to 1961, Joseph Strayer, building on existing strengths and his own initiatives, managed to take a good history department and improve its quality substantially. By the early sixties there were some signs that, despite his estimable achievements, the age of Strayer was coming to an end and the department, intellectually, was at a crossroads. At this point, it was the arrival of Lawrence Stone that injected a needed energy and vision into the department. Where Strayer's strength was his astute recruiting, Stone's contribution was primarily through the program he established for the Davis Center, although Stone, too, was instrumental in recruiting outstanding faculty. Through the topics he selected and the scholars he invited, he made the Davis Center a virtual nerve center of the department and nearly of the historical profession in the United States. Thanks in part to Stone and the Davis Center, by the mid-seventies, the department reinvented itself along the lines of the *Annales School* and cultural history so effectively that in 1987, *The New York Times Magazine* could with confidence again declare it the "hot history department."

---

[1] William Palmer, "Interview with William Chester Jordan," May 27, 2004.

[2] Lynn White, Jr., "History and Horseshoe Nails," in L.P. Curtis, ed., *The Historian's Workshop: Original Essays by Sixteen Historians* (New York, 1970), p. 50.

[3] For Strayer see the brilliant evocation of him as a teacher, scholar, and person in Norman Cantor, *Inventing the Middle Ages: The Lives, Works, and Ideas of the Great Medievalists of the Twentieth Century* (New York, 1991), pp. 245-86; for additional reflections on Strayer, see Cantor, *Inventing Norman Cantor* (Tempe, Ariz., 2002), pp. 42–50; and William Chester Jordan and Teofilo Ruiz, "Joseph Reese Strayer," in Patricia Marks, ed., *Luminaries: Princeton Faculty Remembered* (Princeton, 1996).

[4] Cantor, *Inventing the Middle Ages*, p. 262.

[5] Palmer, "Interview with Gordon Craig," January 4, 1996; for additional information see William Palmer, *Engagement with the Past: The Lives and Works of World War II Generation of Historians* (Lexington, Ky., 2001), pp. 101–2.

[6] Palmer, "Interview with Charles Gillispie," June 4, 2004; and Charles Gillispie, "Apologia Pro Vita Sua," *Isis* 90 Supplement (1999): S84-94.

[7] Marius B. Jansen, "Cyril Edwin Black," in Marks, ed., *Luminaries*, pp. 21–28.

[8] Palmer, "Interview with Craig"; Cantor, *Inventing Norman Cantor*, pp. 34-5.

[9] John Milton Cooper, "Arthur S. Link," in Robert Allen Rutland, ed., *Clio's Favorites: Leading Historians of the United States 1945–2000* (Columbia, Miss., 2000), pp. 112-3; Cooper also describes Link's occasionally edgy relationship with the history department and Princeton administration.

[10] Daniel Kevles, "Eric Frederick Goldman," in Marks, ed., *Luminaries*, p. 90.

[11] Cantor, *Inventing the Middle Ages*, p. 259, Geoffrey Kabbaservice, *The Guardians: Kingman Brewster, His Circle, and the Rise of the Liberal Establishment* (New York, 2004); Jordan and Ruiz, "Joseph Strayer," in Marks, ed., *Luminaries*, p. 202.

[12] Jordan and Ruiz, "Joseph Strayer," in Marks., ed., *Luminaries*, p. 202.

[13] Palmer, "Interview with Raymond Grew," July 7, 2004; none of the younger faculty to whom I talked who were hired at Princeton in the sixties remembered being interviewed for the job. But, at the senior level, both David Donald and John Morton Blum both visited the campus before deciding about whether to accept Princeton's offer.

[14] Material on the lives of junior faculty at Princeton during sixties was obtained through interviews with Raymond Grew, John Gillis, Gary Nash, James McPherson, and Theodore Rabb, and email communications with John Shy.

[15] Palmer, "Interview with Martin Duberman," October 17, 2004.

[16] Cantor, *Inventing Norman Cantor* pp. 34-5. Technically, Cantor left Princeton for Columbia before a tenure decision was reached. But, in *Inventing Norman Cantor* he describes the clear indications from the department, especially Harris Harbison, that he needed to accept Columbia's offer, because he would not make it at Princeton.

[17] Martin Duberman, *Cures: A Gay Man's Odyssey* (Boulder, Co., reprint, 2002), p. 1.

[18] For an interesting discussion of the history of Princeton's graduate school, see Alvin Kernan, *In Plato's Cave* (New Haven, 1999), pp. 205-7

[19] Cantor, *Inventing Norman Cantor*, p. 39; Communication from John Shy, July 7, 2004.

[20] Email Communication from John Shy, July 7, 2004.

[21] Cantor, *Inventing Norman Cantor*, pp. 44, 59; Palmer, "Interview with Gary Nash," July 13, 2004; Gary Nash, "Wesley Frank Craven," in Marks, ed., *Luminaries*, pp. 66. It should be noted that Nash was not referring to Craven in the passage cited here.

[22] The details of Stone's appointment are discussed in John Murrin, "Eminence Rouge?" in A.L. Beier, David Cannadine, and James Rosenheim, eds., *The First Modern Society: Essays in Honour of Lawrence Stone* (Cambridge, 1991), pp. 21-30.

[23] Details on Stone's early career in Oxford, his relations with Trevor-Roper, and the Gentry Controversy can be found in Palmer, *Engagement with the Past*, pp. 112-3, 199–206.

[24] Hugh Trevor-Roper to Wallace Notestein, April 1, 1951; Wallace Notestein Papers, Yale University, Department of Manuscripts and Archives.

[25] Murrin, "Eminence Rouge?" p. 24.

[26] Email Communication from John Shy, July 7, 2004.

[27] Palmer, Interviews with Gary Nash, July 13, 2004; Jerrold Seigal, July 20, 2004; James McPherson, September 15, 2004.

[28] Interviews with Lawrence Stone, June 5,8, 1996; Stone's statement here may qualify as what Cliff Davies has referred to "typical Laurentian hyperbole." While it is true that most Princeton historians, such as R.R. Palmer and Jerome Blum, could do their work from any good university library, there were Princeton historians doing archival work. Strayer, for example, was an archival historian, though by the sixties he was probably no longer working in archives, and Charles Gillispie and James McPherson were certainly doing archival research at this time.

[29] Palmer, "Interview with Jordan."

[30] Palmer, "Interview with John Murrin," May 24, 2004.

[31] For a good discussion of the origins of the Davis Center and of the status of the Princeton History Department in the mid-eighties, see Mark Silk, "The Hot History Department," *New York Times Magazine*, April 19, 1987.

[32] Murrin, "Eminence Rouge?" pp., 28-9.

[33] Palmer, "Interview with Gillispie"; Palmer, "Interview with Robert Tignor," June 19, 2004; John Morton Blum, *A Life with History* (Lawrence, Kansas, 2004), p. 150.

34 Palmer, "Interview with Gillispie"; Palmer, "Interview with Theodore K. Rabb," June 19, 2004.

35 Email Communication with John Shy, July 7, 2004.

36 Palmer, "Interview with Tignor"; Palmer, "Interview with John Gillis," June 24, 2004; communication from Gary Nash, January 7, 2005.

37 Miriam Slater, "'Il Magnifico,'" in Beier, Cannadine, and Rosenheim, eds., *The First Modern Society*, pp. 15–17.

38 Palmer, "Interview with Nancy Malkiel," December 14, 2004.

39 Palmer, "Interview with Maureen Callahan," April 19, 2005; Palmer, "Interview with Christine Lunardini," April 20, 2005.

40 Palmer, "Interview with Tignor."

41 Silk, "The Hot History Department."

42 Carl Schorske, *Fin-de-Siecle Vienna: Politics and Culture* (New York, 1981).

43 Robert Darnton, *The Literary Underground of the Old Regime* (Cambridge, Mass., 1982), esp. pp. 1–40.

44 Idem., "In Search of Enlightenment: Recent Attempts to Create a Social History of Ideas," *Journal of Modern History* 43(1971): 125-7.

45 Natalie Zemon Davis, *Society and Culture in Early Modern France* (Palo Alto, 1975).

46 In the case of Genovese, there is evidence that the failure to offer him a senior position was not entirely the department's fault. In May and June of 1976 there is a fair amount of correspondence about the appointment, the gist of which was that Princeton required a bibliography of Genovese's published works before it could proceed, and Genovese was late in sending it. As Lawrence Stone wrote C. Vann Woodward, "Gene's suspicions about us are groundless, and that he is himself to blame for the disaster, partially because he did not send off the bibliography promptly, and partly because he gave orders that no phone calls from anyone were to be transferred to his office." Lawrence Stone to C. Vann Woodward, June 10, 1976; C. Vann Woodward Papers, Yale University, Department of Manuscripts and Archives.

Chapter Five

The University of California at Berkeley: The Great Battle

The professional department of history emerged first at several eastern private universities, but somewhat more slowly at state universities. Among them, the first examples of their emergence were at the University of California at Berkeley and the University of Wisconsin. It is hard to say where it occurred first. While Wisconsin had begun to build a professional department in the thirties, Berkeley experienced a slightly more dynamic expansion in the fifties.

For the first quarter of the twentieth century, history held a marginal position on the Berkeley campus. It was clearly relegated to secondary status behind classics in terms of a liberal arts education, where knowledge of Latin and Greek remained a prerequisite for a bachelor's degree until 1915. The history faculty at this time consisted of eight men, six in European history and two in American, chaired by Henry Morse Stephens, a prolific scholar, who came to Berkeley from Cornell in 1902. The department was held in contempt by certain faculty in other departments. The classicist Arthur Ryder, upon seeing Stephens at lunch with his colleagues at the faculty club remarked, "there goes a fake giant surrounded by real pygmies."[1]

By the 1930s the department had expanded to fifteen regular members, and had acquired a scholar of distinction, Herbert Eugene Bolton, a Wisconsin undergraduate and University of Pennsylvania Ph.D. Bolton served as department chair from 1919 until 1940 and was elected president of the American Historical Association in 1932. In several ways, he cast a long shadow over the department. As a scholar, he made important contributions to historical study, insisting that the history of the United States be subsumed into the history of the Americas. Bolton's perspective was in part a reaction against what he perceived as an east coast, northern European bias on the part of most colonial historians of the time, most of whom focused on colonial New England, the Puritans, and early Virginia. Bolton believed that the study of the Spanish Americas was an equally important part of the story. And, as the study of colonies, frontiers, and empires has returned to center of historical scholarship, his ideas have enjoyed recently something of a renaissance, receiving a sympathetic reappraisal from scholars.[2]

On a departmental level, Bolton exercised enormous influence. First, the department did not teach a survey course in United States history until Bolton relinquished the chairmanship in 1940; instead, reflecting Bolton's imperatives, it taught "the history of the Americas." Moreover, even earlier than Strayer or Pierson, Bolton was concerned to build up the department. Under his direction, the department had expanded to twenty-one members by 1941. Bolton exhibited a preference for men with degrees from Berkeley, where he trained over one hundred Ph.D. students, or the University of Wisconsin. He hired several of his own students, creating what was essentially an Old Guard of his appointees. This group included Walton Bean, James King, Engel Sluiter, George Hammond, and Lawrence Kinnaird, sometimes pejoratively called "Boltonians."[3]

By the time of Bolton's retirement in 1940 (he came back briefly to teach during World War II when faculty were in short supply), most of the department's faculty, especially those in American history, were Boltonians. It was somewhat harder to recruit historians of Europe, though the two of the most distinguished members of the department were Europeanists who held degrees from outside the Berkeley-Madison pipeline.

The first of these historians was the medievalist Ernst Kantorowicz, a Jew who came to Berkeley just before the outbreak of World War II after fleeing Hitler's Germany. Kantorowicz was already the author of a widely admired book on Frederick I, the first Hohenstauffen emperor. After leaving Germany, Kantorowicz spent a year at Oxford, and, with no job prospects, answered a Berkeley advertisement for a professor of medieval English constitutional history. Kantorowicz had no idea where Berkeley was and knew little about English constitutional history, but he needed a job. The incumbent medievalist at Berkeley had published little, but knew that hiring Kantorowicz would be a major recruiting triumph. Kantorowicz was quickly offered the job, which he was happy to accept.[4]

Kantorowicz and Berkeley were a curious, but agreeable match. A bachelor, Kantorowicz was an extraordinarily learned man, fluent in six languages, and whose scholarship, the political culture and symbolism of medieval kingship, was far ahead of his time. He dressed elegantly, retained his continental accent and manners, and talked in a quirky, sing-song tone of voice. Despite his eccentric qualities or, perhaps because of them, he attracted a devoted following of students. Gathering at his house overlooking San Francisco bay, they comprised an intellectual circle, as they drank wine and listened to Kantorowicz explicate, often word by word, the meaning of classic medieval political texts. His greatest performance was a yearlong exegesis of the meaning and sources for Dante's *De Monarchia*, a modest tract of a little more than one-hundred pages.

A second historian of national reputation in the department was Raymond J. Sontag, a historian of European diplomacy, who had come to Berkeley from Princeton in 1941 to take up the Ehrman chair in European history. Holding a doctorate from the University of Pennsylvania and having taught at Princeton since 1924, Sontag was a product of the kind of elite eastern university that the Berkeley department usually resisted. But Sontag had an outstanding record as a teacher and scholar, and had taken a leading role in building up the Princeton department before coming to Berkeley.[5]

Despite these exceptions, the department continued to look to Madison for its faculty. In 1942 it brought John D. Hicks, a Wisconsin Ph.D. and faculty member, to Berkeley. Hicks was in turn instrumental in recruiting Kenneth Stampp, another Wisconsin Ph.D., to leave Maryland for Berkeley in 1946. In 1948, when Frederick Paxson, who had himself been recruited to a distinguished chair from Wisconsin in 1932, retired, the department sought to replace him with Merle Curti, a Harvard Ph.D., then teaching at Wisconsin. When Curti declined the offer, the department changed its usual pattern, and decided to replace him with Carl Bridenbaugh, a Harvard Ph.D. with an excellent record of publication.

At this time, despite evident improvement in the quality of its faculty, the department was still not highly regarded. When Hicks approached Stampp about leaving Maryland, Stampp had to get out a map to find out where Berkeley was; he initially thought it was in southern California. When he told his friend Richard Hofstadter that he had been offered a job at Berkeley, Hofstadter said, "Surely, you're not going to take it, are you?" When Stampp said that he probably would, but only stay a few years, Hofstadter replied, "Well, I must say, I don't think much of the history department at Berkeley."[6]

If the department wished to improve its reputation, there were several problems that required attention. The first of these problems was that the department's senior faculty, the "Boltonian" wing, claimed little scholarly distinction. Paul Schaeffer, the department's senior medievalist, was reputed to be the brightest Harvard graduate of his generation, but had published little. George Hammond had been director of the Bancroft Library, but no scholar. Nor did many of the others demonstrate more than a passing interest in scholarship, although Walton Bean did produce a good book, *Boss Ruef's San Francisco*.

In addition to its reliance on Berkeley and Madison Ph.D.s, another problem was that power in the department was concentrated in the hands of those who held titled chairs, sometimes called "*baroni*" by the non-chair holders. In the late forties the chair holders included Hicks, Sontag, Bridenbaugh, and Robert Kerner, a historian of Russia. The chair holders sought to preserve their power and influence through the construction of elaborate patronage networks with other faculty. Those who did not hold chairs, like the clients of the great feudal barons, saw the benefits of surrendering their independence in return for the protection of a powerful patron. The patronage ties enabled the chair holders to make most of the important decisions in the department, especially on appointments, often without consulting even the other full professors.[7]

The chair holders' domination often amounted to the crassest kind of cronyism. Students of the chair holders usually received favored treatment for financial aid and teaching positions. Even mediocre students could pass their exams if they enjoyed the protection of a powerful patron. "When I raise my hand in a meeting," Kerner instructed his departmental underlings, "you raise yours."[8]

Occasionally, there were attempts even within the Old Guard to resist the baroni. A fierce rivalry existed between Kerner and Franklin Palm with students caught in the middle. In 1946 six students failed their written Ph.D. examinations. Three of the six were Palm students failed by Kerner; the other three were Kerner students failed by Palm.[9]

The murky waters of California politics during the Cold War years also affected the department. In the late forties and early fifties, popular fears over the spread of Communism around the world began to mount. On February 9, 1950, Senator Joseph McCarthy delivered a speech in Wheeling, West Virginia, charging that not only was Communism spreading around the world, but that it had infiltrated into many of the corridors of power in American life. His main target was Communist penetration of the government and in particular of the State Department, but it was only a matter of time before similar charges of Communists teaching in colleges and universities would be leveled. It was true that many younger faculty at Berkeley and elsewhere dabbled in left-wing politics during the Depression. At Berkeley, Chancellor Robert Gordon Sproul decided that it might be possible to deflect McCarthyite attacks on the university by forcing faculty sign a loyalty oath, phrased in such a way that it would be impossible for a Communist to sign it. Refusal to sign the oath would be cause for termination.

In the summer of 1949, when Kenneth Stampp received his contract for the next year, it also contained a loyalty oath for him to sign. Stampp was infuriated, but, with two small children and a wish not to be fired, he eventually signed. By the time classes began in the fall the oath had become a burning issue.[10]

In late 1950, about twenty-five Berkeley faculty across the university were fired for refusing to sign. In the history department, two faculty members, Ernst Kantorowicz and Gordon Griffiths, the son of one of the trustees, refused to sign the oath. Kantorowicz was one of the twenty-five people who were fired, although Griffiths later changed his mind and signed. Within the department, there were mixed reactions. Several department members, including Raymond Sontag, enthusiastically supported the oath as well as the firing of those who refused to sign. Others, like Stampp, opposed the oath, even though they signed it.

Across the university opponents of the oath formed a committee to raise money to pay the salaries of the non-signers while they tried to find other jobs. In the history department Kenneth Stampp was chosen to collect from those who wished to contribute and turn the money over to the central committee. The list of those willing to contribute and those unwilling exposed the department's fault lines. With a few exceptions, such as James King, Engel Sluiter, George Guttridge, and John Hicks, older faculty and those appointed by Bolton, refused to contribute. On the other hand, younger faculty, like Stampp and Bridenbaugh, contributed.

The termination of Kantorowicz was fraught with irony. Right after World War I, while still in Germany, he had been a member of a quasi-Nazi, right-wing group called the Free Corps, and he insisted that he had shot Communists in 1919. But he objected to the oath on the grounds that imposing limits on freedom of speech sounded eerily like one of the tools that the Nazis used to seize power in the thirties. Kantorowicz eventually found a position at the Institute for Advanced Study outside Princeton. Griffiths was later denied tenure in the department and eventually moved to the University of Washington, which, ironically, had its own McCarthyite scare before his arrival.

In California the legality of the oath was finally settled out of court, but not before it had it caused a major rift in the department. In the middle of the controversy Stampp found himself at a conference with Raymond Sontag where they sat next to each other at dinner. Sontag asked him why he opposed the oath. Stampp replied, "Ray Sontag, you're a devout Catholic. Do you mean to say that you can sign an oath that says you have no commitments that would interfere with the free pursuit of the truth?" Stampp does not remember what Sontag said in reply, but his question clearly implied that he thought Sontag was a hypocrite.[11]

Fortunately, in the fifties, the California economy was expanding and, despite the tensions that existed in the department, money flowed into the university. The opportunity to build a great department beckoned like Ithaca to Odysseus. Perhaps the first step in this process was the appointment of Joseph Levenson in 1950 to teach Chinese history. Before making the appointment, the department wrote John Fairbank at Harvard to ask for the names of his two best students. Fairbank suggested Levenson and Benjamin Schwartz, both young, gifted, and Jewish. Levenson had been a member of the Society of Fellows at Harvard, and Schwartz would soon take up a joint appointment at Harvard in history and political science.[12]

The appointment sparked some controversy. The Communists had just taken over China, and Fairbank was thought to be sympathetic to the Maoist government. Therefore, in the minds of some, his students were suspect. Raymond Sontag, a fervent anti-Communist, urged caution in proceeding with the appointment. Despite the risk, the department elected to go ahead with the appointment, and, mainly at the insistence of Woodbridge Bingham, its incumbent Asianist, also decided that it preferred Levenson. Like many of the Old Guard, Bingham was not himself a serious scholar, but he had no doubt about Levenson's potential.[13] Recruiting Levenson was a major coup, given Berkeley's reputation at the time, and he was the prototype of the kind of junior faculty member often hired at Harvard or other elite eastern universities.

Levenson's appointment was also significant because he was Jewish. The department had hired Jews in the past, including Kantorowicz before World War II and Armin Rappaport in 1949, but a current of anti-Semitism had always existed under the surface at Berkeley. The traditional preference for candidates holding degrees from places west of the Mississippi River may have been one manifestation. Other whisperings occurred. Hicks, reputedly anti-Semitic, detested Kantorowicz. Woodrow Borah, a Jew thought to be Bolton's best student, did not receive a departmental appointment until 1962. Kenneth Stampp suspected that anti-Semitism underlay the opposition of several of his colleagues to Levenson's appointment. And, after Levenson's appointment, several of the older people made anti-Semitic remarks about him.[14]

In the early fifties, two other appointments of importance were made, Robert Brentano in medieval history and Henry May in American intellectual history. Both appointments broke with the department's usual hiring patterns. While May was a Berkeley undergraduate, neither he nor Brentano held a doctoral degree from Berkeley or Wisconsin; in fact Brentano was a Rhodes Scholar who received an Oxford D. Phil., and May's Ph.D. was from Harvard. In May's case, he believed that he was hired because Hicks, who was the chair at the time, thought May was a nice Berkeley boy who would do what he was told.[15]

Another important appointment occurred in 1954 when the department hired Gene Brucker to teach late medieval and early

Renaissance history. Although his first appointment was only a temporary one, Brucker possessed several of the characteristics of the new faculty of the fifties. Like Brentano, he was a Rhodes Scholar with great scholarly potential. And, like several of the other new appointees, he was not connected to either Berkeley or Madison; his Ph.D. was from Princeton. In this case, Brucker's pedigree paid off. Sontag, who taught at Princeton for more than a decade and a half before coming to Berkeley, called Harris "Jinks" Harbison, a close friend from his Princeton days, to ask if Princeton had any students who might be interested in coming to Berkeley, and Harbison recommended Brucker.[16]

But the most contested step in elevating the quality of the Berkeley department was the appointment of Renaissance and Reformation specialist William Bouwsma in 1956. Bouwsma's appointment was closely intertwined with the rise of Carl Bridenbaugh as a powerful force in the department. Bridenbaugh was a Harvard Ph.D. who had written several interesting books on social life in colonial America and had come to Berkeley in 1949 as holder of the Byrne Chair. When the previous holder, Frederick Paxson retired in 1948, the chair holders first turned to Merle Curti, who turned them down. Their next choice was Dixon Wecter, then living in southern California and a reputable scholar. Wecter accepted the position, but died unexpectedly in June, 1950.

Later that summer, Raymond Sontag came to Kenneth Stampp's office and asked him what he thought of Bridenbaugh as a replacement. Stampp replied that while he did not know Bridenbaugh personally, he was a good social historian. Then, without department discussion or even an on-campus interview, Bridenbaugh arrived in September and began teaching. The chair holders simply decided to offer him the position, and he accepted.[17]

During the next few years the chair holders and many of the Old Guard would come to regret the decision. Bridenbaugh was a complex person, bright and energetic, but arrogant and abrasive. He made no bones about his contempt for the department as it then stood, and quickly succeeded in making enemies of Hicks and Sontag. At a meeting of the department's full professors soon after his arrival, Bridenbaugh informed them that the department had a reputation in the east as one of the worst history departments at a major university.[18]

But there were several sides to his personality, including a sensitive one. In the late thirties at the height of the Depression, he helped the unemployed Jack Hexter get his first job at M.I.T. A victim of hard economic times and anti-Semitism, Hexter and his Harvard mentors feared he was unemployable before Bridenbaugh interceded. In the early sixties, Thomas Barnes, the department's Tudor-Stuart specialist, and his family visited the Bridenbaughs not long after Barnes' father had died. Barnes' young daughter took one look at Bridenbaugh, exclaimed "Grandpa," and rushed to embrace him. Bridenbaugh, who had no children of his own, was visibly moved, and tears came to his eyes.[19]

Despite moments of tenderness, however, the central trait of his personality at Berkeley was a relentless determination to upgrade the quality of the department and destroy any obstacle in his way. At one department meeting he viciously denounced James King, the department chair at the moment, and a gentle man. To Bridenbaugh, however, he was one of the enemy, a member of the Boltonian wing loyal to the Old Berkeley, and thus he had to be liquidated. As he walked back to his office after the meeting with Charles Jelavich, a junior member in the department, Jelavich said to Bridenbaugh, "Carl, don't you think you should be easier on King? His wife is dying of cancer." Bridenbaugh replied, "So what? My first wife died of cancer."[20]

But, for all his lack of tact, Bridenbaugh was a driving force in transforming the department from one that claimed little national esteem to one that commanded worldwide respect. In the process he was willing to sacrifice graduate students and junior faculty who failed to meet his standards. At the same time, he was able to rally several of the department's faculty, who called themselves the "Young Turks," to his cause. Bridenbaugh was also willing to put an end to several of the department's traditional power bases. Bridenbaugh was, for example, instrumental in reducing the influence of the chair holders, even though he himself was one. At his urging, by the end of the decade a chair holder possessed no more power than any other full professor.[21]

Some of Bridenbaugh's decisions angered even his allies among the Turks. Bridenbaugh, along with Sontag, Stampp and May, was determined to deny promotion to Gordon Griffiths, even though Griffiths was highly respected by several of the younger Turks. A decade later, Bridenbaugh was also scornful of Carl Schorske's work, even though Schorske was popular enough with the rest of the department that he became chair after only three years at Berkeley.[22]

Bouwsma's appointment became Bridenbaugh's great crusade. Bouwsma, then teaching at the University of Illinois, was, like Bridenbaugh, a Harvard Ph.D. Bridenbaugh was particularly contemptuous of the department's European wing, which he regarded as weak. The department had already taken important steps to improve it, tenuring Robert Brentano, and hiring Gene Brucker. Bouwsma's appointment seemed to be a critical piece of the puzzle, and his dissertation on the French humanist Guillaume Postel was in press with Harvard Historical Studies. Stampp had already heard of Bouwsma's promise from friends of the University of Illinois and had met him while passing through Champaign. At the American Historical Association meeting in 1954, Bouwsma met several of the Berkeley faculty, all of whom came away impressed.[23]

By 1955, however, it may not have been the best thing for Bouwsma to have Bridenbaugh, who had already begun to alienate even his supporters, on his side. The majority of the department, led by Raymond Sontag, who had himself previously supported progressive appointments, now adamantly opposed Bouwsma. They preferred J. Russell Major, a Princeton Ph.D., teaching at Emory University, who had already published a book on the French Estates General.[24]

Opponents of Bouwsma cited several considerations. Some said Bouwsma's brand of intellectual history was too much like philosophy; others said he was a European historian who had never been to Europe. Still others said the department already had Gene Brucker to teach the Renaissance. Most outrageously, John Hicks contended that since Bouwsma's father, who taught at the University of Nebraska, had never published, Bouwsma probably wouldn't either.[25]

The "Young Turks," led by Bridenbaugh, along with George Guttridge and Paul Schaeffer, among the older faculty, remained adamant in their support of Bouwsma. They suspected that Sontag's opposition stemmed from two sources that had nothing to do with Bouwsma's academic qualifications. The first source of opposition was Sontag's mounting hostility to Bridenbaugh personally. And the second source was the fact that Bouwsma was a Dutch Calvinist who would be teaching the history of Christianity and the Reformation, something that Sontag, a devout Catholic, wished to prevent.[26]

When the department voted against offering Bouwsma a permanent position, his supporters appealed to Dean Lincoln Constance to bring Bouwsma to campus on a one-year appointment for 1956-7. Constance approved, and, despite fears that Bouwsma might be insulted by only being offered a one-year position, he accepted. Bouwsma was so eager to take the job that he resigned his position at Illinois, despite having four children and only a one-year appointment at Berkeley. But, even after an impressive performance during his visiting year, Bouwsma was still opposed by the Boltonians.[27]

The issue of Armin Rappaport's tenure, however, afforded Bouwsma's supporters a window of opportunity. Rappaport was a younger faculty member, with a Stanford Ph.D. and a popular teacher who had allied himself with the Old Guard. His record of publication was weak, and he was initially denied promotion. But the Boltonians were willing to trade Rappaport's tenure in return for Bouwsma's appointment, and the deal was made. Rappaport was given tenure, and, a few weeks later, when the decision on Bouwsma was made, Sontag and several of the Old Guard were noticeably absent.[28]

The Bouwsma appointment, sometimes called the "Bouwsma Revolution," was a triumph for the "Young Turks." Bouwsma was a serious and innovative scholar. Moreover, his appointment, supplemented by the retirements of several members of the Old Guard over the next few years, cemented the majority of the "Young Turks" and gave them control over appointments and tenure decisions. At the same time, the state continued to prosper and had a liberal legislature and a sympathetic governor, which made the building of a great department much easier than it would have been a decade before.[29]

Between 1957 and 1963, the faculty who joined the department included David Landes, Charles Sellers, Thomas Kuhn, Martin Malia, Nicholas Riasanovsky, Hans Rosenberg, Richard Herr, Carl Schorske, Lawrence Levine, Robert Middlekauff, Winthrop Jordan, and Adrienne Koch. Among this group, two in particular stood out. Landes was an economic historian of the broadest vision. Kuhn had already published a book on the Copernican Revolution in science, and was at work on *The Structure of Scientific Revolutions*.[30]

Among the most striking features of the group hired in the late fifties and sixties was the high concentration of Jews, including Landes, Kuhn, Schorske, Levine, and Rosenberg as well as Richard Abrams and Samuel Haber. By 1964, several others, including Gerald Feldman, Sheldon Rothblatt, Henry Rosovsky, and Leon Litwack had also joined the department. The decline of the Old Guard and the triumph of the "Young Turks" opened up heightened opportunities for Jews, and the ones who were hired during this period came to rank among the department's most distinguished scholars.

Another important member of that cohort was the appointment of Adrienne Koch, the first woman to hold a faculty position in the department. Koch had a Ph.D. in philosophy and had written a fine book on Thomas Jefferson, whom she admired greatly. She had also taught at the University of Maryland when Kenneth Stampp was there, and, when she first came to Berkeley, her first position was in political science and then in the American Studies program, where she established a reputation as a very good teacher. Henry May, whose field was American Intellectual history, strongly urged that the history department move to appoint her, which it did in 1958.

The appointment was not entirely a success. Koch was the only woman in the department during her time at Berkeley, and several department members, perhaps insensitively, considered her difficult. She was voted tenure, but, she stayed in rank longer than she thought she should have, and left when her husband got a job in Washington in 1965.[31]

The brilliant string of appointments in the late fifties and early sixties also reflected the rise of the great state universities as rivals to the eastern private schools. Times were so flush that when the department was deadlocked between two highly qualified candidates, it was often able to hire them both. When Carl Bridenbaugh departed for Brown in 1962, the department was able to replace him with Winthrop Jordan and Robert Middlekauff, an arrangement that paid off handsomely. Within a few years Jordan had published the prize-winning *White over Black*, which argued that slavery began in part because Europeans were already conditioned by their culture to regard Africans as inferior before they ever laid eyes on them. Middlekauff, through a series of books on education, the Puritans, Benjamin Franklin, and the American Revolution, established a reputation as one of the nation's finest colonial historians.[32]

The department itself offered several advantages. New faculty often found it more open and less hierarchical than the schools where they had received their graduate training. As assistant professors, they were welcomed into a community rather than being permitted to enter an academic food chain at the bottom. Most of the assistant professors hired during this time were ultimately promoted to tenure, and, usually, without as much of the angst and feelings of isolation that usually accompanied being a junior faculty member at other elite institutions. They also became a generational cohort, like the Boltonians of the forties, that formed the core of the department for the next two decades.[33]

Teaching at Cal in the sixties also had its delights. When Carl Schorske came to Berkeley from Wesleyan in 1960, he had to change from the small group discussion teaching at Wesleyan to lecturing to large classes in Berkeley. But he soon discovered that students were hungry for discussion. Early in his time at Berkeley, he finished his lecture course in European intellectual history to a round of applause from the students. But, as he was leaving the lecture hall, he heard one of the students say, "and they call that a dialogue?"

Disturbed by the remark, he realized that he needed to find a way to inject discussion and closer student/faculty interaction into his classes. He decided to use his graduate students to teach discussion sections. The graduate assistants were allowed to choose a topic related to the course material and develop their own readings and assignments that would allow for discussion and afford the opportunity to see the course material from another angle. Schorske particularly admired the course developed by one of his teaching assistants, centering on the theme of "The Costs of Freedom."[34]

Occasionally, when the department attempted to lure outstanding faculty, it suffered some rejections, usually at the senior level. At different times, the department tried to bring in such notable historians as J.H. Hexter in early modern English history, David Brion Davis in American intellectual history, John Pocock in European intellectual history, and Benjamin Schwartz in Chinese history, but without success.[35]

There was also regular socializing among department members. Beverly Bouwsma, wife of William Bouwsma, described the department's social life as "dinner parties, dinner parties, dinner parties all the time. That's what we did. For years I did nothing but have dinner parties." The dinner parties became particularly intense during the period while her husband served as department chair. "If I didn't have a dinner party a week," she recalled, "I wouldn't get around to everybody."[36]

The department's socializing also involved serious drinking. Bouwsma recalled, "we drank so heavily you could hardly believe…you had to have things like Scotch and gin and all those things…sometimes the floor would practically be awash the next morning in spilled stuff, whiskey and things like that."

Heavy drinking led to memorable moments. One of which had Raymond Sontag playing footsie with Beverly Bouwsma under the dinner table. Bouwsma took no offense, even though Sontag had opposed her husband's appointment. More serious was the violent argument that broke out between Bill Bouwsma and another faculty member over moving African-American Studies out of the history department.

The department's social life also reveals much about the place of women in it. Carl Bridenbaugh once tried to organize a group of faculty to meet periodically to read and critique each other's work. The group included Kenneth Stampp, Henry May, Joseph Levenson, and several others. The meetings took place at the homes of the involved faculty and also involved dinner and drinks. The wives would be expected to prepare the dinner and then disappear when the discussion took place. But, at one point, when the faculty arrived earlier than anticipated for one meeting, they were informed by the wife in question, in this case, Rosemary Levenson, that she was not finished with her preparations, and they were not allowed in until she was.[37]

In addition to strengthening Cal's command of established fields, the boom years of the sixties enabled the department to extend its offerings in non-western areas. It already had a good record. It had an Asian specialist in Woodbridge Bingham as early as 1937, and Asian history was strengthened by the appointments of Joseph Levenson in 1950 and Franz Schurman in 1958. In 1946 Delmer Brown arrived in the department to teach Japanese history.

The sixties, however, saw a flood of appointments in non-western areas. Woodrow Borah, reportedly Bolton's best student, taught in the Department of Speech until 1962, when Delmer Brown hired him to teach Latin American history. In the history of India, Thomas Metcalf was added in 1961 and Eugene Irschick in 1964. In 1963 and 1969 Irwin Scheiner and Thomas Smith were added to the faculty teaching Japanese history. At about the same time, Ira Lapidus and John Smith began teaching Middle Eastern history. Raymond Kent arrived in Berkeley to teach African history in 1966, and David Keightly began teaching early Chinese history in 1969.

Unfortunately, the department's prize non-western appointment, that of Joseph Levenson, was destined for tragedy. Levenson was brilliant, charming, and the author of a widely praised book, the two-volume *Confucian China and its Modern Fate*. But, in 1969, he and his son were involved in a boating accident in which Levenson drowned while trying to save his son, an event that devastated the department.[38]

But, if, during the great period of "sturm and drang" the department had taken decisive steps to improve its reputation, some problems remained. One of them was the thorny personality of Carl Bridenbaugh. Bridenbaugh had been a key figure in exhorting the department to improve the quality of its faculty. But his abrasive personality almost ruined the process. By the early sixties, other aspects of that personality surfaced. Bridenbaugh had always dreamed of returning to Harvard. In 1958 the chance to realize the dream opened before him. Samuel Eliot Morison, Harvard's senior colonial historian, retired. Three main candidates emerged as possible successors, including Bridenbaugh, Edmund Morgan then teaching at Yale, and Bernard Bailyn, a junior faculty member at Harvard. When the department couldn't decide between Bridenbaugh and Morgan, it offered the job to Bailyn, who was clearly a star on the rise, but who was still in the early stages of his career and Jewish.

Bridenbaugh had previously revealed an anti-Semitic strain to his personality. Kenneth Stampp remembers him asking, "have you ever noticed that every candidate Joe Levenson supports is Jewish?" Stampp hadn't noticed and didn't think it was important. But many people think that Harvard's decision to appoint Bailyn made Bridenbaugh more visibly anti-Semitic. Not only was Bridenbaugh devastated by missing his opportunity to return to Harvard in glory, but he lost it to a Jew.[39]

Bridenbaugh's anti-Semitism may have played a part in the next great matter before the Berkeley History Department, the promotion of Thomas Kuhn, the historian of science, to full professor. Kuhn was a trained physicist who eventually became perhaps the most renowned figure in the history of science. He came to Berkeley in 1956 along with A. Hunter Dupree, a historian of American science (Kuhn specialized in European science) as well as of technology. Both were able Harvard Ph.D.s, but Dupree was clearly the favored candidate of Bridenbaugh. Kuhn, who was Jewish, however, appeared to be the more promising. Kuhn had been a junior member of the Society of Fellows at Harvard and was the more advanced scholar, having published *The Copernican Revolution: Planetary Astronomy in the Development of Western Thought* in 1957.

Kuhn held a joint appointment in history and philosophy, which put him in an awkward position. He had to please both groups, but his work was too historical for the philosophers and not historical enough for some historians. In 1961 the philosophy department denied his promotion, but suggested that his position be transferred full-time to history.[40]

When the issue of Kuhn's promotion in history was raised in a department meeting, Bridenbaugh offered serious objections to his work. Kuhn was already at work on what is almost certainly the most famous book ever written on the history of science, *The Structure of Scientific Revolutions*. It was soft, Bridenbaugh contended, too theoretical and not really history. Of course this argument closely resembled what he had said about William Bouwsma's work a few years before.[41]

The morning after the meeting, however, several department members, including Henry May, Joe Levenson, and Kenneth Stampp, met in Carl Schorske's office. They thought Kuhn's brilliance was undeniable and were deeply offended by Bridenbaugh's opposition. After some deliberation, they decided to circulate a petition asking for another meeting, which was signed by almost every full professor and presented the next week to Delmer Brown, then the department chair.[42]

On the day it was presented, Bridenbaugh appeared at Stampp's office. Once allies, the two had already been drifting apart, in part over Stampp's divorce from his first wife for which Bridenbaugh had severely chastised him. Before Bridenbaugh could say anything, Stampp said, "Carl, I don't understand what you did last Friday about Tom Kuhn." Bridenbaugh started to reply by saying, "Well, Tom Kuhn is not…" Stampp cut him off. "Carl," he said, "I have to tell you that I have given a petition to Delmer asking for another meeting." Without reply, Bridenbaugh got up and walked out of Stampp's office and never spoke to Stampp again. A week later, another meeting over Kuhn's promotion was held, and it was unanimously approved.[43]

Ironically, despite the triumph, Kuhn would not stay at Berkeley. In 1963 Charles Gillispie, Princeton's historian of science, received an offer from Harvard which gave him leverage to convince the Princeton administration to let him build up the history of science at Princeton and allow him hire another faculty member in the discipline. Gillispie offered the position to Kuhn, who accepted and left Berkeley for Princeton in 1964.

Bridenbaugh's failure to block Kuhn's promotion signaled the beginning of the end of his influence at Berkeley. When he heard that people in the department were highly critical of his actions regarding Kuhn's promotion, Bridenbaugh went to Delmer Brown and demanded an apology, specifically from Stampp and May, whom he regarded as his principal critics. When no apology was forthcoming, he resigned from the department's personnel committee, and, within a year left Berkeley to accept a position at Brown University. Brown labored mightily to convince Bridenbaugh to stay, but later confessed that the more Bridenbaugh talked, "the more I wanted him to leave."[44] After arriving at Brown, Bridenbaugh exacted a small measure of revenge on Berkeley by persuading several of his friends on the Berkeley history faculty, including Bryce Lyon, L. Perry Curtis, and Hunter Dupree, to join him.

In 1963 he delivered his notorious address to the American Historical Association deploring the entry of immigrants unfamiliar with American culture into historical circles, which seemed to be an attack on Jews entering the profession. No one will ever know for certain, but it seems possible, even likely, that Bridenbaugh's remarks stemmed from anti-Semitism, and in particular losing the Harvard job to a Jew and failing to prevent the promotion of another at Berkeley.[45]

At the same time Berkeley was becoming a symbol of the student unrest that characterized the sixties. Despite its increasing national reputation, the Berkeley campus had also come to represent the most visible example of the "multiversity," referring to the transformation of the smaller, more intimate campuses of the pre-World War II years into larger, more impersonal, almost corporate bodies. The university's chancellor, the economist Clark Kerr, had even written a book, *The Uses of the University*, in which he suggested that the university should be run like a business, seemingly justifying the corporate nature of the academic enterprise.[46]

A small group of students found themselves dissatisfied with these developments as they appeared at Berkeley. One of those students, Mario Savio, had spent the summer of 1964 teaching in the Student Non-Violent Coordinating Committee's Mississippi Summer Project. When he returned to Berkeley to start the fall semester, he decided that many of the same power structures used by whites to rule over blacks in the South were also used by university administrators to rule over students. "Last summer, I went to Mississippi to join the struggle there for civil rights," he wrote upon his return to campus. "This fall I am engaged in another phase of the same struggle, this time at Berkeley…the same rights are at stake both places."

Savio was a leader of a group of students who called themselves the Free Speech movement, and their struggle with the university administration began in September 1964, when Kerr banned political recruitment in Sproul Plaza, a popular student gathering place. Savio and other students defied the ban; the administration suspended them or had them arrested. On October 1st, students surrounded a police car in which a demonstrator was being held and prevented it from moving for thirty-two hours. In December the Free Speech Movement seized and occupied the university's main administrative building. Alarmed, Governor Pat Brown sent the state police to remove the students and over eight-hundred people were arrested. In response, irate students shut down classes for several days in protest.

The Free Speech Movement emerged in the broader context of political protest, especially on civil rights, where several members of the department were especially active. Kenneth Stampp helped bring Herbert Aptheker, a historian of slave revolts, to campus. Charles Sellers went to Mississippi as part of the Freedom Riders Movement. Stampp and Lawrence Levine went to Montgomery, Alabama for the famous march on the state capitol. The March included about forty other academic historians, including Vann Woodward and Richard Hofstadter.[47]

After the troubles of the fall of 1964, a Committee on Academic Freedom was established to work with the steering committee of the Free Speech Movement. Kenneth Stampp from the history department was on the committee, and he was sympathetic to student issues. Mario Savio, as the leader of the Free Speech movement, was a central figure in its deliberations, and he regularly threatened to walk out if the things did not go his way. It was his irritation with the committee that led to occupation of university offices and subsequent arrest of students in December, 1964.

The Committee on Academic Freedom had a series of meetings which led to the December 8th Resolutions, concerning political meetings on campus and the rights of students to speak and advocate. The Resolutions were opposed by Clark Kerr and the administration, but, after an intense debate in Wheeler Hall, attended by about half of the university's 1500 faculty members, they were approved. Passage of the resolutions was a victory for the students and the Free Speech Movement.

By 1965 the Free Speech Movement had been overtaken by serious protests against the War in Viet Nam. These protests became increasingly violent. The next issue as far as faculty were concerned was whether or not the Academic Senate, the main faculty body at Berkeley, should take stands on political issues. One group of faculty wanted it to take stands, deploring the war, for example, as a similar faculty body at Harvard did; another group thought that academic bodies should only take stands on issues that pertained to academic matters.

Like almost every history department in the country, the Berkeley department was bitterly divided over student protest. Several, such as Charles Sellers and Carl Schorske, were strong supporters of the students. Others, like Stampp, were sympathetic to the issues raised by students, but were eventually repelled by their extremism. The students, for example, wanted the freedom to bring in speakers sympathetic to their political viewpoints, but opposed bringing speakers who opposed them. Still others had no sympathy for the students and wished the administration would take a harder stand. Raymond Sontag and Martin Malia fell into this category. Others even left the department over protests. After one incident, David Landes said, "this really does it. I'm getting out." He left for Harvard and was soon followed by Henry Rosovsky. William Bouwsma also left the department to go to Harvard in 1969, but he returned to Berkeley two years later.[48]

In the period between 1966 and 1968, the course of events took some curious turns. Violence escalated. Thomas Barnes, the department's Tudor-Stuart specialist, was serving as an interim assistant dean in the fall of 1964, landing in the middle of student anger and what he called "the interminable talk, the glut of writing, the hyperbole, rhetoric, incitement, resolutions, rallies, the constant positioning and unpositioning." He also described the surreal quality of being a faculty member at one of the country's finest institutions of higher learning and looking out his office window at a campus blanketed with tear gas and a full-scale battle raging between a thousand insurrectionists and half as many police, with a hundred casualties, and, after years of exposure, finding himself almost unmoved.[49]

Gene Brucker also recalled a similarly surreal experience of being in a graduate oral exam in May, 1969 when the campus was occupied by the National Guard. While the candidate, whose field was medieval history, responded to questions, heliocopters hovered overhead and tear gas swirled around the campus. William Bouwsma was manhandled by black militants, though the only injury was to his dignity. After his office window was smashed by demonstrating students, Joseph Levenson placed a plastic statue of Chairman Mao in the window as a talisman and escaped further student reprisal.[50]

There were some points of agreement between students and faculty. In January 1967 the regents fired Clark Kerr, under the urging of then Governor Ronald Reagan. At another huge, widely attended faculty meeting, radical leaders secured the passage of another set of resolutions deploring the regents' actions in firing Kerr. The resolutions claimed support across the political spectrum.

In 1967 the issue of developing a program in Black Studies was raised by Walter Knight, the dean of the College of Letters and Science. The issue placed the history department in a dilemma. One of the department's strength's was its cluster of outstanding faculty, including Stampp, Charles Sellers, Lawrence Levine, Winthrop Jordan, and Leon Litwack, who had published books in black history, several of which won awards. But they were all white, and several, including Stampp, felt that the best way to teach black history was to integrate it into all American history courses, rather than create a separate department to teach only black history. Despite their reservations, the historians who taught black history, bowed to the inevitable, and an African-American studies department was created.[51]

In the spring of 1970 American military forces expanded the war in Southeast Asia into Cambodia, and demonstrations, violence, and tear gas returned to the Berkeley campus. Since the Cambodian incursion came late in the academic year, administrations at many universities were able to deflect student anger by allowing faculty a great deal of latitude in accommodating student protestors. In the history department, many instructors dismissed their classes and allowed students to take the grades they had earned so far in the course or just gave them all "A's," if they wanted to go out and work for peace.

Several department members were offended, since it seemed a complete abdication of academic standards. Students were going to get grades without completing all the work; faculty who dismissed their classes were going to get paid without finishing their teaching. Moreover, graduate students who were teaching assistants in cancelled classes were not going to get paid.[52]

The department entered the seventies aware that the heady days of departmental expansion were coming to a close. Not only was the California economic boom slowing down, but the student disturbances had given the campus a bad reputation. The days when the department, deadlocked between two impressive candidates for a position, would be allowed to hire them both, were gone, as well as the days when the department could make a fair number of its appointments at the senior level. Governors friendly to higher education, like Pat Brown, had been replaced by critics like Ronald Reagan. One observer noted that in one sense, without the student troubles, Reagan would not have become president of the United States. The student troubles allowed him to become governor of California, and, without that experience, he could never have been president.[53]

The department had improved its standing dramatically, although opinions differed on where precisely it should be ranked. When Nicholas Riasanovsky spent a year as a visiting professor at Harvard, he and Robert Lee Wolff, one of Harvard's Russian historians, regularly discussed the merits and defects of various departments, concluding that the top two were Harvard and Berkeley. When Riasanovsky and Bernard Bailyn discussed the issue, Bailyn gave Harvard a slight advantage only because it required less of its faculty in the way of committee service; Harvard's only committees involved appointments. However, when Riasanovsky visited with George Pierson at Yale over the possibility of taking a position there, Pierson's only point of reference was Yale versus Harvard. Berkeley did not figure in his assessment.[54]

One positive note, amidst all the difficulties facing the department and university in the early seventies, was the return of William Bouwsma in 1971. Bouwsma accepted an offer from Harvard in 1969, eager to escape the increasingly irate demands of radical students. But he found other problems at Harvard and became disenchanted soon after his arrival. He deplored the department's hierarchy and lack of community, as well as its treatment of the junior faculty, particularly after one episode when the junior faculty were not invited to the department Christmas party. "I am increasingly aware," he wrote to Gene Brucker, "that Harvard lacks the human riches of the Berkeley department." He was even chastised for keeping his office door open for students, though he did acknowledge that Harvard offered him greater opportunity to pursue his scholarship than he had ever enjoyed anywhere else.[55]

He had not, however, let on to his friends in Berkeley the extent of his unhappiness. But a series of unforeseen events brought him the opportunity to return to Berkeley. The death of Joseph Levenson opened up the Sather Chair. Gene Brucker, acting chair of the department at the time, had gone the A.H.A. meeting in Boston. While at the meeting, he paid a visit to the Bouwsmas. Later, at lunch with Herbert Mann, one of his publishers, the subject of the Bouwsmas came up. Brucker ventured that they seemed happy at Harvard. Mann informed him that, on the contrary, they were miserable.[56]

Sensing an opportunity to lure Bouwsma back, Brucker quickly contacted as many of the senior members of the department as he could and sounded their opinions on Bouwsma's suitability for the Sather Chair. The response was overwhelmingly positive, though certain financial considerations had to be negotiated before the deal was finalized. Bouwsma wondered, for example, if Berkeley could afford him. His salary at Harvard in 1971 was $25,000.[57]

In the seventies, the department also faced the need to add blacks and women to its faculty and how to integrate courses on women and African American history into the curriculum. In the search for a black historian, the department first approached

Nathan Huggins, who, as a Berkeley undergraduate, seriously considered the possibility of remaining there for graduate study so he could work with Kenneth Stampp. Despite that attraction, Huggins accepted a fellowship offer from Harvard where he worked with Oscar Handlin. After he finished his degree, his first job was at Long Beach State, and, noting his promise after his first years there, the department offered him a one-year, visiting appointment. During Huggins' time at Berkeley, the department voted to offer him a position, but he took an offer from Columbia instead and later returned to Harvard.[58]

Subsequently, the department approached John Blassingame at Yale and Sterling Stuckey at Northwestern, without success. It was not until 1980, when the department was hired Waldo Martin, that it was able to secure a black faculty member, although African American Studies already had several.

The department was also dealing with the entry of women. It had already hired and promoted Adrienne Koch in the late fifties and mid-sixties. The next woman to join the department was Natalie Zemon Davis in 1968. Davis had been pursuing a career as a gypsy scholar since the early fifties. Her husband, Chandler Davis, was a mathematician, who refused to sign loyalty oaths often required in academic life in the fifties and, thereby found himself effectively blacklisted, able to get only temporary appointments. Thus, Davis bounced around from place to place as her husband moved from job to job. Despite the nomadic nature of their lives, they were able to start a family, and Davis was able to take some steps toward an academic career. She earned a Ph.D. from the University of Michigan in 1959 while her husband was teaching there. After they left Ann Arbor, she was able to do research and began publishing a series of innovative articles on sixteenth century French social and cultural history.[59]

By 1967, she decided she needed a regular job, even if it meant being separated from her husband, who had finally found a permanent position at the University of Toronto. At the 1967 meeting of the American Historical Association, she ran into Bill Bouwsma, whom she knew from her days as a Radcliffe undergraduate and who was familiar with her work. She mentioned to him that she was trying to get a regular job.[60]

Davis returned to Toronto and, to her surprise, found a letter from the department wanting to know if she wished to be considered for an appointment. Accepting a position at Berkeley would mean leaving her husband and Toronto where they had a home, children in school, and many friends. But Berkeley and the opportunity to have a full-time position was too tempting. She remembers sitting with her husband in front of warm fire in their Toronto home and deciding to accept it.

The position had many advantages for her. She came in the wake of the student troubles, and wrote one of her most famous articles, "The Rites of Violence," during the first year she was at Berkeley, admittedly influenced by the heady discussions of rebelliousness and turning the world upside down. She found it a pleasure to work with her fellow early modernists, Bouwsma, Gene Brucker, and Randolph Starn, and many of the other history faculty.

The department also enjoyed a great reputation, and there were opportunities for interdisciplinary exchange. Although the journal *Representations* would not be founded until after she left Berkeley, its leading figures, including Stephen Greenblatt, Svetlana Alpers, Katherine Gallagher, David Wright, and the historians Thomas Laqueur and Randolph Starn, were already meeting. She met all of them and shared their interest in adopting approaches from other disciplines, such as art history, to study the importance of representational forms, and also to applying the anthropological perspectives of Clifford Geertz and Mary Douglas.

But, like all jobs, the position at Berkeley had curiosities. She thought the department was superb, but that it was a brotherhood composed of male, egalitarian aristocrats. They were not snooty or arrogant, but they were aristocratic in the sense of respecting good work and wanting the department to be the best. Several of the established faculty, however, were not interested in her work and were skeptical of its interdisciplinary orientation.

There was also the issue of being the only woman. One man in particular made it clear that he wished she would leave. When Davis would stride down the hallway in high heeled shoes, he said it was like having his mother as a member of the department. Another man said he could not vote tenure for a woman. Still another had a reputation for sexual harassment. Davis feared that the brotherhood covered up for him. Things became easier when Diane Clemens was hired the next year, and, later, when Lynn Hunt came.

Davis' role in the department's active social life was also difficult, since her husband, still teaching in Toronto, was rarely in Berkeley. The awkwardness of her situation sometimes surfaced in the group she helped organize for graduate students and faculty in early modern Europe. With Davis, Bouwsma, Brucker, and Starn, the department was particularly strong in this field, although Bouwsma did leave briefly for Harvard. Davis and the other early modernists organized a regular dinners for students and faculty where there would be regular reading of papers and discussions of issues of importance to early modernists. The dinner did mean, however, that in the traditional Berkeley manner, the wives, in this case Beverly Bouwsma and Francie Starn, would do most of the work preparing the meal, while Davis and the men, busy teaching, would only arrive later.[61]

Divisions between the department male and female faculty also emerged at a meeting in which the department considered the promotion of Lynn Hunt, a brilliant young historian of the French Revolution, to associate professor. Her promotion should have been automatic, but when a department member known to have made unfortunate remarks about women, voiced his support for her, a major argument erupted and more than one of the department's fault lines was exposed. One of the department's women exclaimed that since the male faculty member was not allowed to vote, he should not even be allowed to speak.[62]

The department's course offerings also reflected changing times. Many of the traditional national histories and courses framed around time period remained, but a range of new offerings appeared. Most of them dealt with issues involving race, gender, and class, but an intriguing mix of other offerings appeared, including courses in deviance, criminality, childhood, historical memory and identity formation, and colonial ideologies.[63]

Among history departments, the course of events in the Berkeley department, is the most clearly defined. Before the mid-fifties Berkeley was dominated by an Old Guard of Bolton students and powerful chair holders. Largely at the initiative of Carl Bridenbaugh, and younger faculty, like Kenneth Stampp and Henry May, the department was transformed into a powerhouse. While there had been several progressive appointments in the early fifties, the appointment of William Bouwsma in 1956 cemented the dominance of the "Young Turks" and cleared the way for increasing numbers of progressive appointments in the late fifties and sixties. The department hired many Jews and took critical steps to improve its faculty in non-western areas.

Like most departments, it struggled to understand the students of the sixties and to reach agreement about how they should be treated. The student troubles cost the department several important faculty and also contributed to public disgust with the university. Much harder to deal with, however, was the contraction of support for higher education in the seventies. Public anger at the students and a declining economy reduced the funds available for higher education in California, and the department was effected.

---

[1] Gene A. Brucker, "History at Berkeley," in Gene A. Brucker, Henry F. May, and David A. Hollinger, *History at Berkeley: A Dialog in Three Parts* (Berkeley, 1998), p. 3.

[2] David A. Hollinger, "Afterward," in Brucker, May, and Hollinger, *History at Berkeley*, pp. 37-9; for Bolton as historian, see David J. Weber, "Turner, the Boltonians, and the Borderlands," *American Historical Review*, 61, 1(February, 1986): 66–81.

[3] John Francis Bannon, *Herbert Eugene Bolton: The Historian and the Man, 1870–1953* (Tucson, Ariz., 1978); Hollinger, "Afterword," pp. 38-9.

[4] Kantorowicz's story is told in Norman Cantor, *Inventing the Middle Ages: The Lives and Works of the Great Medievalists of the Twentieth Century* (New York, 1991), pp. 96-9.

⁵ See Chapter Three in this volume for Sontag's role at Princeton.

⁶ Kenneth Stampp, "Historian of Slavery, the Civil War, and Reconstruction, the University of California at Berkeley, 1946–1983," an oral history conducted in 1996 by Ann Lage (Regional Oral History Office, the Bancroft Library, University of California at Berkeley, 1996), p. 121.

⁷ Ibid., p. 160; Brucker, "History at Berkeley," pp. 6–7.

⁸ Nicholas Riasanovsky, "Historian of Russia, University of California at Berkeley, 1957-1994," An oral history conducted by Ann Lage (Regional Oral History Office, the Bancroft Library, University of California at Berkeley), p. 97.

⁹ Delmer Brown, "Professor of Japanese History, University of California at Berkeley, 1946–1977," An oral history conducted by Ann Lage (Regional Oral History Office, the Bancroft Library, University of California at Berkeley, 1996).

¹⁰ For the oath controversy, I follow Stampp, "Historian of Slavery," pp. 144-6.

¹¹ Stampp, "Historian of Slavery," p. 146.

¹² Brown, "Professor of Japanese History," p. 108.

¹³ Stampp, "Historian of Slavery," p. 158.

¹⁴ On Hicks' anti-Semitism, see Robert Brentano, "Historian of Medieval Europe, University of California at Berkeley, 1952–2003," An oral history conducted by Ann Lage (Regional Oral History Office, the Bancroft Library, University of California at Berkeley, 2003), p. 52; and Palmer, "Interview with Stanley Kutler," September 10, 2005; on Borah, see Palmer, "Interview with Gene Brucker," October 25, 2005; for the department in the late forties, see Stampp, "Historian of Slavery," pp. 158-9; on anti-Semitism among older faculty in the department in the fifties, see Henry F. May, "Intellectual Historian, University of California at Berkeley, 1952–80," An oral history conducted by Ann Lage (Regional Oral History Office, the Bancroft Library, University of California at Berkeley, 1995), p. 87.

¹⁵ May, "Intellectual Historian," p. 90.

¹⁶ Gene Brucker, "Historian of Renaissance Europe, University of California at Berkeley, 1954–1991," An oral history conducted by Ann Lage (Regional Oral History Office, the Bancroft Library, University of California at Berkeley), p. 102.

¹⁷ Stampp, "Historian of Slavery," pp. 160-1.

[18] Ibid., p. 162.

[19] William Palmer, *Engagement with the Past: The Lives and Works of the World War II Generation of Historians* (Lexington, Ky., 2001), p. 26; Palmer, "Interview with Thomas Barnes," October 28, 2005.

[20] Riasanovsky, "Historian of Russia," p. 100.

[21] Brucker, "History at Berkeley," pp. 6-7; Hollinger, "Afterward," pp. 38-9; Stampp, "Historian of Slavery," pp. 162-4.

[22] Brucker, "Historian of the Early Renaissance," p. 143-5.

[23] Stampp, "Historian of Slavery," p. 151. Bouwsma's book was published as *Concordia Mundi: The Career and Thought of Guillaume Postel, 1510–1581* (Cambridge, Mass., 1957).

[24] Palmer, "Interview with Brucker," October 25, 2005; Major's book was *The Estates General of 1560* (Princeton, 1950). A second book, *Representative Institutions in Renaissance France* (Madison, Wis., 1960) would be published a few years later.

[25] Stampp, "Historian of Slavery," p. 153; Bouwsma, "Interview with Lage," p. 57.

[26] For a shrewd analysis of the process, see Hollinger, "Afterward," pp. 40-3. It should be noted that Carl Schorske, who was not a member of the department at the time, but who knew Sontag well, believes that the idea that Sontag opposed Bouwsma because of Bouwsma's Dutch Calvinism is "nonsense." Palmer, "Interview with Carl Schorske," November 5, 2005.

[27] Hollinger, "Afterward," pp. 40-1.

[28] Stampp, "Historian of Slavery," p. 155; Hollinger, "Afterward," p. 42.

[29] Hollinger, "Afterward," pp. 42-3.

[30] Brucker, "History at Berkeley," p. 7; Hollinger, "Afterward," p. 42; Thomas S. Kuhn, *The Structure of Scientific Revolution* (Chicago, 1962).

[31] Stampp, "Historian of Slavery," pp. 165-6; Brown, "Professor of Japanese History," p. 124; Beverly Bouwsma, "A Wife's Perspective," p. 215.

[32] Brucker, "History at Berkeley," p. 9.

[33] Ibid., p. 8.

[34] Carl E. Schorske, "A Life in Learning," p. 10.

[35] Brucker, "Historian of the Early Renaissance," p. 137.

[36] The account of the department's social life in the sixties come from Bouwsma, "A Wife's Perspective," pp. 148-50, 155, 181-2, 197

37 Brentano, "Historian of Medieval Europe," p. 57.

38 For a discussion of *Confucian China and its Modern Fate*, see Levenson's essay, "The Genesis of *Confucian China and its Modern Fate*, in L.P. Curtis, ed., *The Historian's Workshop: Original Essays by Sixteen Historians* (New York, 1970), pp. 277-91.

39 Stampp, "Historian of Slavery," p. 169. The part about Bridenbaugh and Harvard is speculation on my part.

40 The story of Kuhn's promotion is recounted in Hollinger, "Afterward," pp. 43-5; and Stampp, "Historian of Slavery," p, 228.

41 In fairness, it should be added that Bridenbaugh was not the only one who was skeptical about Kuhn's work. Robert Brentano lived near Kuhn and often walked home with him in the afternoon. During the course of those walks he heard Kuhn discuss extensively the ideas in *Structure* ("Tom Kuhn never listened; he always talked," Brentano recalled) and thought they were rather ordinary. Brentano, "Historian of Medieval Europe," p. 80.

42 Stampp, "Historian of Slavery," p. 228.

43 Ibid., p. 229; Bouwsma, "Interview with Lage," p. 66.

44 Riasanovsky, "Historian of Russia," p. 97

45 Hollinger, "Afterward," pp. 43-4; for Bridenbaugh's speech, see "The Great Mutation," *American Historical Review* 67(January, 1963).

46 For a good account of the student troubles, see W. J. Rorabaugh, *Berkeley at War: the 1960s* (Oxford, 1989).

47 Stampp, "Historian of Slavery," pp. 231-3.

48 Ibid., pp. 239-41.

49 Thomas Garden Barnes, "Largely Without Benefit of Prior Conceptualization," in Curtis, ed., *The Historian's Workshop*, pp. 125-49.

50 For Brucker and Levenson, see Brucker, "History at Berkeley," p. 11; for Bouwsma, see William Bouwsma to Gene Brucker, March 1, 1969, Collection of letters available in the Regional Oral History Office, Bancroft Library, University of California at Berkeley.

51 Stampp, "Historian of Slavery," p. 245.

52 Ibid., p. 248.

53 Palmer, "Interview with Brucker," October 25, 2005.

54 Riasanovsky, "Historian of Russia," p. 117.

55 Bouwsma to Brucker, May 27, 1970;

56 Brucker, "Historian of the Early Renaissance," p. 123

57 Bouwsma to Brucker, February 16, 1970.

58 Stampp, "Historian of Slavery," pp. 247-8; Brucker, "Historian of the Early Renaissance," p. 146.

59 Robert Harding and Judy Coffin, "Interview with Natalie Zemon Davis," in Henry Abelove et al, eds., *Visions of History* (New York, 1983), pp. 99–122.

60 Davis describes her Berkeley career in her interview with Ann Lage, (Regional Oral history Office, the Bancroft Library, University of California at Berkeley) unpaginated.

61 Beverly Bouwsma, "A Wife's Perspective," p. 217.

62 Brentano, "Historian of Medieval Europe," p. 137.

63 Brucker, "History at Berkeley," pp. 13-4.

Chapter Six

Wisconsin: History as a Calling

Situated on an isthmus, the University of Wisconsin combines a campus of remarkable beauty with winters whose numbing cold defies description. The city of Madison is also appealing, once celebrated for its charms by a visiting Henry Wadsworth Longfellow. In the thirties Madison had a population of about 75,000 people and also served as the state capital. The community was known for its radical politics, and, despite the administration's efforts to keep them out, many of the university's undergraduates were out-of-state students attracted to the campus by its highly political atmosphere.[1]

The Wisconsin history department embraced a tradition of excellence dating back to the late nineteenth century and Frederick Jackson Turner. Turner, who had grown up in rural Portage, Wisconsin, was a Madison undergraduate who went to Johns Hopkins University for graduate work. Hopkins was then one of the centers for historical study in the United States, having adopted the German model, advanced by Leopold von Ranke, for the scientific study of history. Ranke advocated, among other things, objectivity in approach, extensive research in primary sources to discover the truth, and the graduate seminar as a means of teaching the writing of history.[2]

Hopkins also reflected the east-coast bias of most historians of the United States at the time. Such historians believed that most American institutions were derived mainly from English models. At Hopkins, Herbert Baxter Adams contended that American democratic institutions, particularly those in New England, could be traced to British and European roots. "It is just as improbable," Adams wrote, "that free local institutions should spring up without a germ along American shores as that English wheat should have grown without planting." Turner, with his Middle Western origins, was frustrated by Adams' attitude. "Not a man I know here," he wrote, "is either studying or is hardly aware of the country behind the Alleghenies."[3]

In 1889 Turner returned to Madison to take up a position in the history department. At the time of his arrival, he held the department's only position; a year later, he was able to appoint Charles Homer Haskins, a medievalist and close friend who had also taken a Hopkins doctorate, to an instructorship in European history.

In 1893 Turner delivered his famous paper on "The Significance of the Frontier in American History," at a Chicago fair to celebrate the four-hundredth anniversary of Columbus' arrival in America. Contrary to his Hopkins mentors, Turner argued that distinctively American institutions and character had emerged only as Americans encountered the frontier. The first settlers who arrived in the American colonies were Europeans in thought, culture, and dress. But, to survive on the frontier, they had to adapt to the harsh and unforgiving terms it imposed. In the process, Europeans were transformed into Americans. "The true point of view in the history of this nation is not the Atlantic coast," he insisted, "it is the great West."[4]

In time Turner's insistence on the primacy of the frontier in American history would amount to a crusade, and he would later leave Madison to teach, far from the frontier, at Harvard. But his view of the significance of the West would come to shape to a high degree the Wisconsin history department. A large portrait of Turner hung for many years in the history department office, and, department members would sometimes refer to themselves as the "*Turnerverein*." Coming to Madison in 1956, George Mosse thought that the department approached American history from the vantage point of South Dakota, where, in fact, one of its leading figures, Merrill Jensen, had grown up.[5]

The influence of Charles A. Beard, the noted progressive historian, also pervaded in Madison, and the members of the history department were legendary in the reverence for him. Through his stress on the importance of economic motivation in historical events and the relative nature of historical truth, Beard effected what amounted to a revolution in the study of history in the early twentieth century. Between 1910 and 1930, his work attracted enormous popular attention as he appeared frequently on the lecture circuit and on radio. His *The Rise of American Civilization*, written with his wife, Mary, detailed his view that economic interest lay at the heart of almost everything in American history, and reached the homes of thousands of educated Americans across the country.

Even by the fifties, when Beard's reputation had begun to wane, he was still regarded as a deity in Madison. Warren Susman, then a graduate student, reported back to Paul Gates, his undergraduate teacher at Cornell, on the order of worship in the department. "We have gotten to the point," wrote Susman, "where we can admit some failings in Turner, but Beard looms as even a larger task. Even Bill Hesseltine, who thinks nothing of damning and even laughing a little at Parrington, allows nothing of this when it comes to CAB. With Merle [Curti] the mention of Beard or of John Dewey evokes a kind of sign of the cross." At about the same time, the Jacksonian specialist Lee Benson was convinced that he lost whatever chance he had of getting a job at Wisconsin when, at an AHA meeting, Howard Beale overheard a conversation in which Benson had criticized Beard.[6]

The arrival of Paul Knaplund, a specialist in the British Empire, in the early 1920s was a significant step in the department's development. Knaplund was a Norwegian immigrant who scarcely spoke a word of English when he came to the United States. But he managed to earn an undergraduate degree at St. Olaf College and a Ph.D. in history from Wisconsin. He became department chair in the early thirties and served on and off in that capacity for the next seventeen years. Knaplund could be highly authoritarian, but he possessed a sharp, critical cast of mind. William Appleman Williams described Knaplund as "Madison's John Quincy Adams," and a man who "liked a good dialogue with first-rate radicals. He gave Harvey Goldberg "A's, read all my books, discussed them with great verve and intelligence."[7]

Knaplund also ran the history department with an iron hand, and his wife was an equally powerful social arbiter among the faculty wives. But he played a critical role in improving the department's quality. While the department already possessed several outstanding faculty, Knaplund was instrumental in the appointments of John D. Hicks and William B. Hesseltine in 1932, Merrill Jensen in 1937, Merle Curti in 1942, and Fred Harvey Harrington in 1943.[8]

These hires formed the core of what would become an "Old Guard" of respected scholars and formidable personalities who would exercise an enormous amount of influence over departmental affairs for the next quarter century. With the exception of Curti, these men also comprised the rough equivalent of the gentleman's club that existed at most Ivy League departments in the forties and fifties. The Wisconsin history faculty were all male, with, for a long time, no Jews, Catholics, blacks, or women. Several members of the group, along with others, like William Sachse in English history or the classicist Charles Edson, lunched regularly at the all-male University Club, where even other members of the department were not always comfortable in their presence.

Before the appointment of George Mosse in 1956, the department did not have Jewish faculty. Both Hicks and Knaplund were reluctant to hire Jews even though other departments at Wisconsin were already hiring them. The economist Selig Perlman, who attracted many Jewish graduate students from history, often asked them, "what are you doing over there with all those Anglo-Saxons?"[9]

But Knaplund's appointees established the department's strong reputation in American history. Hicks' field was the populist movement; Hesseltine taught the Civil War; Jensen was a colonialist; Curti specialized in American intellectual history; and Harrington taught American diplomatic history. The appointments also gave the department a left-wing orientation. Hesseltine had been a socialist before coming to Madison. Jensen had published an article in *Science and Society*, a Marxist journal, for which the department's other colonial historian, Curtis Nettels, served as an editorial associate. Jensen was famous for extolling the Articles of Confederation as the only truly democratic document produced in the aftermath of the American Revolution before its genuinely egalitarian principles were subverted by the Constitution. Curti was a civil rights activist sympathetic to pacifism. Harrington was not afraid to challenge either conventional historical wisdom or the State Department.

Of these men, Curti enjoyed the greatest reputation outside Madison. A Nebraska native and the son of a Swiss-American pacifist, he took both his undergraduate and graduate degrees at Harvard, where he studied with Turner and Arthur Schlesinger, Sr. supervised his dissertation. While teaching at Smith and Columbia, Curti made his scholarly reputation with studies of American peace movements and John Dewey. He was accorded numerous honors. Shortly after coming to Wisconsin in 1942, he received a Pulitzer Prize for his *Growth of American Thought*. In the years between 1952 and 1954, he served as president of the Mississippi Valley Historical Association, the American Historical Association, and the American Studies Association.[10]

Curti was a committed egalitarian. As president of the Mississippi Valley Historical Association, he forced its council to cancel a planned meeting in New Orleans when the contracted hotel refused to give rooms to black members. As a Wisconsin faculty member, he championed the appointments of Jews and women, and led a campaign to open the University Club to black graduate students.[11]

For many students, Hesseltine was the most dynamic presence. He was short, rotund man, with a deep gravelly voice, and a curved, Sherlock Holmes-style pipe perpetually in his mouth. His style was decidedly intense. He insisted that to be a good historian it was necessary "to eat, drink, and sleep history." Kenneth Stampp was a graduate student at Wisconsin in the thirties and terrified of Hesseltine, but drawn to southern history by the brilliance of Hesseltine's teaching.

But, like many brilliant people, Hesseltine could also be abrasive and arrogant, and he delighted in saying outrageous things and scoffing at conventional wisdom. "Doing intellectual history is like trying to nail jelly to a wall," was his most famous one-liner. While admiring Hesseltine greatly, Stampp occasionally chafed under his tutelage and, with enormous ability himself, sometimes could not overcome the urge to reply in kind. The two developed a close, but tense relationship.

Part of their problem stemmed from a misunderstanding early in Stampp's graduate career. At Wisconsin graduate students attached themselves to a particular professor and attended that professor's courses and seminars. After a year of taking all of Hesseltine's offerings, Stampp felt that he had learned all he could. He and Richard Current, another Wisconsin graduate student, asked Hesseltine if they could be excused from further attendance in his classes in the spring of 1938 while they studied for their qualifying exams. They thought that Hesseltine agreed. Later, however, Hesseltine exploded at them in his office, asking, "who do you guys think you are, not coming to my seminar?" And he did not support Stampp for the extension of his assistantship.

The relationship between Stampp and Hesseltine continued to be stormy and heated, but they did manage to cooperate well enough for Stampp to complete his dissertation under Hesseltine's direction in December 1941, and receive his doctorate in March, 1942. But traces of hostility remained. Years later, after the publication of Stampp's famous book on slavery, *The Peculiar Institution*, Hesseltine wrote a churlish review of it for the *Milwaukee Journal*, Stampp's hometown newspaper, where Stampp's friends and relatives would be sure to see it.¹²

The relationship between Stampp and Hesseltine was not the only contentious one in the department. Among the department's stars, who were sometimes known as "the Murderer's Row," after the batting order of the great New York Yankee baseball teams of the twenties and thirties, there existed several strong personalities. Even at its best, wrote one observer, the department was "intensely political, full of aggressive types, self-promoters, and empire builders." Hesseltine, always iconoclastic, was suspicious of Curti and intellectual history. Curti incurred Knaplund's wrath when, shortly after his arrival at Wisconsin, he hired Howard Beale to teach the Progressive Era while Knaplund was on leave.¹³

Beale, as it turned out, was probably the most contentious member of the department. George Mosse remembers him as "pugnacious, self-righteous, and inconsistent in his attitudes." Mosse also recalled an episode in which Beale began a quarrel with Merle Curti as he was driving Curti to the airport. In the middle of the argument Beale became so incensed that he stopped the car in the middle of the road, jumped out, pulled the handles from the car doors, and left Curti locked up in the car while he stormed off.¹⁴

In the years immediately after World War II, Wisconsin still had the feel of a small college. The college president, E.B. Fred, often waited outside of classroom buildings as classes were changing, to visit with students and obtain information about who the best teachers were. Fred had previously served as Dean of Agriculture at Wisconsin, and when George Mosse came for his interview in 1956, Fred asked him what he thought about the artificial insemination of horses. Mosse said he had no idea. Fortunately for Mosse, this turned out to be the right answer. E.B. Fred did not want pompous, long-winded faculty who would waste his time spouting opinions on subjects they knew nothing about.¹⁵

The post-war years were good for the department. In American history, with its galaxy of stars, the department rivaled Harvard in quality, if not in size. And it continued to attract outstanding graduate students. In the thirties, such scholars of future distinction who were graduate students at Wisconsin included Kenneth Stampp, Richard Current, and Frank Freidel. In the late forties and early fifties, the list of graduate students included William Appleman Williams, Herbert Gutman, David Noble, George Rawick, Richard Kirkendall, John Higham, Warren Sussman, and many others. In 1949 the department awarded a Ph.D. to Jackson Turner Main, grandson of the greatest figure from its past.

But one problem loomed. The department's prestige in European history did not match that of its Americanists. In the mid-fifties the department began taking steps to correct the discrepancy. The first step in this direction was the appointment of George Mosse in 1956. Mosse was a Harvard Ph.D. who had been teaching at the University of Iowa, where he had established a reputation as a dynamic teacher and had published books on subjects as diverse as the struggle for sovereignty in seventeenth-century England and the Protestant Reformation. Mosse's achievements had been noticed by Merrill Jensen, who recommended him to the department. The Iowa department in the fifties was very good, and Iowa City was an attractive place, but Wisconsin was more high-powered intellectually, so Mosse decided to leave.[16]

Mosse's appointment had significance beyond enhancing the department's stature in European history. Mosse was the first Jew appointed to the Wisconsin history department. He was also a homosexual and initially somewhat amused at the department's deification of Turner and Beard, but he soon found the department to be a congenial place. He steered clear of the fiercer rivalries, and formed close friendships with Merle Curti and with another new faculty member, William Appleman Williams, a Wisconsin Ph.D. who returned to Madison in 1957. If anyone noticed or was offended by his faith or sexual orientation, Mosse never knew.[17]

The appointment of Theodore Hamerow in 1958 was another move to strengthen the European wing of the department. Like

Mosse, Hamerow was a Jew already holding a position at another university, in this case the University of Illinois. In the fifties Illinois had several Wisconsin Ph.D.s on its faculty, including Frank Friedel and Richard Current. Fred Harrington liked to visit places where Wisconsin Ph.D.s had landed, and he made occasional trips to Champaign. At the time of Harrington's visit, the department was looking for a German historian and, while in Champaign, Harrington heard about Hamerow, a Yale Ph.D. who had already published a book, and asked him to come to Madison and give a lecture. Hamerow was quickly offered a job, and, after some negotiation, accepted it, becoming the second Jew on the department's faculty.[18]

Another appointment designed to enhance the European wing of the department was that of Harvey Goldberg. Goldberg had done his graduate work in French history at Wisconsin in the forties, and had won the admiration of Harrington and Jensen. After receiving his Ph.D. in 1949, he taught at Oberlin and Ohio State before returning to Madison in 1963. While he published comparatively little, an anthology of American radical writing and a biography of the French historian and socialist Jean Jaures, he was an electrifying presence in the lecture hall. For his first class he was given a small room with space for about thirty students. By the next semester a large lecture hall was required to accommodate the hordes of students who wished to take his classes.[19] Soon he was conducting his classes in one of the university's largest lecture halls, the enormous auditorium in the Agriculture Hall on the west end of campus.

Goldberg's classes were so popular that they required about half of the department's teaching assistants and, in any given semester, roughly ten per cent of all history majors were enrolled in at least one of his courses. He was equally appealing as a thesis director, supervising forty-nine Ph.D. dissertations in French history before his death in 1988.

There were several secrets to Goldberg's success. The first was his radicalism. An historian of the French left, he was an unapologetic and unabashed Marxist just at a time when students were looking for one. His themes were class conflict and the impulse of the powerless toward freedom and liberation. But he was never doctrinaire and welcomed intellectual challenges from students with opposing views.

He was also a classic campus guru. A masterly storyteller, he treated each lecture as a dramatic performance, and he knew how to extract every ounce of pathos from it. He waited in the wings until the students were seated, and then strode to the lectern. Pale, almost cadaverous looking, he took off his glasses and, after a glance around the room, he pointed a finger at his audience and began, "the point is …" Faultlessly intense and immersed in his subject, he could not be approached either immediately before or after one of his lectures.

He also enjoyed out-of-class friendships with students and was perfectly comfortable meeting with groups of them in a bar or coffeehouse in the evening. When word reached him of the assassination of John Kennedy a few minutes before the beginning of one of his lectures, he dismissed class on the spot and invited students to meet with him in a coffee house where they could talk as equals.

In some ways, however, he disappointed his students. After being inspired by Goldberg's burning sense of social injustice, many students expected him to lead the revolution, which he would not. "I start revolutions," he once declared, "I don't finish them." He addressed many student rallies, exhorting them to action, but was rarely present when the moment for action finally appeared.

Yet another part of his appeal was his bohemianism. Like Mosse, he was a Jew and a homosexual, but, unlike Mosse, he was comfortable living in cheap housing in the student sections of town. Later on, he made an arrangement with the university in which he spent half the year in Madison, the other half in Paris. "I teach in Madison," he said, "but I live in Paris."

The appointment of Robert Kingdon in 1965 was another attempt to bolster European history. A Reformation specialist, Kingdon had already written a book, *Geneva and the Coming of the Wars of Religion in France, 1555–1563*, and received a strong recommendation from Roland Bainton of Yale, a biographer of Martin Luther and perhaps the leading American student of the Reformation at this time. Kingdon was one of several Wisconsin historians, including Mosse and Allen Bogue, recruited away from the University of Iowa. Because of his record of publication and recommendation from Bainton, Kingdon had already proven himself. When he came to Madison for his interview, he didn't have to convince them of his worth. The interview was mainly devoted to persuading him to come. Other appointments in European history during this time included Rondo Cameron in modern Europe, David Herlihy in the Middle Ages, and Edward Gargan in French history.[20]

As the European wing was developing, the department did not neglect its American roots. In 1957 it offered a position to William Appleman Williams, one of its own Ph.D.s, who, like Harvey Goldberg, had been teaching at Ohio State. Williams had been a student of Fred Harrington, and accepted Harrington's view of the essentially imperialist and economic basis of American foreign policy. Like Harrington, Williams was also interested in the Far East because it seemed to be the perfect example of the hidden agendas that drove American imperialism. Arriving one year before, George Mosse thought that Wisconsin's diplomatic historians stood Turner on his head. Where America's noblest aspirations, they thought, were realized on the frontier, its more ignoble ones were exposed after they decided to expand beyond it.[21]

Williams fit in perfectly; he was opinionated and radical, consistent with the department's self-image. Like most of the department's stars, with the exception of Curti, he was indifferent and even hostile to the historical establishment. Williams also echoed Hesseltine, who became a close friend, in his desire to eat, drink, and sleep history. Regarding diplomatic history as the epicenter of historical study, Williams argued for the broadest possible approach. Diplomatic history was too important to be limited to diplomacy. Understanding it required knowledge of social and political theories from Thomas Hobbes to Franklin Roosevelt, and the integration into its narrative of politics, economics, and social change. In his work and conversation Williams could summon authorities as diverse as Marx, Sartre, John Quincy Adams, and the science fiction writer Arthur Clarke.[22]

During a remarkably creative period between 1959 and 1961, Williams published two powerful syntheses of American history, *The Tragedy of American Diplomacy* and *The Contours of American History*. The first explored the expansion of American imperialism from the 1890s to the Cold War. In it, Williams contended that the American conception of empire emerged as a response to the social crises of late nineteenth century industrial America, and was conceived mainly in a defensive sense, to curtail expansion by other imperialist powers. This defensive posture, Williams argued, allowed the United States to present itself an anti-colonial power while still reaping the benefits of colonialism. Williams concluded that "the tragedy of American diplomacy is not that it is evil, but that it denies and subverts American ideals. The result is a most realistic failure, as well as an ideological and moral one." And he further contended that it was time to stop saying that "all the evil in the world resides in the Soviet Union and other Communist countries."[23]

Initially, *Tragedy* received a respectful response from traditional diplomatic historians. The age of student protest had not yet begun nor had the Viet Nam War raised deeper questions about the implications of American foreign policy. Most reviewers praised the original thinking in the book, while expressing reservations about the heavy emphasis on economic motivation. The laudatory reviews Williams received in high visibility periodicals, such as *The New York Times* and *New York Review of Books*, gave him a national reputation. Politicians wanted to talk with him; national journals solicited his opinions.

But he encountered murkier waters in dealing with the government. In 1960 he was offered a position in the Kennedy administration, as an advisor on Latin American affairs.

Mistrusting the Kennedys, he turned down the offer. Whether there was a connection to this refusal is not clear, but, in the early sixties he was investigated by the Internal Revenue Service, and the House Committee on UnAmerican Activities demanded to see the manuscript of Williams' next book. While HUAC was not the omnipotent force in had been a decade earlier, it was still capable of seriously disrupting the lives of the people it targeted. Williams' mentor, Fred Harrington, by then president of the University of Wisconsin, assured Williams that his job was safe, but also urged him to go to Washington to defend himself in person before the committee. Friends at the Wisconsin law school put him in touch with Paul Porter, a prominent Washington lawyer with ties to the labor movement. In the end, upon the advice of one of Porter's junior partners, Williams appeared before the committee and, in his words, "paid his respects" to it, by which he apparently meant that he convinced them that he was not a dangerous radical, just a harmless academic. The strategy worked. The subpoena for his manuscript was dropped and Williams left Washington without further difficulty.[24]

Despite his difficulties with the government, Williams proceeded with the publication of *The Contours of American History*, an even more ambitiously radical book. If *Tragedy* offered a synthesis of American foreign policy from the Gilded Age to the sixties, *Contours* offered a synthesis of the entire sweep of American history. Both books explored the idea of "corporate liberalism," by which Williams meant that the great theme of recent American history was the merging of interests between government and big business. Both groups realized that it was in their interest to stabilize capitalism by reducing the volatility of business cycles through protective legislation, expanding overseas markets, and generally using government and foreign policy to further business interests. It was a provocative thesis, and defending it was a risky enterprise. "If you are right," George Mosse told him, "you will be as famous as Beard or Turner; if you are wrong you will simply be written off as another sign of the times."[25]

Williams boldly divided American history into three distinct economic phases which in turn affected foreign expansion. During the first phase, which Williams called "mercantile phase" and which covered 1720 to about 1828, policymakers followed patterns inherited from Great Britain by attempting to regulate trade and economic growth. This period was followed by a second, from around 1820 to 1900, which Williams called "laissez nous faire," in which economic regulation was replaced by an aggressive capitalism that allowed ambitious individuals to accumulate a great deal of wealth and expansion became a device to solve internal problems. The final phase, which Williams called "corporate capitalism," characterized the first half of the twentieth century in which government business cooperated not to make the world safe for democracy, but to make the world profitable for American corporations. Following this principle, in Williams' eyes, Woodrow Wilson became as big a counterrevolutionary as Metternich, committing the United States to intervention in Mexico and Russia, and elsewhere in Latin America, but ignoring genuinely democratic rebels, such as the Chinese nationalists.

Underscoring the whole book was Williams' intellectual stance as a committed Christian socialist, where his point of view seemed to echo nineteenth century reformers, like William Morris, who mourned the loss of skilled craftsmen and the replacement of communal values with an individualist ethos. By the mid-twentieth century, history, Williams seemed to be saying, had reached a great turning point. The superpowers now possessed the ability to destroy the world. Humanity required cooperation and community to survive, not a continuing struggle about who will control the world. Recovery of utopian ideals, Williams wrote, was "necessary if men were to move beyond the enervating and ultimately dehumanizing stalemate of existence."

Published in 1961, *Contours*, like *Tragedy*, received a highly critical response. Oscar Handlin, writing in *Mississippi Valley Historical Review*, thought it was so outrageous that the possibility that it had been written as an elaborate hoax could not be excluded. Others quarreled with Williams' lack of interest in black history. But it was not until the seventies, after the war in Viet Nam provoked a storm of debate not only about the war but about America itself that Williams' work came under the most intense fire. At the time that *Tragedy* and *Contours* were published American involvement in Viet Nam was slight, and Williams had not discussed the conflict in either book. By the seventies, however, his work indirectly gave credence to the New Left view that the war in Viet Nam was not an aberration, but simply the extension of American policies and values that had been in existence for decades.

The most aggressive attack on Williams' work was contained in Robert J. Maddox's *The New Left and the Origins of the Cold War*, published in 1973, after Williams had left Madison for Oregon State. Maddox had once been a student of Williams at Wisconsin, but had twice failed his comprehensive exams. With Williams' help, he transferred to Rutgers. In his book Maddox analyzed the way Williams and six other leftist scholars had treated a critical, fourth-month period in 1945 and succeeded in uncovering many discrepancies between what was said in the documents and what appeared on the pages of the revisionists' books, including Williams'.[26]

Those who believed that the New Left's view of the Cold War and American foreign policy was too extreme bored in for the kill. Arthur Schlesinger, Jr. and Oscar Handlin immediately congratulated Maddox for destroying what they considered the evidentiary base for revisionist history on the origins of the Cold War. Others viewed Maddox as a mere pedant and someone who had merely succeeded in locating a large number of mirror errors rather than completely overturning an older view.

Williams, for his part, conceded that he had made some mistakes, but attributed most of them to the fact that he wasn't a very good proofreader. There were no real winners in the debate, but in 1972 when John Lewis Gaddis published his Bancroft-prize winning *Origins of the Cold War*, he assigned primary responsibility for the Cold War to the Soviet Union, but he also made significant concessions to New Left historiography.[27]

Williams also made several other major contributions to the history department. While he was not a spellbinding lecturer in the manner of Harvey Goldberg, he was an excellent teacher and attracted a loyal following of left-leaning students. Thomas McCormick, one of Williams' graduate students and later a department member, thought that when Williams was teaching it was a chance to watch "a world-class intellectual thinking on his feet. You could see the wheels turn and grind and mesh." Williams also repeatedly fascinated graduate students during the open forums he held on Friday afternoons for discussion of historical issues, on which he always seemed to have a unique slant. Another one of his graduate students, Walter Lafeber, remembered watching Williams on those Friday afternoons and "understanding for the first time that this was what a teacher was supposed to do."[28]

Williams was also an inspirational force for *Studies on the Left*, which was founded in Madison in 1959 mainly by his graduate students. In its opening editorial, "The Radicalism of Disclosure," the editors dismissed the traditional notion of historical objectivity, pleading instead for a history that would enhance the "reconstruction of society." Many of the articles in *Studies* used, much in the manner of Williams' work, the contrast between the expressed goals of American policymakers and their actual policies to question American's role in the world. *Studies* only stayed in Madison for four years, but it provided an early outlet for scholars seeking alternative explanations in American history.

Williams' return to Madison in 1957 was the beginning of another trend in the department's hiring practices; it was hiring increasing numbers of its own Ph.D.s. In addition to Williams, the department's appointments during this time included Richard Current, David Cronon in intellectual history, David Shannon, and Irvin Wyllie, all of whom earned Wisconsin Ph.D.s and had gone away to teach before returning. The pattern of hiring Wisconsin Ph.D.s did not last, but, for a brief period, Wisconsin resembled Harvard in hiring its own students after they had been sent away to prove themselves.[29]

Students also benefited from interdisciplinary opportunities. In the twenties and thirties the labor economist John R. Commons and his students had compiled an extensive collection of documents relating to American labor movements. Commons' work was continued by the labor economist Selig Perlman, who attracted many history graduate students. In the fifties and sixties the role of interdisciplinary *eminence de grise* was assumed by Hans Gerth. Gerth was a German refugee known for his translations of Max Weber and for his connection with the Frankfurt School of sociologists and philosophers. He recognized the possibilities that might be realized from combining history and sociology. Williams and C. Wright Mills were both among his protégés and were inspired partly by Gerth to develop their critiques of the way corporate values had come to control American life.[30]

The sixties were generally a prosperous time for the department. Like almost all large state universities, Wisconsin's enrollment increased dramatically, and state support for higher education probably reached its peak. The history department flourished even more when Fred Harrington was chosen president of the university in 1962. Between 1964 and 1970 the department expanded from about twenty-five to seventy faculty members.

One compelling enticement to new faculty was the expansion of the funds provided by the Wisconsin Alumni Research Foundation, or WARF. WARF consisted of money that had been raised through inventions and processes patented by Wisconsin faculty. Most of the inventions and processes came from agriculture and the sciences, and WARF money was originally limited to scientists. Under the presidency of Fred Harrington, however, WARF funds became available to all faculty in all departments. The university had no regular policy concerning sabbatical leaves, but WARF grants were generous enough to enable faculty who received them to take a semester off every third year for research and writing. Moreover, the funds were not limited to paying for time off; they could also be used for travel to archives, to hire a research assistant, or any reasonable kind of assistance. WARF was invaluable tool in recruiting and retaining quality faculty. When

Allan Bogue arrived in Madison in 1964, he was told by Merrill Jensen that if he continued to work seriously at his research, the department could pretty much guarantee him a semester off every third year.[31]

By the sixties the department's graduate program had reached epic dimensions. No one was quite certain how many history graduate students there actually were. In 1969 the history department had about 650 registered graduate students, though not all of them were in residence. Admission was basically determined by individual professors, and several faculty members were exceedingly generous, some admitting as many as forty students. While some might wonder if it was possible for graduate advisors to do justice to that many students, it is clear that many Wisconsin advisors did. Merle Curti directed over eighty dissertations. As we have seen, Harvey Goldberg supervised forty-nine completed dissertations; and, in only eleven years in Madison, Bill Williams supervised thirty-seven.[32]

The department also developed a stunningly efficient system, sometimes called "the Big Red Machine," for finding jobs for its Ph.D.s. In the sixties, as the department's graduate program expanded, jobs were plentiful, and, in the days before affirmative action and advertising, word of vacancies spread in several different ways, most often through "old-boy networks." A chance encounter in a hotel lobby during a major historical meeting might determine someone's future. A graduate student or new Ph.D. might find that their advisor, graduate placement director, or even another faculty member had found them a job without them even being aware of it. On the other hand, Wisconsin produced so many new Ph.D.s that hiring institutions often wrote to the department inquiring about the best candidates.

The department would rate its recent Ph.D.s in various subfields. The top candidate on the list would be offered their pick of the best positions in their field, and Wisconsin faculty members attending meetings would know who to recommend if they encountered a friend in another university looking to hire someone. Or, if the position was still open to Ph.D.s from other institutions, the department's graduate director and the student's major advisor would write letters on their behalf. During his year as placement director in the late sixties, Allan Bogue helped find positions for sixty-two students, and, during this time, Wisconsin Ph.D.s swarmed like locusts into history departments across the country.[33]

Howard Schoenberger, who earned a Wisconsin Ph.D. in 1968 under the direction of Bill Williams, was presented a list of five places, including the University of Maine and Hampden-Sydney, where he could have a job without so much as an interview. The only thing the department asked in return was that he let them know when he had made his decision so it could offer the remaining opportunities to the next person on the list.[34]

By the mid-sixties, then, a department of exceptional quality had emerged. The American wing was superb; progress had been made to strengthen the European side; several of the social and religious obstacles to hiring the most qualified candidates had been eliminated, and the department was bulging with talented graduate students who found it an exciting place to study. At the same time, the department had also emerged as a leading center for the study of the histories of non-western areas.

Before World War II, the department's commitment to non-western areas was weak. Like most departments under consideration here, its offerings were strongest mainly in American and European history, although there were a few non-western offerings. Fred Harrington occasionally taught Latin American history, and, shortly after World War II, the department hired Clifton Kroeber to teach Latin America, and, Eugene Boardman to teach Asian history.

The most decisive step, however, was taken in 1956, when Philip Curtin arrived from Harvard as a Caribbeanist. Curtin was a specialist in the British Empire who replaced Knaplund in that field after Knaplund retired. Curtin became, however, less interested in studying the empire from the point of view of London, and more interested in studying from the point of view of the imperial possessions. He emerged innovative scholar of the

African slave trade and was encouraged to try to build up the African history. Along with Jan Vansina, who came to Madison in 1960 and was also trained in anthropology, Curtin helped establish African history as a legitimate field of study and Wisconsin as one of the premier places to study it. Vansina would later win one of the coveted MacArthur "genius" grants.

Among his many published works, Curtin's studies of the Atlantic slave trade between 1600 and 1800 were particularly innovative. In 1968, for example, he published an article on "Epidemiology and the Slave Trade," in the *Political Science Quarterly*, which examined the health problems which tormented the slaves while crossing the Atlantic. While scholars were aware that slaves suffered grievously during their time in transit, no one had studied their health problems quite as thoroughly, and Curtin succeeded in bringing medical history to the forefront of the history of the slave trade.

Curtin was also a tireless and uncompromising advocate for more coverage of non-western areas and not just in Africa. In the late sixties the department also hired the Turkish historian Kemal Karpat and added another Chinese historian and a Middle Eastern specialist.

The inclusion of non-western areas did not come easily. Resisted even by the radical American historians as "swamp history," non-western history at Wisconsin was the subject of heated debate in the department. To a certain extent, Curtin was himself an empire builder whose singleness of purpose occasionally rubbed others the wrong way. Fortunately, he had the support of Fred Harrington.

At the same time, an era was coming to a close. The "Murderer's Row," the cohort of historians hired in the thirties and forties had reached the end of their careers. Hesseltine died in 1963; Harrington became president of the university in the same year; Curti retired in 1968, although Jensen taught on. Williams, somewhat younger than the others, left Madison for Oregon State in 1968. These departures left a huge hole in the department's American wing.

In response the department made a series of strong appointments in American history. In 1962 David Cronon returned to Madison. In 1965 Richard Sewell replaced Hesseltine in the Civil War, and Allan Bogue replaced Vernon Carstenson. Stanley Katz and Stanley Kutler taught legal and constitutional history, and Paul Conkin replaced Curti in American intellectual history. It took several people to replace Williams, including John DeNovo and Thomas McCormick. The department's reputation helped immensely with its recruiting. Stanley Kutler, who had been teaching at San Diego State in 1964 before receiving an offer to join the department, recalled, "I would have walked to Madison to take that job."[35]

It was, in the minds of many faculty from that time, the department's golden age. In addition to its strong appointments and breath of coverage, many members also took particular pride in the department's tradition of outstanding teaching. Where most departments usually assigned their junior faculty to introductory courses in order to free senior members for graduate teaching and thesis direction, in accordance with long standing tradition, the Wisconsin department inverted the order. Many in the department believed that introductory courses were too important to be left to younger faculty because good teaching in them led students to take upper-division courses. So senior faculty regularly taught introductory courses and took pride in their success with them.[36]

But signs of change were on the horizon. The first of these concerned students. In the mid-sixties the campus was beginning to experience student disruptions. Protest was always different in Madison because the brutal winters limited demonstrations to fall and spring. Anti-war teach-ins began at Wisconsin the spring of 1965, and Bill Williams was a speaker at one of them. The government, he informed a crowd that had waited until after midnight to hear him speak, was in the process of subverting America's highest aspirations, and it was the duty of the assembled to bring the government back in lines with American ideals.[37]

By the spring of 1967 the students, longer satisfied with teach-ins, turned their energy to protest. One of their first targets was the Dow Chemical Company, producer of napalm, the terrifying jellied gasoline dropped into jungle areas infested with Viet Cong and which frequently hit civilians instead. Dow officials frequently came to campus to recruit, and a small group of protestors, many of them history students, launched a campaign against the company. They founded a campus newspaper, *Connections*, to deplore the university's complicity with Dow and the war, repeatedly urging university administrators to sever their ties with Dow and other companies profiting from the war.

The protestors soon realized that the university was connected with other objectionable activities, including permitting and benefiting from research designed to hurt civilians and cooperating with intelligence engaged in human rights abuses. For their part, university officials proclaimed their record in defending campus protestors' freedom of speech against attacks from conservative state legislators demanding a crackdown on campus radicalism.

In October 1967 Dow recruiters arrived on campus in the midst of a national "Viet Nam Week." Madison protestors organized a peaceful sit-in in front of the building in which the interviews were to be held to appeal for continued non-violent protest against Dow. Dow officials insisted on conducting the interviews and local police, perhaps eager for a confrontation, decided to clear the area by any means necessary. An ugly episode ensued in which police officers clubbed demonstrators and fired tear gas and mace into a group of shocked onlookers.

Angry students proposed a strike. After a heated discussion of the issue in the Memorial Union Auditorium, faculty in attendance voted not to support the strike. As the faculty left the Union, they were greeted by students singing "Solidarity Forever," with some of them calling out "shame, shame." Harvey Goldberg later addressed a crowd of disappointed students with a fiery speech.

Other reactions to the students were surprising. Bill Williams became increasingly disenchanted with them. For all his radical views and the inspiration he provided to radical students, he was still a proud graduate of the United States Naval Academy and a World War II veteran. While he opposed the war, he deplored the extremism and anti-patriotic sentiments of the protestors. As the father or stepfather of several teenage children, he was increasingly concerned about the effect that the sixties counter culture of drugs and illicit sex, was having on children, including his own. After the faculty meeting over the student strike, from which he was conspicuously absent, Williams sat down with a *New York Times* reporter. After a few drinks, he denounced the protestors as "the most selfish people I know." In 1968 he left Madison to go to Oregon State.[38]

The late sixties saw steady stream of student protest. The most regrettable incident occurred when protestors set off a bomb in Sterling Hall, the physics building, which also housed the Army Mathematics Research Center. The saboteurs timed their explosion for the early morning hours, in the mistaken conviction that the building would be empty, but the explosion killed a post-doctoral student in physics who happened to be working late.

At about the same time, history students demanded a greater role in the department, proposing that they be allowed to go participate in department meetings and be involved in curricular decisions. When members of the department resisted, the students threatened to disrupt classes. Debates about how to handle the students tore the department apart. Some faculty urged a hard line; others proposed selective concessions; still others avoided department meetings and business altogether. New faculty arriving in the seventies learned that it was unwise to bring the issue up. Students were eventually allowed to participate in several departmental activities, but when they discovered that a considerable amount of departmental business is tedious, their interest waned.[39]

Despite difficulties with the students, the department entered the seventies in an enviable position. It was large, with numerous prominent scholars, and a Ph.D. program so large that by itself it came close to producing as many Ph.D.s in a year as there were job openings. The department had also succeeded in addressing several of its most pressing recruiting needs. It had found capable replacements for the "Murderer's Row," and developed an impressive European wing. Even more impressive, the department's coverage of areas outside the west, once a weakness, had been transformed into a major strength. Not only did the department cover most of the world, but it often had two people covering certain areas. African history sometimes had as many as four or five. And the department also had two Latin Americanists, John Phelan and Thomas Skidmore.

The creation of the Institute for Research in the Humanities also benefited the department. Over the years it was directed by several historians, including David Cronon and Robert Kingdon. Like WARF, though probably not quite as beneficial, it provided money to allow faculty to work full-time on their research, and brought a steady stream of scholars and recent Ph.D.s, many with interdisciplinary interests from outside Madison to the campus.[40]

Nevertheless, some problems loomed. The department still had no blacks or women and faced administrative pressure to hire people from both groups. The first black faculty member hired in the history department was William Brown, a Wisconsin Ph.D. who had been a Curtin student.

In 1971 Diane Lindstrom was the first woman hired in the department on a tenure-track position. When the department invited her to come to Madison for an interview, Lindstrom, a Ph.D. candidate at the University of Delaware, already had two job offers, one from Boston University, the other from the University of Virginia. So she initially told the department that she was not interested. They persisted, so she decided to at least go to Madison for a visit. Even though the department consisted of approximately sixty men and the temperature in Madison on the day of her arrival was thirty degrees below zero, she was impressed. After refusing an initial offer due to a low salary, she accepted a second, improved, offer.[41]

During her time as a junior faculty member, Lindstrom found a great deal to like about Wisconsin. While some faculty were clearly not happy with her appointment, most were supportive, and some were wonderful. She was also pleased to discover that she taught the same amount as everyone else and that most people in the department wanted her to succeed. A year later, the department hired a second woman.

There were of course annoyances. The brand new Humanities Building in which the history department was housed initially had no female restrooms. Faculty housing was not open to single people, which she was at the time, and the university was still developing a policy on maternity leave. Still, the positive aspects of her situation at Wisconsin far outweighed the negatives.

But, on a broader scale, like other universities in the seventies, Wisconsin was compelled to face changing times economically. State universities are particularly vulnerable to economic downturns, and, in the seventies, Wisconsin had to face the reality that the great academic boom of the sixties was coming to an end. Enrollments leveled off, and the free flow of money from the legislature ceased. The state also diverted money to create several regional campuses around the state. At Madison, these changes meant smaller budgets. By the mid-seventies it was clear that the department would never be able to hire in the numbers that it had earlier, that it would never again be allowed to make so many of its appointments at the senior level, and that the department's chairs would have to fight much harder to justify replacing those who left. By 1982 the size of the department had been reduced to forty-seven.

The end of the academic boom had implications for the department's graduate program. Where Wisconsin history Ph.D.s once found jobs easily, sometimes without even applying for them, by the mid-seventies the job market in history had tightened considerably. There were no longer as many positions available for historians, although there were still large numbers of candidates seeking them. The "Big Red Machine" could no longer deliver jobs for Wisconsin Ph.D.s the way it had a few years earlier.

The department was also forced to make major cutbacks in its graduate program. Its gargantuan size was primarily a function of allowing individual professors to admit whatever students they wished. By the end of the sixties, graduate students were no longer admitted at the whim of individuals; they were admitted into the college on the basis of a competitive process. At the same time, the department was increasingly unable to match the financial aid packages offered by other schools to promising graduate students.[42]

The department's morale also suffered. Younger faculty had started their graduate training with the expectation that the prosperous, upwardly mobile era of the sixties would extend to them. Without lifting a finger, they would have job offers from universities even better than Wisconsin. Instead, they found that the once robust job market had dried up. Senior faculty, while in a better position, also recognized that the golden days of the previous decade had also vanished.

Nevertheless, the department maintained a reputation for being a place where junior faculty would receive more humane treatment than they would at other universities. Almost all the junior faculty who came to Wisconsin in the seventies were on tenure-track positions. While other departments in the university occasionally hired two assistant professors in the same subfield and gave them five years to prove who was better, that was never the case in history. Junior faculty were welcomed with the expectation that they would succeed. "We want you to prove us right," was the attitude held by the senior faculty.[43]

This does not mean, however, the experience of the junior faculty member at Wisconsin was always cheery. A certain anxiety always accompanied being a junior faculty member in the department. Wisconsin was a premier history department that was not inclined to let just anyone in, but, like all departments, it sometimes made mistakes. More than thirty years later, several faculty from the time remained bitter about the department's failure to promote Peter Kolchin, who later established himself as a leading scholar of slavery and a prize-winning author of a book comparing slavery in the American South to serfdom in czarist Russia, and who even learned Russian on his own to write it.

The department also began to lose some of its most distinguished faculty to other schools. Before the seventies, the department had relatively few of its most distinguished faculty leave for other jobs. Merle Curti turned down several offers to leave. Except for Bill Williams' departure for Oregon State in 1968, the department rarely lost a senior star. But in the seventies, there were several major departures, although they were not necessarily connected to any dissatisfaction with the department.

In 1972 David Herlihy left Wisconsin to take up an appointment at Harvard. While at Madison, he turned down senior positions at Berkeley and Penn, but Harvard's call was a siren's song he could not ignore. Ironically, he would come to regret the decision to leave. In 1980 he left Harvard for Brown when his wife, a Russian historian, was offered a job there. But, at the time, Herlihy's departure was a serious blow to the prestige of the Wisconsin department. "Herlihy was irreplaceable," one department member recalled.

Another serious blow occurred in 1975 when Philip Curtin left Madison for Johns Hopkins. He was a star in a rising field and would be hard to replace. He was also leaving for a department that, while it was very good, was not considered quite at the level of Wisconsin. Hopkins did, however, offer an excellent department, a much higher salary, and a significantly reduced teaching load. In 1979 Paul Conkin left Madison for Vanderbilt, where he had been a student.

The evolution of the Wisconsin history department follows a pattern fairly typical of the process at other leading departments. Like most of them, the Wisconsin department in the thirties and forties was a gentleman's club, although there were certainly some high-powered scholars, particularly in American history. Several of the department's other wings, however, were relatively weak and Jews, Catholics, blacks, and women were conspicuously absent. Some observers even detected a perceptible anti-Semitic strain.

It was not until the mid-fifties that significant progress was made. The European wing was expanded, largely by hiring Jews and Catholics, and in 1956, Philip Curtin arrived as a formidable scholar and a John the Baptist for non-western areas. Between 1956 and 1965, a department with a strength in American history is transformed into a body with impressive coverage of the entire world.

Most of what happened at Wisconsin reflects similar developments at other universities and results from the unprecedented expansion of universities in general. The department's first-rate coverage of non-western areas was possible because there was a lot of money, and, unlike other departments, adding positions in those areas did not usually require sacrificing one in United States or Europe.

However, beginning with the clashes with students of the late sixties, the department entered an age of diminished expectations. The academic boom subsided, and issues that were easily settled in the sixties become battlegrounds. The decision to hire in one area, for example, now meant not hiring in another.

More seriously, the department could not always pay high enough salaries to keep their ablest faculty at either the junior or senior level. It adopted two strategies to deal with changing times. In the absence of senior appointments, the department tried to make advanced junior appointments when possible, and it tried to promote its reputation as a more congenial place for young faculty as a tool for recruitment and retention, with mixed results. By 1980, it was still a formidable body, but not at the level of what it had been in the sixties.

---

[1] Paul H. Buhle and Edward Rice-Maximin, *William Appleman Williams and the Tragedy of Empire* (New York, 1995), p. 45.

[2] Ray Allen Billington, *Frederick Jackson Turner: Historian, Scholar, Teacher* (New York, 1973), pp. 62–5.

[3] Ibid., p. 74.

[4] Ibid., pp. 127–31.

[5] George Mosse, *Confronting History: A Memoir* (Madison, Wis., 2000), p. 152.

[6] Susman and Benson are quoted in Peter Novick, *That Noble Dream: Objectivity and the American Historical Profession* (Cambridge, 1987), pp. 346–7.

[7] William Palmer, "Interview with David Cronon," January 22, 2005; for Williams' remarks about Knaplund, see Paul Buhle, ed., *History and the New Left: Madison, Wisconsin, 1950-1970* (Philadelphia, 1990), p. 267, n. 1.

[8] Palmer, "Interview with Cronon;" and John D. Hicks, *My Life with History* (Lincoln, Neb., 1968), p. 157.

[9] Palmer, "Interview with Stanley Kutler, September 15, 2005."

[10] Paul Conkin, "Merle Curti," in Robert Rutland, ed., *Clio's Favorites: Leading Historians of the United States, 1945-2000* (Columbia, Mo., 2000), pp. 23–29.

[11] Ibid., p. 29.

[12] "Historian of Slavery, the Civil War, and Reconstruction: An Interview with Kenneth Stampp," (Bancroft Library, University of California at Berkeley, Oral History Project, 1996), p. 29.

[13] Conkin, "Curti," p. 27; Palmer, "Interview with Cronon."

[14] Mosse, *Confronting History*, p. 154.

[15] Ibid., p. 152.

[16] Ibid., pp. 148–51.

[17] Ibid., pp. 157–8.

[18] Palmer, "Interview with Theodore Hamerow," January 19, 2005.

[19] Material on Harvey Goldberg can be found in Buhle, ed., *History and the New Left*, pp. 241–5; Buhle and Rice-Maximin, *William Appleman Williams* (New York and London, 1995), pp. 148–50; Mosse, *Confronting History*, pp. 160–1.

[20] Palmer, "Interview with Robert Kingdon, September 6, 2005."

[21] Mosse, *Confronting History*, p. 156.

[22] Buhle and Maximin, *William Appleman Williams*, p. 107.

[23] William Appleman Williams, *The Tragedy of American Diplomacy* (Cleveland, 1959). For good discussion of *Tragedy* and its significance, see Buhle and Maximin, *William Appleman Williams*, pp. 108–14.

24 Ibid., pp. 115-16.

25 Mosse, *Confronting History*, p. 158; William Appleman Williams, *The Contours of American History* (Cleveland, 1962); a good summary of *Contours* and its reception can be found in Buhle and Maximin, *William Appleman Williams*, pp. 124-39.

26 Robert J. Maddox, *The New Left and the Origins of the Cold War* (Princeton, 1973).

27 John Lewis Gaddis, *The United States and the Origins of the Cold War* (New York, 1972).

28 For Williams as a teacher, see Buhle and Maximin, *William Appleman Williams*, pp. 105-7.

29 Palmer, "Interview with Allen Bogue," September 13, 2005.

30 For Gerth, see Buhle, ed., *History and the New Left*, pp. 252-63.

31 Palmer, "Interview with Bogue;" Almost every department member with whom I talked testified to the importance of WARF.

32 Palmer, "Interview with Cronon."

33 Palmer, "Interview with Bogue."

34 This anecdote comes from a conversation I had with the late Howard Schoenberger while I was a graduate student at the University of Maine in the early eighties.

35 Palmer, "Interview with Stanley Kutler," September 15, 2005.

36 Hicks, *My Life in History*, p. 157; Palmer, "Interview with Stanley Kutler."

37 For a good narrative of campus radicalism at Wisconsin, see Buhle, ed., *History and the New Left*, pp. 33-7; Buhle and Maximin, *William Appleman Williams*, pp. 156-64.

38 Buhle and Maximin, *William Appleman Williams*, p. 160.

39 Palmer, "Interview with David Cronon;" Palmer, "Interview with Richard Sewell, September 7, 2005."

40 Palmer, "Interview with Robert Kingdon."

41 Palmer, "Interview with Diane Lindstrom," September 25, 2005.

42 Palmer, "Interview with Allen Bogue;" Idem., "Interview with Diane Lindstrom."

43 Palmer, "Interview with Stanley Kutler."

Chapter Seven

Chicago: The Serious Place

The University of Chicago is unique among universities in American higher education. Before one can understand the development of the history department at Chicago, one must understand several aspects of the university's culture and approach to higher education. The University of Chicago was founded in 1890 by the American Baptist Education Society and oil magnate John D. Rockefeller. The campus, constructed on lands in the Hyde Park area of Chicago donated by department store magnate Marshall Fields, featured elegant, Oxford-style buildings with towers, soaring spires, and gargoyles. The style, however, did not command universal approval. Thorstein Veblen and J. Franklin Jameson, both early members of the university's faculty, thought that the buildings were pretentious. In the words of Veblen, it was an outrage to house "the quest of truth in an edifice of such false pretences."[1]

But faculty fears that the impressive buildings disguised intellectual mediocrity proved to be without foundation. William Rainey Harper, Chicago's first president, was committed to building a great university, intending to combine the liberal arts education of a small, private college with the research expectations of a great university. Despite the Rockefeller money, however, the university was never on entirely secure financial foundations.

Harper had to work hard to raise money from Chicago's wealthiest families. "It is all very well to sympathize with the working man," Harper once remarked, "but we get our money from those on the other side, and we can't afford to offend them."

From its beginnings, the university embraced an ethos of intellectual commitment, and many observers regarded it as the most serious of America's great universities, both for students and faculty. Among the faculty, there was little of the tweediness, gentleman's club atmosphere, and concern about breeding that characterized Ivy League history departments before World War II and, for some, even after. To be sure, the history department occasionally had members more comfortable at the faculty club than the university library, but there were probably fewer of them at Chicago than in other history departments.[2]

The anti-Semitism prevalent at most universities was almost non-existent at Chicago. From the beginning, the university had large numbers of Jewish students and faculty. The history department hired Louis Gottschalk in the twenties and Daniel Boorstin in 1944, and, by the fifties, half of the university's students were Jewish. Edward Levi, Chicago's president in the seventies, once remarked, "Chicago is a Jewish university. Not everyone will admit it, but everyone is Jewish."[3]

There was also a sharp distinction at Chicago between the undergraduate college and the graduate school, with separate appointments for each. Those hired to teach in the undergraduate college taught undergraduate courses; those hired in the graduate school taught graduate students, although they could teach undergraduates if they chose. By the sixties, the line of division between college and graduate school became increasingly blurred. When Karl Weintraub was turned down for tenure in the history department in the early sixties, his chair told him not to worry. Keep coming to the meetings, Weintraub was told, you can be tenured elsewhere.[4]

If Harper succeeded in laying the foundation for the university he envisioned, the imprint of a subsequent president, Robert Maynard Hutchins, proved to be equally enduring. A philosopher who was chosen president in 1929 at the age of thirty, Hutchins introduced much of the innovative curriculum for which Chicago is known today. Hutchins denied that vocational education had any place at a liberal arts college; he believed that education should be broadly based, with a concentration on the origins and transmission of the great ideas of western culture and the development of critical and logical thinking. With the assistance of another philosopher, Mortimer Adler, Hutchins developed a new curriculum for the university, based on a series of interdisciplinary courses with an emphasis on discussion rather than lecture.[5]

The courses were intense and rigorous. When William McNeill, later a Chicago history professor and eventually a president of the American Historical Association, entered the university as a freshman in 1933, he followed Hutchins' new curriculum, which meant that he took four required survey courses, one each in physical science, biological science, social science, and the humanities. Each course was a revelation for McNeill, enabling him to "put together the universe in a way that would not have occurred otherwise." Decades later, McNeill could still claim some security in the sciences, and he continued to read and take an interest in fresh developments.[6]

But the humanities course, created by the historian Ferdinand Schevill, was the most critical to his intellectual development. It combined art, history, and literature within the framework of the western world from the Greeks to the twentieth century. It was, McNeill said later, "the central experience of my late adolescence; I was sixteen years old when I took the course."

But Hutchins had little respect for history, and it played only a minor role in his vision of Chicago's curriculum. He was interested in truth, and he thought that philosophy, not history, was the surest path to it. Thus, while there were several noted historians at Chicago in the thirties, including William E. Dodd, Bernadotte Schmidt, John U. Nef, Avery Craven, Louis Gottschalk, and Schevill, the members of the history department felt a constant need to defend the value of their discipline and even its existence at Chicago.[7]

By the end of World War II, however, things were changing. Hutchins retired in 1945, and historians were not alone in the conviction that World War II affirmed the importance of history as opposed to detached reflection on great ideas. In the immediate aftermath of the war, Chicago was an exciting place. The faculty now included a substantial number of European refugees, many of whom were exceptionally distinguished. Hutchins' departure and the influx of new faculty created a different climate of opinion about what constituted the best curriculum. While the undergraduate core courses continued to be taught, the rest of the curriculum was now the subject of intense discussion.

In the forties the department recruited several new historians. Daniel Boorstin came to Chicago in 1944. In 1945 Edmund Morgan was hired to teach English composition and the core course in Social Science, which was, in his mind, basically a course in American history. While Morgan did not stay long at Chicago, he did enjoy the heady intellectual atmosphere of change, recalling that it was like "being goosed all the time."[8]

Most importantly, in 1947 William McNeill returned to Chicago. After completing his undergraduate studies and also receiving a master's degree from Chicago, he had gone to Cornell in 1939, where he began work on his Ph.D. After military service and a year back at Cornell to finish his dissertation, McNeill wrote a letter to Hutchins asking for a job. Since McNeill had been a luminous Chicago undergraduate, once voted Chicago's "man of the year," Hutchins appointed him to a position as an instructor teaching core courses to undergraduates beginning in the fall of 1947. McNeill would stay at Chicago for the next forty years.

Already a publishing scholar, McNeill as much as anyone embodied Chicago's seriousness, which for him also included his attitude toward teaching. While McNeill enjoyed teaching the core courses, he came to resent the resistance to history that lingered at Chicago. Hutchins' influence lived on in the person of Richard McKeon, the philosopher in charge of the core. McKeon, like Hutchins, believed that history, being an assemblage of facts and dates, was the least philosophical of the social sciences.

Accordingly, history figured in the curriculum as a form of literature, studied in the Humanities seminar by reading excerpts from the works of a handful of famous historians.⁹

But when it turned out that Chicago graduates had no idea whether Martin Luther came before or after the Declaration of Independence, or whether Cicero and Plato were contemporaries, graduate departments in the humanities and social sciences protested. To correct that defect, McNeill, along with historians Christian Mackauer and Sylvia Thrupp, was appointed to a committee to help organize a new course known as History of Western Civilization.¹⁰

The committee consisted of faculty members from several other disciplines, and there were many tense arguments about how the new course should be structured. At one point, a member of the English department, brandishing a copy of Aristotle's *Poetics*, cited it as an authority that poetry was superior to history. Nevertheless, they did manage to construct a course, and the course they conceived still thrives at Chicago.¹¹

The new course explored the high points of the European past, from ancient Greece to the twentieth century, and at regular staff meetings, the instructors debated which readings should be used, how they should be taught, and the possibility of finding other texts. McNeill particularly enjoyed teaching Ernst Troeltsch's essay, "Renaissance and Reformation," a controversial interpretation of the early modern period. McNeill also wrote a textbook, *The Handbook of Western Civilization*, still in circulation, to provide background.

McNeill, however, also wished to teach graduate students, and he made a point of cultivating friends in the history department, particularly its chair, Louis Gottschalk. Not long after he arrived at Chicago, McNeill was invited to join the history department and start teaching graduate students, although he did keep a foothold in the college and continue to teach undergraduates.

The development of the Western Civilizations course at Chicago was a critical step in the department's evolution. Before its implementation, the department clearly held only secondary status in the eyes of the administration; at one point Hutchens had even frozen appointments in history. But with a small-group discussion course in western civilization required of every Chicago undergraduate, there would be a continuing need to hire historians, particularly those who specialized in European history, to teach it. As they got tenure, they could teach graduate students, but the salary line would stay in the history department.

The department as it stood then had several impressive figures, including Daniel Boorstin. But Louis Gottschalk was the senior historian at Chicago, and, like McNeill, a Cornell Ph.D. who had studied with Carl Becker. He specialized in the French Revolution, but early in his career had suffered a terrible setback from which he never recovered. Gottschalk had decided to write a biography of Lafayette in which he aspired to exhaust all available sources, but he had been denied access to some of Lafayette's papers by an elderly woman who held them. At the same time, over the years, he reportedly assigned each of his graduate students to study one day in Lafayette's life. Since Lafayette lived a very long life, his graduate students were able to make little headway into his day-to-day activities.[12]

For several reasons, then, Gottschalk's Lafayette biography was in shambles. Looking for an alternative project, he agreed to edit a volume in the UNESCO-sponsored series in *Scientific and Cultural History*, which aspired to be worldwide in its coverage. Thus engaged with world history, Gottschalk encouraged McNeill to consider a global project.

The American historian Walter Johnson succeeded Gottschalk as chair, and, between about 1955 and 1961, he began recruiting new faculty. Karl Weintraub in early modern Europe, Eric Cochrane in the late Renaissance, and Charles Gray in the Renaissance were among them. It was certainly an eclectic group. Weintraub earned a reputation as a fine teacher of undergraduates, although he was not a serious scholar. Cochrane was both a serious scholar and a dedicated teacher.

Charles Gray brought his wife, Hannah Holborn Gray, also a Harvard history Ph.D., to Chicago in 1960, even though at first there was no position for her. But, after a year as a fellow at the Newberry Library, she joined the history department and began teaching in the college. There were already female historians at Chicago, including Bessie Louise Pierce and the medievalist Sylvia Thrupp, both of whom had begun teaching in the forties. Thrupp was a serious scholar, but her entry into the history department had been blocked by a senior medievalist. She became a member of the Committee on Social Thought, but had little connection to the history department. Gray was thus the first woman to be a full-time member of the department. She would leave Chicago to pursue a career in university administration at Northwestern and Yale. But in 1978, she returned to Chicago as president of the university.[13]

As the only woman in the department, Gray had some odd experiences. In the early sixties she was the chair of a search committee for a medieval historian. When she presented the short list to a senior male colleague, he said, "I hope you didn't put any women on the list. They make such difficult colleagues." Then, realizing he had committed a mild *faux pas*, he tried to correct it, although his correction only made matters worse. "Oh, but Hannah," he said, "you're not a woman."

By that time McNeill had emerged as one of the department's leading scholars, and his research interests would help shape the department's structure and direction. In 1963 McNeill published *The Rise of the West*. He had been encouraged to think globally by Gottschalk, but the idea for the book actually pre-dated his appointment to the Chicago faculty. When McNeill was a graduate student at Cornell, he stumbled by accident upon the first three volumes of Arnold Toynbee's *A Study of History*, while casually perusing the stacks of the White Library. A few years before, he had read the work of the other great metahistorian, Oswald Spengler, but Spengler left him unimpressed. Toynbee, on the other hand, was an epiphany.[14]

McNeill spent the next three days in a comfortable chair in the central bay of the reading room of the library devouring

Toynbee's first three volumes. It was as if he had encountered his double. With his interest in the rise and fall of civilizations and panoramic vision, Toynbee wrote the history that McNeill dreamed he could write one day. "His thoughts were my thoughts, or so it seemed to me when I first read him in my twenties," McNeill later recalled.[15]

Toynbee's verdict on history was highly idiosyncratic. Writing in the aftermath of the Great War and in the midst of the Depression, he saw the West on the verge of collapse. He admired the unity of the Middle Ages, and believed the fragmentation of the medieval Catholic Church was a disaster from which the West had never recovered. The loss of religious unity, Toynbee believed, was also the key to understanding the collapse of other leading civilizations. For Toynbee, the Protestant Reformation, the Scientific Revolution, and the Enlightenment, regarded by many as significant steps in the development of religious and intellectual freedom, were tragedies, further steps in the destruction of religious unity.

McNeill was less attracted to Toynbee's conclusions than he was to Toynbee's Olympian vision. In 1947 McNeill was able to meet the man himself, and the two became friends. They talked at length about history and the importance of a world perspective, hiked together, even getting lost at one point. In 1950 McNeill spent some time in London and met often with Toynbee to discuss the final volumes of *A Study of History*. While continuing to admire Toynbee's erudition, McNeill was less captivated than he had been as a graduate student, and often expressed his reservations about Toynbee's arguments. For the eighth volume, McNeill provided Toynbee with a careful, written critique of specific problems in the text, and was surprised when Toynbee included a direct transcription of McNeill's remarks in a footnote without taking any account of them in the text.[16]

Disappointed with Toynbee's conclusions, McNeill began working on his own synthesis, *The Rise of the West*. Writing in the fifties, McNeill was also influenced by the temper of the times. The book was written while the West was still rising.

The 1950s saw the United States reach the summit of industrial and economic power. *The Rise of the West* may be seen in some sense as the expression of the triumphant American imperialism of the time. McNeill's theme was that civilizations fall when they close themselves off from contact with other cultures. Thus, the book also emphasized the need for Americans to grasp the importance of continuing contact and dialogue with other parts of the world if they wished to maintain that place.[17]

McNeill's ambition in *The Rise of the West* was vast. Like Toynbee, he aspired to write a history of the world and was interested in the comparative consideration of the rise and fall of civilizations. Toynbee's perspective was broad, identifying twenty-one developed civilizations and several "arrested civilizations," such as the Eskimos, the Spartans, and the Ottoman Empire. McNeill's was even broader, comprehending Chinese dynasties, the Mogul and Ottoman Empires, Mongolia, India, the central Asian steppes, North American indigenous cultures, and Japan, as well as the West.

While McNeill was primarily interested in the ability of cultures to absorb new ideas, *The Rise of the West* ranged widely over a multitude of subjects and disciplines. McNeill's exposure while at Cornell to the *histoire totale* of the French *Annalistes* was revealed in his emphasis on the vitality of agricultural innovation in early civilizations. He also discussed common patterns behind the expansion of government in early societies, such as the growth of bureaucracy, professional armies, legal systems, and religion, and tax collection.

The rise of the West, however, remained his central theme, and McNeill identified several reasons for Europe's emergence. Among the most important was the relentless tenacity and utter ruthlessness of the European soldiers and adventurers in the Western Hemisphere who behaved toward indigenous peoples as if they had been absolved from ordinary standards of morality. Europeans also developed a superior maritime technology that enabled them to navigate the immense distance required to explore the world and to chart with reasonable accuracy their discoveries.

Finally, the Europeans unwittingly introduced into the Western Hemisphere their most potent ally, disease. At the time, Cortez assumed that his conquest of the enormous Aztec civilization with just a few hundred men was attributable to his own moral and cultural superiority. But it is now clear that the invisible killers of smallpox and influenza, for which the indigenous population had little resistance, did most of the damage. The swift and brutal conquest of the Western Hemisphere along with the goods appropriated from indigenous populations, facilitated the development of a market economy. The final stages of the triumph of the West commenced with the emergence of the twin forces of the democratic and industrial revolutions.

Ironically, upon completion, McNeill's work was a clear contrast with Toynbee's. McNeill saw the story from the point of view of the winners; Toynbee saw it from the point of view of the losers. According to Toynbee, studying the history of the Western world in recent times was like watching a train in reverse. In his view the West had been in decline since the Renaissance because of the unwarranted destruction of the religious unity of the Middle Ages. McNeill saw it the other way around. New ideas and change were the *élan vital* that sustained great civilizations.

At the time of its publication, *The Rise of the West* had little impact on the historical profession. McNeill even doubted whether members of his own department at Chicago read it or took it seriously. The book was long, and the discipline of history had already acquired a high degree of specialization by which historians tended to concentrate on relatively narrow fields and periods. But, despite its focus on the West, it did convince McNeill of the narrowness of his Chicago education and of his department, both of which concentrated on the ancient world, modern Europe, and the United States, at the expense of the rest of the world.

Even before *The Rise of the West* was published, he was in a position to correct these deficiencies. In 1961 McNeill became chair of the history department. He assumed the chairmanship at a precipitous moment. The fifties had been a difficult time for the university, with money tight and clear signs of urban decay increasing apparent in the surrounding neighborhoods. In the early sixties, there were serious discussions about moving the entire university to another location, perhaps in Chicago, perhaps elsewhere. McNeill was also appointed with the support of the department's Old Guard, which thought they could control him and trust him not to rock the boat.[18]

Given these circumstances, few would have expected decisive change to occur while McNeill was chair. But McNeill benefited from a sudden change in circumstances. By the time he became chair, the university's financial position had improved, and granting agencies, like the Ford Foundation, were at their most generous. Moreover, the leadership of the university had changed. It was no longer led by Hutchins or his disciples. Not only were the new leaders of the university, President George Beadle and Provost Edward Levi, more sympathetic to history, but they were McNeill's close friends, as was the Dean of the College, Dale Johnson. McNeill's great triumph was to convince Chicago's top administrators that the opportunity to create a first-rate department of history had presented itself, an opportunity that should not be squandered.

With the interest in global history he had pioneered in *The Rise of the West*, McNeill's main goal to strengthen the department's coverage of non-western areas. The department already had several faculty members teaching in these areas. Donald Lach, the author a three-volume study, *Asia and the Making of Europe*, had been at Chicago since the thirties, and there were also faculty members teaching Japan, Southeast Asia, and Russia.[19] But McNeill was committed to expanding the department's coverage of non-western areas much further, with the ultimate goal of having two people with linguistic competence in each of the world's major areas. At the same time, the university was deepening its commitment to the concept of offering courses in the world's great civilizations, including new courses in Latin American and Russian civilizations, which made it easier for him to convince the administration to fund the positions.

McNeill worked extremely hard and sometimes autocratically to bring this expansion about. "In those days," remarked a department member from the time, "chairmen were chairmen."[20] McNeill was also shrewd enough to take full advantage of the circumstances. Among the appointments made during his chairmanship were Ping-ti Ho in China, Bernard Cohn in Southeast Asia, and Bentley Duncan in Latin America. McNeill did not neglect other areas. In American history, he helped bring in Barry Karl, Neil Harris, Richard Wade, John Hope Franklin, and Arthur Mann. In European history, he played a key role in hiring Richard Hellie, Emmett Larkin, Karl Morrison, Peter Novick, and Leonard Krieger.

Hiring Krieger away from Yale in 1965 was a major triumph for the department. Krieger had been a celebrated student at Yale, reportedly Hajo Holborn's best student ever in German history. His brilliance was obvious enough that he was a rare Yale Ph.D. to be promoted and tenured at a time when Yale was beginning to look elsewhere for its junior faculty. McNeill's ability to lure such a highly regarded scholar away from Yale was a major coup for the department.

McNeill not only had a vision, but he pursued it relentlessly. In 1966, when the department was searching for a historian of modern Britain, McNeill flew to Massachusetts to interview Emmett Larkin, who was then teaching at M.I.T. Even when it came to Europeanists, McNeill wanted scholars who had reach. After reviewing the applications of many prospective British historians with narrow research interests, McNeill was attracted to Larkin by Larkin's plan to write a history of the Roman Catholic Church in Ireland from the eighteenth to the twentieth century. McNeill spent five or six hours with Larkin to make certain of his breadth as a scholar.[21]

In 1967, when he stepped down as chair, McNeill had succeeded in improving the quality and breadth of the department. The department had nearly doubled in size and was truly comprehensive, no longer just a collection of talented individuals. By 1967 its strengths included expanded coverage of non-western areas and thematic approaches to such fields as black history, intellectual history, and social history. Moreover, many of those hired to teach in these areas were leaders in their fields.

But the expansion of the department, like Paul Kennedy's concept of imperial overstretch, whereby great empires decline in part because they expand beyond their ability to manage their conquests, caused problems. At least from McNeill's point of view, the expansion of the department doomed attempts to manage it, and often led to friction among those who felt they were not valued enough. Like several other leading departments, the Chicago history department became a somewhat disparate body, where only a few of its members felt they had a common ground.[22]

More seriously, the department's place in the historical pantheon depended upon careful reading of resumes and books when it came to appointments and promotions. In the years that followed his chairmanship, McNeill believed that many of the faculty involved in these decisions, whether due to devotion to their own work or indifference to the department, failed to do their homework.[23]

One manifestation of departmental tensions was the unusually large number, for a leading history department, of associate professors who been in rank for a long time. Every appointment and tenure decision is of course a guess about the level of commitment a candidate has to the department and profession. While everyone makes mistakes, the best departments are those who make the fewest. Chicago appears to have appointed many people, both in McNeill's time and for a while afterward, who did enough scholarship to receive tenure but who did not remain very dedicated to scholarship after receiving it. In the view of one faculty member from the time, the department did not always realize how much of a junior faculty member's first book, usually a revised dissertation, might be attributable to their advisor rather than the faculty member.

By the mid-sixties Daniel Boorstin had also emerged as a scholar of national reputation, although he was sometimes more of a cultural critic than a historian. His basic approach could be detected in a book, *The Lost World of Thomas Jefferson*, he published in 1948, several years after his arrival in Chicago. The book helped establish Boorstin's reputation as a sensitive interpreter of American thought and set down several of the basic premises that would inform his later, more celebrated work. He suggested that Jefferson's contribution to early American history was not, as some thought, as the spokesman and articulator of the ideas of the European Enlightenment. For Boorstin the key to understanding Jefferson was grasping his practical, pragmatic approach to problems.[24]

The theme of pragmatism, originally conceived in *The Lost World of Thomas Jefferson*, was developed on a grander scale in Boorstin's next and most important book, *The Genius of American Politics*. Its stated purpose was to explain why the United States has never produced a political philosopher or political theory comparable in quality to those produced in Europe. But Boorstin ended up offering an assessment of the American character along with his ideas about the absence of political theory in America, and he introduced a new concept, "giveness," to explain them. By "giveness" Boorstin meant that certain aspects of American history were determined by immutable facts of geography and history, such as American's isolation from the rest of the world and its immense natural resources. "Giveness" especially helped explain American exceptionalism, by which Boorstin meant why America had developed differently from Europe and why American experience was not likely to be repeated. Moreover, linked with economic abundance and natural resources "giveness" dictated an American consensus whereby most American were in general agreement about the direction and values of the nation.

Like Tocqueville, Boorstin saw America as the exception to the ordinary flow of history, a startling contrast to a Europe buried in a bitter and superfluous ideological discourse, wisely eschewed by most Americans. America, according to Boorstin, was founded by an unrevolutionary "revolution without dogma," and even the

Civil War did not lead to any substantive overhaul of society or institutions.²⁵

In a remarkable series of books, including *Americans: The Colonial Experience*, *The Americans: The National Experience*, and *The Americans: The Democratic Experience*, Boorstin elaborated on the themes developed in *The Genius of American Politics*. Displaying a particular gift for amassing carefully sifted facts and for citing the telling example, Boorstin delighted in repeatedly exposing the non-European elements of American society and culture and extolling the virtues of innovators, boosters, and investors. One innovator Boorstin admired was Frederick Tudor of Boston, the "Ice King," who refused to be denied in his efforts to figure out how to ship ice to Europe and Asia. Boorstin also admired the boosters who by canny promotion helped turn wilderness into civil society, and the investors who produced such things as condensed milk and the Pullman car. All of the volumes in the series won coveted prizes. *The Colonial Experience* won the Bancroft Prize in 1959. *The National Experience* received the Parkman Prize in 1966. *The Democratic Experience* was awarded the Pulitzer Prize in 1974.

Boorstin has sometimes been classified as part of the "consensus school" of American historians, who, led by Louis Hartz, have stressed the continuity of the American experience and the general agreement of most Americans about values. And indeed, before the work of Hartz and Boorstin, the debate on the American character centered on the dreary, Prufrocklike threnodies of sociologists, like David Riesman or C. Wright Mills, about the ominous signs of conformity in American culture. In the hands of Hartz and Boorstin, the debate was extended to a discussion over the existence and meaning of an American consensus.

Boorstin exerted a powerful influence over the Chicago history department, particularly on the Americanist side. His attitude was similar to those who guarded the gates at Harvard. In Boorstin's view it was better to deny tenure to those you are not sure about. If you make a mistake, you can always hire them back. On the other hand, if you make a mistake by tenuring them, you're stuck with them. During his time at Chicago, several promising junior

Americanists were either denied tenure or let go. Often, it seemed, the junior faculty in question had ideas about American history that clashed with those Boorstin expressed in his books.

In 1955 Stanley Elkins and Eric McKitrick were hired at Chicago with the understanding that they would receive two, three-year contracts, with no possibility of tenure. For Elkins and McKitrick, who were Ph.D. candidates at Columbia, working on their Ph.D.s, it was a wonderful opportunity. Good friends, they could remain together a while longer. Better yet, they would be able to teach at a great university while they finished their dissertations. At Chicago they were even allowed to teach graduate students.

Elkins, however, ran afoul of Boorstin. At Columbia, under the supervision of Richard Hofstadter, he had begun a dissertation on the sociology of the slave experience. When he presented a paper based on the dissertation to a Chicago faculty seminar, Boorstin was offended. Boorstin's books had espoused a pragmatic, optimistic view of American history, and slavery was neither pragmatic nor an optimistic chapter of the American past.[26]

Boorstin decided that neither Elkins nor McKitrick should be renewed for a second, three-year term, although they were given an additional year after the first, three-year term expired. Boorstin's decision appeared to be based wholly on ideological reasons and incurred the wrath of not only of Hofstadter but of C. Vann Woodward, who, while serving a visiting term at Columbia, had taught Elkins and McKitrick, and thought highly of them. More shockingly, there was nothing in McKitrick's work that was objectionable to Boorstin; McKitrick seems to have been tainted only by his close friendship with Elkins. Ironically, both Elkins and McKitrick would go on to distinguished careers elsewhere, and Elkins' book on slavery would become a classic.

Jesse Lemisch was another junior Americanist who fell from grace with Boorstin. In 1963 Lemisch was a Yale Ph.D. with an innovative dissertation on popular radicalism during the American Revolution, testing the job market in the early sixties. His initial prospects were not good. There was no junior position for him at Yale, and he was interviewed by Carl Schorske for the position in colonial history at Berkeley for which Robert Middlekauff was hired. Fortunately, when a position opened up at Chicago, he had an advantage. Edmund Morgan at Yale was a close friend and former Harvard pupil of Boorstin, and he helped Lemisch get the job.

When Lemisch arrived in Chicago, he did not think the department's quality was comparable to Yale. But, Lemisch recalled that he was told by William McNeill that he would be hired for a three-year term, which would be renewed for a second three-year term, unless "he did something awful." Yet even though Lemisch did not do anything awful, he was not renewed for a second, three-year term, meaning that he was essentially fired.[27]

Accounts vary on the reasons why. From Lemisch's point of view, he was doing the things a beginning assistant professor who wanted to move up the academic ladder should do. He won a fellowship from the American Council of Learned Societies, delivered several papers, attracted a student following, and willingly assumed several departmental duties.

On the other hand, he was active in campus politics, and his research seemed to rub people the wrong way. When he showed Boorstin one of his papers, Boorstin said, "It's very nice, but why do you have to talk about class all the time?" After his contract was not renewed, Boorstin explained to Lemisch that "your convictions get in the way of your scholarship," a charge, ironically, that had been often leveled at Boorstin. In his autobiography, McNeill contended that Lemisch cultivated a circle of radical students, while neglecting the necessity of getting his dissertation into print.[28]

While many people remember Boorstin as a curmudgeon, several of his graduate students remember him fondly. By the sixties he was teaching almost entirely graduate students. "Boorstin was the smartest man I ever met," recalled Richard Beeman, a Boorstin student at Chicago in the mid-sixties. The vastness of Boorstin's learning and agility of his mind were both thrilling and terrifying to students, and some tried, usually without success, to emulate his style. While some were intimidated by his brilliance, he was remarkably open to questions and new ideas. His goal seemed to be to invite students to think about the process of doing history. If a student said something that impressed him, he would take out a pad of paper and write it down, which could be flattering to the student, but Boorstin could also make it clear when he had lost interest.[29]

John Alexander, another Chicago graduate student in the sixties, though he was not one of Boorstin's, witnessed a firsthand example of Boorstin's openness and intellectual honesty. Taking Boorstin's course in eighteenth-century American intellectual history, Alexander was asked on the final examination to write a critique of either Vernon Parrington's *Main Currents of American Thought* or Boorstin's own prize-winning *The Americans: The Colonial Experience*. Alexander was already aware through the graduate student grapevine what his choices would be for the final examination and had actually lain in ambush for the question on *The Colonial Experience* all semester. He decided that while the book was brilliant and exciting, it was also based on a highly selective reading of the evidence. Taking his graduate school future in hand, he chose to critique *The Colonial Experience* and handed in a savage attack, fully expecting Boorstin to exact a brutal retribution. To his surprise, Boorstin praised his essay, gave him a grade of "A-," and invited Alexander to stop by his office to talk about it.

Boorstin took his responsibilities to graduate students seriously. Students often went to Chicago having been dazzled by his books, and Boorstin made many efforts to accommodate them. He threw elegant parties for them at which there would be other people of interest and at which he was an unfailingly gracious host. He was a conscientious supervisor of dissertations, reading student work carefully and offering valuable suggestions about style and content. And his interest did not stop at the completion of the degree. He wrote letters by the score on behalf his students and guided them to job leads.

Boorstin's teaching sometimes closely paralleled his own work. He talked in class about the things that presently engaged him and, as in his own work, had little use for debates with other historians. In discussing books, students were rarely asked to summarize the book's argument or determine where it fit into historical debates. Instead, Boorstin tossed out general comments about the books usually designed to make students think about how the book could be used to deepen historical understanding and assist students in arriving at their own conclusions.

One of the department's success stories in the sixties was the hiring of John Hope Franklin. Franklin had been teaching at Brooklyn College since 1956 and was a well-respected Reconstruction scholar as well as the author of the groundbreaking survey of black history, *From Slavery to Freedom*. In the fall of 1962, he was serving as Pitt Professor of American History at Cambridge. In January, 1963 he received a letter from McNeill informing him that there was an argument among the Chicago history faculty that only Franklin could resolve. Could McNeill come visit him in Cambridge to discuss the matter? Puzzled by the request, Franklin decided it must be a major department crisis to compel McNeill to travel all the way from Chicago to seek his advice.[30]

When McNeill arrived, the problem turned out to be quite simple. What were Franklin's plans for the future? The Chicago department wished to invite Franklin to join them, but, some members of the department were certain that Franklin was planning to leave academic life to take a position in the Kennedy administration, on the recommendation of his friend Arthur Schlesinger, Jr.; others insisted that Franklin would never leave his teaching and research. Before the department could offer him a position, it required assurances that Franklin intended to stay in academic life.

Franklin informed McNeill that, given several of his experiences as a black man dealing with the United States government, he had little interest in joining it, and he remained deeply committed to a career of teaching and research. McNeill expressed his appreciation for Franklin's time and candor and returned to Chicago. A few days later, Franklin received a letter from McNeill informing him that the Chicago history department had voted to invite him to join their ranks at his convenience. As he considered the invitation, a barrage of letters from various Chicago faculty arrived, urging him to accept the invitation and describing the benefits he would receive from being at Chicago.

Franklin and his wife discussed Chicago's offer at length. Their main concern was the effect that leaving Brooklyn College would have on their son, Whit. While Whit could attend the famous Chicago Laboratory School, and they thought he would receive better treatment in Chicago's Hyde Park neighborhood than he did in Brooklyn, they also worried about his adjustment to a new city, neighborhood, school, and circle of friends.

There was no question, however, that Chicago represented an extraordinary opportunity for Franklin. Even though he was a Harvard Ph.D. and a scholar of international reputation, he had never been offered a job at a university with the reputation enjoyed by Chicago. Brooklyn College was a good school; but it could not match the prestige and resources of the University of Chicago.

When Franklin decided to accept Chicago's invitation and begin teaching there in the fall of 1964, Walter Johnson told him that the department had held a celebration. *Time* magazine carried an announcement of Franklin's move, and mentioned several other appointments that were enhancing Chicago's reputation.

Franklin's move was made easier when Alan Simpson, one of Chicago's deans, left the university to become president of Vassar College. Franklin and his wife wanted to live near the Chicago campus. Daniel Boorstin wrote Franklin to tell him that Simpson and his wife were vacating a fine, old house in the vicinity of the campus. The university owned the house and offered the Franklins very reasonable financial arrangements. After a trip to Chicago to see the house, the Franklin agreed to take it.

When Franklin finally arrived in Chicago, he was delighted to find the department to be as good as his new colleagues had described it. Everyone was congenial. On the quarter system he taught two courses in the fall and winter, and in the spring supervised research. While Franklin could have elected not to teach undergraduate courses, he chose to do so. Franklin elected to teach a section of the undergraduate survey of American civilization, teaching the part covered the antebellum through Reconstruction.

Undergraduate teaching did bring some surprises. Although the section usually had an enrollment of 50 or 60 students, instructors did not normally use teaching assistants to grade papers. But, finding himself extremely busy one quarter, he asked his research assistant to grade his papers. He discovered that Chicago students were offended since they expected "Professor Franklin to grade his own papers." He in turn respected them for demanding the best the university had to offer. He was also surprised one quarter when he inadvertently scheduled a class meeting on Labor Day, but all the students showed up.

Franklin arrived at Chicago in the midst of social upheaval. When Martin Luther King, Jr., and other civil rights leaders organized a march from Selma, Alabama, to the state capitol at Montgomery, the marchers, their heads bowed in prayer, were attacked by mounted state troopers armed with clubs and tear gas. King and his followers then began organizing a larger march.

At this point, Walter Johnson, the former chair of the Chicago history department, suggested that members of the department should participate. Johnson and several others issued a call for historians at other universities to join the march. Several Chicago historians went, including Franklin, Johnson, Roger Shugg, and Mark Haller, as well as a former member, Bernard Weisberger, who had recently left for Rochester.

The march was emotionally trying. After gathering in Atlanta, the historians took a bus to Tuskegee. En route, the driver took a corner too fast and nearly rolled the bus. Richard Hofstadter called out to the driver, "if your driving leads to an accident that kills us all, you will set back the liberal interpretation of American history for a century."[31] During the march into Montgomery, the historians were aware that other demonstrators had been subjected to vicious attacks and wondered what would happen to them. Before they returned to Atlanta, Viola Liuzzo, a white woman from Detroit who had volunteered to transport marchers from Montgomery back to Selma, had been murdered.

In 1967 McNeill stepped down after six years as chair of the department. University provost Edward Levi asked Franklin to succeed him as chair. After eight years of administration at Brooklyn College, Franklin was reluctant to accept, especially since there were already signs that he would be serving during troubled times. Levi offered the usual inducements, including a reduced teaching load and improvements in the chair's office. Franklin was not persuaded to take the job, however, until he encountered Daniel Boorstin at the entrance of the Social Science Building. Franklin asked how the family was doing. Boorstin said that his wife was not sleeping well. When Franklin asked why, Boorstin said that she was afraid that Franklin would not accept the chair position.[32]

The appointment garnered national attention. Franklin was the first African American to chair a first-tier university history department. The celebratory atmosphere, however, was short-lived. Within months the campus was caught up in a variety of student protests. In addition to the common student protests about Viet Nam and Civil Rights, but the 1968 democratic convention was held in Chicago, and all of the issues agitating protestors in the late 1960s were brought into focus. Police seemed all too eager to attack crowds of demonstrators.

On campus, students became increasingly militant, demanding a voice in such things as the hiring and firing of faculty. At Chicago the issue concerned the administration's decision not to reappoint Marlene Dixon, an assistant professor of sociology. Dixon was popular teacher, but had published little. Students not only rallied to her cause, in the conviction that she was being discriminated against because of her gender and radical politics, but asserted their general right to have an equal voice with faculty in appointments. A university committee, chaired by Hanna Gray of the history department, approved the termination of Dixon, on the grounds that the decision had been reached in accordance with the university's existing standards of appointments, but recommended a one-year extension of her position on the Committee on Human Development.³³

The students who supported Dixon called the Gray Committee's recommendation a "whitewash" and urged all students to go out on strike. After some deliberation, the students voted to hold a sit-in in the administration building, which continued for three weeks. When, despite their presence in the main offices, the university continued to operate, the students become frustrated turned to performing minor bits of sabotage, including pouring ketchup into the typewriters and rifling personnel files.

The student protests at Chicago led to a long period of soul-searching among the faculty. Several department members watched with amazement the transformation of former department chair Walter Johnson, once a pillar of the establishment, into a man drafting resolutions denouncing American imperialism and the murder of the Black Panthers for the A.H.A.'s radical caucus.³⁴ Most Chicago faculty, however, sympathized with the students' positions on the war in Viet Nam, Civil Rights, and the authoritarian nature of many aspects of American life. They denied, however, that the students enjoyed equal status with the faculty and feared that the manner of their dissent, including the occupation of a building and destruction of university property, threatened free inquiry.

Wisely, the Chicago administration elected not to summon local police for help in dealing with the protestors. But it also insisted that students who usurped the rights of others by occupying property that did not belong to them and damaging it should be held responsible for their actions. Many of the students who were involved in the sit-ins were summoned to the university faculty-student discipline committee and suspended or expelled.

Within the department, the most prominent target of student anger was Daniel Boorstin. Boorstin was vulnerable on several counts. He had briefly been a member of the Communist Party while he was an undergraduate at Harvard in the thirties, which might have been reassuring to student radicals. But he had later named names of his friends who had been Communists in the thirties, including Richard Schlatter, one of his roommates at Harvard, to the House Un-American Activities Committee. At the same time, he had written books celebrating American greatness and had used them as part of his defense to the House committee. He was also blamed by radical students for the denial of tenure to Jesse Lemisch, and he sometimes seemed aloof.[35]

In short he seemed to epitomize to students many of the things about the establishment that they disliked. Students disrupted his classes and left anti-Boorstin slogans and pronouncements in his classrooms. Disgusted by student insolence and the coarsening of discourse in the halls of learning, Boorstin left Chicago in 1968 to accept a position director of the National Museum of History and Technology of the Smithsonian Institution in Washington. Whatever his defects, Boorstin was the department's brightest star in American history and an irreparable loss.

At the beginning of the seventies, the department's future looked promising. It had enjoyed an almost decade long "Golden Age" of expansion. While its expansion created a somewhat disconnected collection of individuals, this was true of most other elite departments, and the Chicago department had emerged as an elite body. The department also benefited from being the editorial base of the *Journal of Modern History*. The journal, devoted to European history since 1500, had been founded in the 1920s by historians from the Middle and Far West who had been alienated by what they considered the east coast bias of the profession and of the *American Historical Review*. Published by the University of Chicago Press, it was usually edited by the Chicago history faculty.

By the early seventies, it no longer had any anti-establishment mantra, but its reputation was improving. As publication increasingly became the way to make one's way up the ladder of the profession, an article published in a journal edited by the University of Chicago history department became more and more prestigious.

In 1971 William McNeill took over as editor, a position he retained until 1979. He found that submissions far outnumbered the amount of space he had available for articles, so that he could pick and choose. He even initiated a series of supplements to the journal, in which worthy articles that did not appear in the print edition of the journal could be purchased by mail.

As editor, he wielded enormous power to determine what got in and what didn't. He could reject certain submissions out of hand; he could see that others were sent to readers likely to be sympathetic or hostile to them; or he could commission articles or even entire issues himself.[36]

Among the high points of his tenure were two issues he commissioned, one on Fernand Braudel, the other on A.J.P. Taylor. Both issues had the intent of connecting the work of each historian with his life. Braudel was initially reluctant to contribute, but eventually he did, at the urging of his wife. The highlight of the Braudel issue was a brilliant critical analysis of his work and intellectual outlook by J.H. Hexter. The Taylor issue attracted a great deal of attention, although in the end McNeill was disappointed. Taylor produced a predictably perverse essay, arguing for the importance of accident in his life and in history, and none of the supplementary pieces about him were as engaging as Hexter's piece on Braudel.

When McNeill retired as editor in 1979, the editorship was assumed three younger Chicago historians, John Boyer, Julius Kirshner, and Keith Michael Baker. The new editors made several changes. The supplemental series was discontinued. And, while the journal continued to publish a great deal of traditional scholarship, it also took an intellectual turn. In the late seventies and eighties, the traditional Marxist interpretation of the French Revolution came under attack. In the hands of historians like Francois Furet, language replaced class as the engine of the revolution. With the influence of Keith Baker, a specialist in Old Regime France, Furet came to teach at Chicago, published articles in the journal, and the journal became known as a leading place to publish the most innovative, new scholarship on the Revolution.

But the hopeful atmosphere that existed as the department entered the seventies did not last long. Like almost every university in the United States, Chicago had expanded in the sixties as if the flow of money would never stop. But prosperity turned to austerity almost overnight, and the university began to feel the effects of declining enrollment and a constricting economy. Equally important, the grant and foundation money on which much of the history department had been built was cut off, and, to keep the positions generated by grant support, the university now had to raise the money itself. When Karl Morrison became department chair in 1971, one of his first duties was to tell the faculty that the grant money was no longer available.[37]

Richard Hellie, a Chicago undergraduate and Ph.D. hired in 1967 to teach Russian history, could date the moment the crisis arrived precisely. In 1971, as a junior faculty member who had published a book, he had been advised that he should try for early tenure. He was surprised when he was denied. When he went to discuss it with his dean, he was told that the administration decided that it needed to retain financial flexibility, and, since it did not need to make a decision on him, it would not do so.[38]

So began more than a decade of financial agony. Administrators initiated numerous fund-raising campaigns and budgetary tricks to keep the size of the shortfalls from becoming known and to appear smaller than they really were. The budget deficits exposed several of the university's fault lines. One was that Chicago undergraduates did not remember their experience as fondly as many students in other universities did. Chicago was a serious place, and it did not play big-time sports. Few of the alumni returned for reunions, and, not surprisingly, they were unwilling to donate large of amounts of money.

At the same time, the neighborhoods around the university continued to deteriorate. Where once perhaps eighty percent of the university's faculty could walk to work, a fact that was an important recruiting inducement, that number shrank steadily. Late in his career William McNeill was mugged outside his house on his way home from work one wintry evening. While the university wanted its faculty live in the neighborhood around the university and introduced reduced mortgage programs and university-run schools to make it worth their while, it was increasingly hard to do.[39]

Graduate students faced special difficulties. There was little money available for them, and Chicago did not offer teaching assistantships, so when they entered the job market they were often at a disadvantage because they didn't have teaching experience. Moreover, they often faced indifference from some of the faculty. One faculty member told a student that he was giving her a "B" so she "could have a job with the sales girls."[40]

Chicago also allowed faculty to take research leaves whenever they could raise the money to do so. The result was that often key faculty members were unexpectedly absent, and the graduate students were unable to take the courses they needed. At one point, the situation was serious enough that graduate students asked for a meeting with the faculty over the shortage of course offerings. One senior member of the department declared that he didn't think that the shortage of course offerings posed a problem; in fact it was an opportunity. Students could just spend the year reading and thinking great thoughts.

Certainly not all of the Chicago history faculty were insensitive to student concerns. One interesting exception was William Sewell, appointed as an instructor in 1969, and promoted to assistant professor in 1971, after he received his Ph.D. from Berkeley. In 1968 he was in Marseilles working on his dissertation when he received a letter from his dissertation advisor, Hans Rosenberg. Peter Stearns had just left Chicago, and Rosenberg had received a call from Hannah Gray asking if Rosenberg knew anyone who could replace him. Rosenberg recommended Sewell, and Chicago hired him, sight unseen.[41]

Sewell brought a Berkeley aura with him. In contrast with the senior faculty of the department who wore suits and ties, Sewell wore long hair and blue jeans. Some students thought he looked like Frank Zappa. But he was friendly with the graduate students which clashed with the department's usual behavioral norms.

More importantly, he brought a new intellectual dimension to the department. Despite several illustrious members and its broad coverage of the world, the Chicago department, at the time of Sewell's arrival, was still a fairly traditional department in the sense of its commitment to political, diplomatic, and intellectual histories. Sewell, however, was deeply versed in the new social history, both in its quantitative and theoretical dimensions. His dissertation, published in 1980 as *Work and Revolution in France: The Language of Labor from the Old Regime to 1848*, was regarded by many observers as one of those rare books that redefined a field.[42]

Despite his outward differences with the senior faculty, Sewell thought the department was an excellent place to be, particularly because it had made so many recent junior hires. Among the faculty who had been hired just before his arrival were Richard Hellie, Ralph Austen, Keith Baker, Julius Kirshner, and Peter Novick. Several other junior faculty, including John Coatsworth in Latin America, Neil Harris in American social history, and Friedrich Katz, a socialist who specialized in Latin American history, were equally engaged with the new social history. But it was Ronald Inden, a specialist in the history of India, however, who was most important for Sewell. Inden worked on importance of kinship and was himself deeply versed in the literature of the new social history.

It was fortunate for Sewell that he found the junior faculty congenial, because the senior faculty were largely aloof. There was little socializing between the junior and senior ranks at Chicago. The junior faculty had their own dinner party circuit, joined on occasion by one of the rare senior faculty interested in the juniors, Bernard Cohn.

But, if the senior faculty were distant, there were other important benefits to being a junior member of the department. Junior faculty were real colleagues, participating in department deliberations and voting on new appointments. And junior faculty had a realistic chance of getting tenure at Chicago. During Sewell's time at Chicago about half the junior faculty were granted tenure.

Sewell's contribution, however, was not always recognized. In 1971-2, he had been a visiting fellow at the Institute for Advanced Study. In 1974 Clifford Geertz, the director of the Institute, invited him to take a three-year appointment at the Institute. When the department decided that it could not afford to lose him for three years, the Institute improved its offer to five years. Sewell took the offer and simply resigned from Chicago. Interestingly, after his appointment at the Institute and teaching at the University of Michigan, Sewell returned to Chicago in 1991.

The hiring of female faculty also slipped. While the department had female faculty, such as Sylvia Thrupp and Hannah Gray, before other leading departments, by 1972, it had none. After Gray's departure, the department did not hire another female faculty member until it appointed Kathleen Niels Conzen in 1978.

One thing that helped the history department maintain its high level of quality, despite the difficult times of the seventies, was its relationship with the College. As long as the College needed instructors for its western civilizations courses, the department was able to hire new people. They often taught the civs until they received tenure, at which time, they could begin teaching graduate students. Even those hired in the graduate school were expected to teach civs. Several of Chicago's best appointments in the seventies, including John Boyer in the Hapsburg Empire, Jan Goldstein in modern European intellectual, and Constantin Fasolt in the late Middle Ages, were told at the time of their appointment that they would be teaching civs.

By 1980 Chicago had experienced a pattern common to most departments of the time. It experienced a golden age in the sixties and had become a highly regarded department. But the golden age did not last forever, and the university fell into financial austerity in the seventies. The news was not all bad. The department retained its strong reputation. Junior faculty still clamored for the chance to work there. It was both a sign of its problems and of its strengths that, by the eighties, Harvard was raiding its ranks for senior faculty, including two presidents of the American Historical

Association, Akira Iriye and John Coatsworth, as well as Philip Kuhn and, later, Mark Kishlansky.

---

[1] Background on the University of Chicago can be found in "A Brief History of the University of Chicago," on the university's website. See also the works of John Boyer, a member of the history department and presently dean of the college, on the university's history. See especially, Boyer, *Three Views of Continuity and Chance at the University of Chicago* (Chicago, 1999) and *The Organization of the College and the Divisions in the 1920s and 1930s* (Occasional Papers on Higher Education, VIII, published by the College of the University of Chicago, 2001).

[2] William Palmer, "Interview with Peter Novick," December 9, 2005.

[3] Palmer, "Interview with Richard Hellie," December 12, 2005.

[4] Palmer, "Interview with Novick."

[5] William H. McNeill, *Hutchins' University: A Memoir of the University of Chicago, 1929–1950* (Chicago, 1991).

[6] Idem., *The Pursuit of Truth: A Historian's Memoir* (Lexington, Ky., 2005), pp. 12–25.

[7] William Palmer, "Interview with Hannah Holborn Gray," December 8, 2005.

[8] William Palmer, *Engagement with the Past: The Lives and Works of the World War II Generation of Historians* (Lexington, Ky., 2001), p. 98.

[9] McNeill, *Pursuit of Truth*, p. 58.

[10] Ibid., pp. 58–9.

[11] Palmer, "Interview with Hannah Gray."

[12] McNeill, *Pursuit of Truth*, pp. 64–5; Palmer, "Interview with Novick."

[13] Palmer, "Interview with Gray."

[14] McNeill, *Pursuit of Truth*, pp. 60–2.

[15] Palmer, *Engagement with the Past*, p. 39.

[16] McNeill, *Pursuit of Truth*, pp. 60–2.

[17] William H. McNeill, *The Rise of the West* (Chicago, 1963); for an analysis, see Palmer, *Engagement with the Past*, pp. 285–7.

[18] Palmer, "Interview with Karl Morrison," January 24, 2006.

[19] McNeill, *Pursuit of Truth*, pp. 77–8.

[20] Palmer, "Interview with Morrison."

[21] Palmer, "Interview with Emmett Larkin," February 4, 2006.

[22] Ibid..

[23] Ibid., p. 77.

[24] Daniel Boorstin, *The Lost World of Thomas Jefferson* (Chicago, 1948).

[25] Idem., *The Genius of American Politics* (Chicago, 1953); for an analysis of the book, see Palmer, *Engagement with the Past*, pp. 180–2.

[26] William Palmer, "Interview with Stanley Elkins," December 20, 2005.

[27] William Palmer, "Interview with Jesse Lemisch," December 15, 2004.

[28] McNeill, *Pursuit of Truth*, p. 78; Palmer, "Interview with Lemisch."

[29] For the recollections about Boorstin as a teacher, see Palmer, *Engagement with the Past*, pp. 156-7.

[30] John Hope Franklin, *Mirror to America: The Autobiography of John Hope Franklin* (New York, 2005), 206-08.

[31] Ibid., p. 238.

[32] Ibid., p. 241; for Franklin as chair, see pp. 240-5.

[33] Franklin, *Mirror to America*, pp. 242-3.

[34] Peter Novick, *That Noble Dream: The "Objectivity Question" and the American Historical Profession* (Cambridge, 1988), p. 437.

[35] Palmer, *Engagement with the Past*, p. 164; Franklin, *Mirror to America*, pp. 245-6.

[36] McNeill, *Pursuit of Truth*, pp. 78-9.

[37] Palmer, "Interview with Morrison."

[38] Palmer, "Interview with Hellie."

[39] McNeill, *Pursuit of Truth*, pp. 105-6; Palmer, "Interview with Hellie."

[40] Palmer, "Interview with Jonathan Sperber," January 18, 2006.

[41] Palmer, "Interview with William Sewell," February 2, 2006.

[42] William Sewell, *Work and Revolution in France: The Language of Labor from the Old Regime to 1848* (Cambridge, 1980).

Chapter Eight

Columbia: Reinventing a Department

The pattern of professional development at Columbia closely parallels that of Harvard. In the early twentieth century Columbia already possessed several outstanding historians, including James Harvey Robinson, Charles Beard, Dixon Ryan Fox, Herbert Osgood, and William A. Dunning. With the exception of Osgood, all served as presidents of the American Historical Association.

James Harvey Robinson was an especially important figure in the profession. In 1912 he published *The New History* in which he attempted to redefine history as a discipline. Disliking historian's traditional emphasis on political and diplomatic history, Robinson believed that historians should explore all aspects of human behavior and employ all the tools available for their study, including those appropriated from other disciplines. Robinson was the American Braudel in his outlook, if not his achievement, believing in a *histoire totale*.[1]

Even more important was Charles Beard, perhaps the most influential historian in the United States in the first half of the twentieth century. Through his stress on the importance of economic motivation in understanding historical events and the relative nature of historical truth, Beard had triggered a revolution in historical thought in the early twentieth century. In Beard's most famous and contested work, *An Economic Interpretation of the Constitution of the United States*, published in 1912, he rejected the idea that the American constitution represented the triumph of an epochal American struggle for liberty. For Beard, it was the product of a series of backroom deals by which various interest groups negotiated the political system they wanted and could control, with only an occasional nod to altruism and principle. In *The Rise of American Civilization*, he interpreted the entire span of American history in the same manner. While not everyone agreed with his emphasis on economic motivation, historians in the formative stages of their development before World War II knew they had to confront him.[2]

By the thirties, the department had also added such scholars as Merle Curti in American intellectual history, Dumas Malone, the great if admiring biographer of Thomas Jefferson, Jacques Barzun in European intellectual history, Garret Mattingly in the Renaissance and Reformation, Shephard B. Clough, and Carlton J.H. Hayes, both in modern European history. The progressive nature of the department can be illustrated by its strengths in several areas not usually covered by other departments. Salo Baron was an outstanding scholar of Jewish history, Harry Carmen taught agricultural history, and Lynn Thorndike was an international leader in the history of science. The department also had an Asianist, Carrington Goodrich, and a Latin Americanist, Frank Tannenbaum. And it had also hired Allan Nevins, a productive scholar in American history, even though he did not hold a Ph.D. and sneered at what he regarded as the "dry as dust" style of most professional historians.

There was occasionally some of the gentleman's club atmosphere that pervaded in other departments. Robert Livingston Schuyler, a descendant of an old Dutch Knickerbocker family, was probably the closest representative of that culture, although he spoke in a Brooklyn accent. As a one-time ambassador to Spain, Carlton J.H. Hayes could be described as a gentleman. And Allan Nevins also possessed a level of gentlemanly demeanor.

When Henry Graff, a graduate student at Columbia in the early forties, told Nevins he had been drafted after America's entry into World War II, Nevins replied, "Splendid, I hope you see action."³

History was not the only department that prospered at Columbia before World War II. During the long presidency of Nicholas Murray Butler (1903-45) Columbia emerged as a nationally prominent university. The famous School of Journalism was established in 1912, and Columbia could claim among its ranks faculty who were the leading figures in several different disciplines. Franz Boas was considered the father of modern anthropology, and Thomas Hunt Morgan was a pioneering geneticist. By the thirties, Columbia's faculty included such stars as the sociologist Paul Lazarsfeld, as well as Mark Van Doren and Lionel Trilling in the English department.

Actual encounters with some of the great men of the Columbia faculty, however, were not always satisfying. As a Columbia undergraduate in the thirties, Carl Schorske got a first-hand view of two of Columbia's leading lights, Beard and Lionel Trilling. As an undergraduate, Schorske had eschewed a history major, concentrating on a self-designed humanities curriculum, centering on great books seminars. Nearing graduation, he decided that history was the discipline that interested him most, but he had some reservations about his preparation. Since his Columbia seminars had mainly involved discussion, he wondered if he could succeed at an leading graduate school without any experience in writing papers.

At the 1935 meeting of the American Historical Association in New York City, Schorske managed an audience with Beard and explained his doubts. Pontificating from his bed in a steamy room in the Hotel Pennsylvania as though his words should be handed down on tablets, Beard dismissed the profession in which he had achieved so much renown. "Choose a commodity," he told Schorske, "like tin, in some African colony. Write your first seminar paper on it. Write your thesis on it. Broaden it to another country or two, and write a book on it. Your place in the esteemed halls of learning will be assured."

Schorske also approached Trilling, who had been one of his teachers in the great books seminars, about the wisdom of pursuing an academic career. The results were not encouraging. Trilling sneered at the folly of Schorske, a Jew, for contemplating an academic career at the height of the Depression.[4]

Fortunately, others had better experiences. Fritz Stern was a Columbia undergraduate during World War II. Not only did he befriend the poet Allen Ginsburg, but he had the good fortune to enroll in classes taught by Trilling and Jacques Barzun, an experience that was by turns edifying and humbling. Barzun and Trilling were both not only brilliant and learned, but taught Stern a great deal about writing. Struck by the force of their teaching, Stern abandoned his original plan for a career in medicine, turning to history and literature instead.[5]

The seminars in which Schorske had enrolled as an undergraduate were a unique component of the Columbia experience. Like Chicago and Johns Hopkins, Columbia had separate faculties for undergraduates and graduate students, although both were hired and tenured by the faculty in the graduate wing of the department. Those hired in the Graduate College taught only graduate students, unless they chose to teach undergraduates. Those hired in Columbia College taught undergraduate history courses and in Columbia's core curriculum.

The core curriculum had been established in 1919 with the introduction of two courses, Literature Humanities, or "Lit Hum," as it was popularly known, and Contemporary Civilization, or "C.C," as it was usually called. Both courses were great books courses, surveying a range of great books and ideas from western civilization, and centered on intense, small-group discussions.

The two-tiered system of instruction led to some division in the department. The bulk of Columbia's budget, whether in the history department or elsewhere, was devoted to the graduate enterprise, including the graduate programs and professional schools. The history department was housed in two different buildings, Fayerweather Hall for the graduate faculty and Hamilton Hall mainly for the college faculty.

When the Renaissance specialist Eugene Rice was hired at Columbia in 1964, he thought that there was a clear line of division within the department between the college and graduate faculty. Rice had been hired away from Cornell after his predecessor at Columbia in early modern Europe, Garrett Mattingly, died unexpectedly while teaching in Oxford. Shortly after his arrival, Rice was taken aside by Shepherd Clough and told, "you're responsible for Renaissance and early modern history at the graduate level; your counterpart in the college will assist the undergraduates." The same arrangements existed in other subfields. For many years William Leuchtenberg taught graduate students in modern American history, while Walter Metzger instructed the undergraduates.[6]

In the late fifties, there was a bitter fight in the department over the promotion of James P. Shenton, a teacher of legendary dramatic power. Shenton taught in Columbia College and offered courses in nineteenth-century American history to undergraduates, while Eric McKitrick taught the graduate students in nineteenth-century history. Shenton devoted himself to teaching and students, probably teaching twice as much as he had to, but neglecting his scholarship. One department member who was on the graduate faculty refused to support the promotion unless he was assured that Shenton would never teach a single graduate student.[7]

It was not necessarily the case that the most distinguished faculty across the university taught in the Graduate College. Such luminaries as Lionel Trilling in English, C. Wright Mills in sociology, and Jacques Barzun in the history department taught in the college and disdained graduate teaching. Nor was it true that graduate teaching involved less work. William Leuchtenberg, who never taught a single undergraduate in thirty years at Columbia, often faced graduate classes of over one-hundred students. He and Richard Hofstadter would often ruefully note that they were each teaching more graduate students than the entire history faculty at Princeton.[8] Even in European history, the numbers were staggering. In the sixties Peter Gay taught an introductory course in European historiography to over one-hundred students.

Merle Curti, one of Columbia's stars in the thirties and forties, left Columbia for Wisconsin because he thought that graduate teaching at Columbia was too time-consuming.

Teaching at Columbia was further complicated by its relationships to other parts of the university, such as Barnard College and Columbia's Teachers College. In both cases the history department hired and tenured the historians who taught at Barnard and the Teacher's College. But it also meant that the department was divided in still more ways. James Gilbert remembered a story told by a friend, who held an appointment in the Teachers College, about attending the department's annual dinner. The seating arrangements seemed to reinforce Columbia's hierarchy. The graduate faculty were seated at the main table at the center of the room with Richard Hofstadter at the head of the table, while the table for the Teachers College faculty was practically out in the hallway.[9]

Columbia resembled Harvard in that its appointments were made not solely by the department making the hire, but in conjunction with a university *ad hoc* committee on which no historian sat. To receive a tenured position at Columbia, it was necessary to survive the scrutiny of both a department and a university committee.

Another unique feature of Columbia was its location in New York City. While Columbia has no direct affiliation with the city, its official title is "Columbia University in the City of New York," and one of its powerful attractions was its location in the middle of the city's intellectual and artistic vitality. Perhaps the person most affected by the city's energy was Richard Hofstadter. In 1937 Hofstadter arrived at Columbia, in the words of Alfred Kazin, as "the All-American, blonde collegian just in from Buffalo with that unmistakable flat accent."[10]

While a student at Columbia, Hofstadter and his wife, Felice Swados, attended Communist Party meetings, and they also became involved with union activism. In 1938 Hofstadter joined the Communist Party, although he did not seem fully committed to it. But he preferred working at the Trotskyite *Partisan Review* to party activities, and he slowly began to conceive of a view of America consistent with that of H.L. Mencken, especially regarding those parts west of the Hudson River. Under the influence of his friends at the *Review*, Hofstadter became convinced of the truth of Mencken's analysis of small town buffoonery and ignorance. At the same time, he began to perceive deeper and more sinister implications for the power of anti-intellectual forces in American life, a concept that would inform much of his later work.

Oddly, some of Hofstadter's early work at Columbia displayed some sympathy for farmers, and it also combined his radicalism with historical analysis. His master's thesis, written in 1938, represented a Beardian approach to the plight of southern sharecroppers. Hofstadter exposed the total inefficiency and hypocrisy of New Deal agricultural policies, where the money ostensibly appropriated to relieve the suffering of poor sharecroppers went preponderantly to large landowners while the sharecroppers' plight worsened. The thesis was a bitter condemnation of the Roosevelt administration's farm policies. Like so many others of his generation, Hofstadter was deeply influenced by Beard's work. "Beard was the really exciting influence on me," Hofstadter later remarked.

But Hofstadter soon began to distance himself from Beard. Beard paid minimal attention to ideas, regarding them as mere ideological camouflage for economic motivation. Hofstadter by contrast found an increasing attraction to American social thought and to ideas as forces in their own right. This interest was encouraged through Hofstadter's association at Columbia with Merle Curti, a leading figure in American intellectual history. In 1943 Curti won a Pulitzer Prize for his *The Growth of American Thought*. By 1939, according to Felice Swados, Hofstadter and Curti had formed a "mutual admiration society."

Despite his obvious abilities, Hofstadter encountered considerable difficulty during his early years at Columbia. For three consecutive years, despite his intellectual promise and the early publication of an article in the *American Historical Review*, he was denied financial aid. He nursed a continuing sense of resentment over this slight, remarking acidly that "the guys who got the fellowships are little shits who never accomplished or published anything."

The reasons for Hofstadter's difficulties in the Columbia history department are not clear, especially since he had the distinguished Merle Curti as his advisor. But, Lionel Trilling's remarks to Carl Schorske about anti-Semitism, however discouraging they were to Schorske, had the ring of truth. The department did have Jewish members, such as Baron and Tannenbaum, and it had a large number of Jewish graduate students. Yet several observers thought that the department's growth had been stunted by the anti-Semitism of Carlton J.H. Hayes and the ancient historian William Westermann. Thus, while the department's record on hiring Jewish faculty was good by the standards of the time, a graduate student could never be sure when anti-Semitism would rear its head.[11]

To survive at Columbia without aid, Hofstadter was forced to seek teaching jobs. In the spring of 1940 he began teaching evening classes at Brooklyn College. A year later, he found a full-time position at a downtown branch of City College.

In 1944 Hofstadter published his dissertation as *Social Darwinism in American Thought*, and accepted a position at the University of Maryland. While at Maryland, Hofstadter found bright, engaging colleagues, including Kenneth Stampp, Frank Freidel, and C. Wright Mills. Nevertheless, he yearned to return to Columbia and for the intellectual atmosphere of New York City, which he regarded as far superior to that of the Washington area.

Despite his radical convictions, he also exhibited a tendency to shy away from active participation in left-wing causes, perhaps because he feared that notoriety might jeopardize his chances of returning to Columbia. In 1944 Hofstadter joined Stampp and Freidel in signing a petition opposing the candidacy of Carlton J.H. Hayes for the A,H.A.'s presidency, on the grounds that Hayes had expressed pro-fascist views. But Stampp and Friedel were later disappointed when Hofstadter backed away from further protest, saying that his grievances were really against the fascist governments not with Hayes. Stampp and Friedel, who believed that they had put their careers on the line to oppose Hayes, thought that Hofstadter had betrayed them. Hayes was a prominent member of Columbia's history department, and Hofstadter was not about to antagonize him further.

The Hofstadter family suffered a personal tragedy when his wife became ill with cancer in 1944. As she lay dying in a darkened hospital room, he began writing *The American Political Tradition*, the book that would secure his early reputation and allow him to escape from Maryland to Columbia.[12] Felice Swados died in 1945, but *The American Political Tradition* was immediately hailed in historical circles as a masterpiece of unusual vision and imagination.

In 1945 the chance to return to Columbia opened up. In the words of Henry Steele Commager, who had joined the department, Columbia needed "someone who could really take hold of intellectual history." The department first tried to lure Curti back from Wisconsin, but he declined. Then, in a close call, it decided that it preferred Hofstadter to Arthur Schlesinger, Jr.[13]

Over the years, Hofstadter would emerge as the department's most celebrated member. Two of his books, *The Age of Reform*, published in 1955, and *Anti-Intellectualism in American Life*, published in 1963, won Pulitzer Prizes. Of the two, *The Age of Reform* was probably Hofstadter's greatest book, and it is in many ways firmly grounded in his experience at Columbia.

In 1946, after finishing his first book, *The American Political Tradition* and getting the job at Columbia, Hofstadter undertook an intensive period of interdisciplinary reading, especially in the fields of sociology, psychology, and literary criticism. And he benefited immensely from the fact that many of the leading figures in these disciplines were his colleagues at Columbia. These included the literary critic Lionel Trilling, the sociologist Robert K. Merton, and another leading sociologist, C. Wright Mills, whom Hofstadter had known while both of them were teaching at the University of Maryland.[14]

Yet another important influence came from Karl Mannheim, whose book, *Ideology and Utopia*, became central to Hofstadter's work in the 1950s. Where conventional Marxist thinking reduced ideology to mere "superstructure," or the reflection of economic realities, Mannheim sought to redefine the concept by showing the way its influence could appear in other ways. Ideology, for Mannheim, could develop from specific day-to-day experiences and from self-perceptions that did not necessarily correspond to economic realities.

Over the years, Hofstadter had been gradually breaking away from Charles Beard, his most profound early influence, and Mannheim provided the final nails for Beard's coffin. Where Beard understood the political motivation of groups and individuals primarily through their personal finances and economic circumstances, Hofstadter explained their behavior with the use of new tools, drawn from his interdisciplinary reading, to explain other aspects of motivation, including status, myth, transference, conspiracy, and alienation. Under the influence of Mannheim and his colleagues at Columbia, Hofstadter began to see psychological issues, both individual and collective, as having as much explanatory force as economic motivation.

The insights that Hofstadter received from his interdisciplinary reading and his growing dissatisfaction with Beard were at the core of *The Age of Reform*. In his introduction, he thanked Mills and another sociologist, David Riesman, and the book is infused with sociological explanations, particularly in terms of how groups develop their ideas from idealized visions of the past. In *The Age of Reform* Hofstadter investigated the reform impulse in American history from the 1890s through the New Deal, with particular attention to the populists. It was here, with the help of his interdisciplinary reading, that Hofstadter finally exorcised the ghost of Beard. Where earlier scholars, especially the Progressive historians, admired the grassroots, back-to-the-people style of popular agitators, Hofstadter took a very dim view of populism. In *The Age of Reform* Hofstadter portrayed the populists as anti-Semitic bigots, who clung to an irrational, mythic view of themselves as self-reliant farmers, at a time when the world had moved into the industrial age and who embraced a conspiracy as an explanation for the forces that threatened them.

While Hofstadter had shed Beard, he was still a child of Mencken, another of his early idols. Hofstadter, like Mencken lived in fear of the "boobus Americanus," the archetypal rural American who Hofstadter feared was not only bigoted and ignorant, but used numerical superiority to intimidate spineless politicians into doing the will of the masses. Arthur Schlesinger Jr. has emphasized the fact that Hofstadter was one of the first major American historians to emerge from the cultural life of New York City, and, this fact, according to Schlesinger, who himself reveled in the vitality of the city, accounts in significant measure for the character and direction of his work. Moreover, Hofstadter was also an academic who received his first full-time job at CCNY after forty teachers had been fired or forced to resign after a legislative committee investigated subversive influences within the city colleges. And, as a man who had lived through the McCarthy era, Hofstadter had more reason than most to fear popular government and to long for a principled leader.

Other parts of *The Age of Reform* revealed Hofstadter's generally hostile attitude toward rural America. For a farmer, Hofstadter suggested, "it was bewildering and irritating to think of the great contrast between the verbal deference paid them by almost everyone and of the real status and real economic position in which he found himself." At the same time, many rural supporters of Populism, noted Hofstadter, believed that there was an East-coast, big-city, conspiracy against them. The willingness to explain things by conspiracy, suggested Hofstadter, "frequently occurs when political and social antagonisms are steep. Certain audiences are especially susceptible to it, particularly, I believe, those who have attained only a low level of education, whose access to information is poor, who are so completely shut out from access to the centers of power…[that] when conspiracies do not exist, it is necessary for those who think in this fashion to invent them." In these assertions Hofstadter described what he called the "rural mind," which, he contended when confronted with immigrants and the city, often responded with shock. Even the hostility shown toward immigrants, according to Hofstadter, was the result of small-town people who had moved to big cities. Hofstadter's distaste for rural America culminated in *Anti-Intellectualism in American Life*, published in 1963, in which he bemoaned a persistent opposition in American life toward creativity and independent thought, which again he traced to the ignorant, particularly the southern and mid-western masses. Hofstadter appeared not to notice that possessing the education and erudition that rural Americans so manifestly lacked, he subscribed to his own version of conspiracy, this one emanating from the ignorant, rural masses.

But Hofstadter was not the only star in the department's galaxy. In the post-war era, its size and quality improved steadily, with the appointments in American history of such scholars as David Donald, John Garraty, Henry Graff and William Leuchtenburg. In European history, the department was able to add the medievalists John Hine Mundy and J.M.W. Bean, the Renaissance specialist Eugene Rice, Istvan Deak in eastern Europe, Fritz Stern in modern Europe, Peter Gay in European intellectual history, Marc Raeff in Russian history, and Jacob Smit in the early modern low countries. An unusual but important appointment was that of the historical sociologist Sigmund Diamond who bridged not only history and sociology but the European colonization of North and South America. The department also developed its ability to offer non-western areas by appointing Hans Bielenstein in early China, Ainslee T. Embree in South Asia, Jacob Hurewitz in the Middle East, Graham Irwin in Africa, and Herschel Webb in modern Japan.

Several of these appointments were Jews, including Hofstadter, Graff, Diamond, Stern, and Gay. When William Leuchtenberg began teaching at Columbia in 1951, he thought a whiff of the department's earlier anti-Semitism existed. But, it was also clear to him that, with the new appointments, it had all but vanished. By the early sixties, nearly half the department was Jewish.[15]

Money was clearly not the primary incentive to join the department. Before returning to Columbia in 1953, Fritz Stern taught for two years at Cornell, where he was offered $3600 and the promise of tenure to stay. But when Columbia offered $3000 with no promise of tenure, he quickly accepted. Later, still feeling his salary unnecessarily low after years at Columbia, he consoled himself with the thought that he was a member of a department that included Richard Hofstadter, William Leuchtenberg, Jacques Barzun, and many others of distinction.[16]

Appointments were usually made in the casual manner of the time. In 1952 David Donald was a doctoral student at the University of Illinois who had held a Social Science Research Grant. Shepherd Clough was on the SSRC board and read Donald's report on how he had utilized the grant. Donald was in the process of writing to as many schools as possible about job openings. He received favorable replies from ten or twelve, including the University of Colorado. One day a letter appeared on his desk from Columbia offering him a job for a year at $3,000, with the possibility of a second year at $3,600. Clough had read Donald's report and was impressed enough to persuade the department to offer Donald a job.[17]

While Donald was pleased to have a job at Columbia, he also found some problems. There was little social life in the department. Alan Nevins and his wife entertained occasionally, but, Donald, a bachelor at the time, was forced to find other sources of entertainment and amused himself by shooting pool with students. Salaries at Columbia were also low. Donald knew that at some point he wanted to have a family, and it was clear that it would be difficult to do on a Columbia salary.

Donald also noticed an undercurrent of hostility toward women. At the time, there was one woman, Elizabeth Bancroft, teaching as an adjunct faculty member, in the history department. She was regarded as a lightweight by most of other faculty, but one year the students rated her as the best teacher in the department.

When the department was looking for a modern Europe specialist, Donald suggested Barbara Tuchman. Several people opposed her appointment on the grounds that the history department offices were on the sixth floor of Fayerweather Hall, but the only women's rest room was on the first floor, in their eyes, making Tuchman's appointment impossible. Years later, when he told Tuchman the story, she remarked, "how utterly absurd men are."

The department did offer a position to a woman, the Oxford medievalist Beryl Smalley. In Donald's opinion, the offer was simply a token gesture to give the appearance of interest; the department made the offer fairly sure that Smalley would not accept. They could, in Donald's opinion, save appearances by making it look like they were interested in making a female appointment.

By the end of the 1950s the department was riding high. While Donald departed for Princeton in 1959, the department was still strong in American history, with Hofstadter, Leuchtenberg, Morris, and McKitrick. New York City, with the New York Public Library, the New York Historical Society, and Columbia's own superb library, offered unique advantages to those in American history.

The number of graduate students entering the program was staggering, usually around one-hundred a year. Even though many of them were teachers, not necessarily interested in pursuing a Ph.D., it was still a remarkably high number of students.

There were a number of oddities about the program. The department had minimal admission standards, but rigorous standards for those who wished to continue. The result was that many students, admitted without deep preparation, were overwhelmed by what was expected of them. The large numbers of students also meant that the Columbia graduate program in history had a self-directed quality, which left many students wanting more.

No department member exuded this quality more than Richard Hofstadter. Many of the students who flocked to Columbia to study history in the fifties and sixties came to study with the brilliant winner of two Pulitzer Prizes who seemed to understand America better than anyone else. But those who expected a Pied

Piper found a distant and aloof man, who stayed in his office while his secretary guarded the gates to his time and wisdom.[18]

To be sure, had Hofstadter elected to become intensely involved with all the students who wanted his counsel, he could have been swallowed up. But he seemed to go out of his way to put up barriers. It was sometimes said that he wanted to see his graduate students twice, when they had a dissertation topic and when they were finished. He normally called students by their last names and was notorious for reading his mail while listening to their research problems. "Do you really like working with graduate students?" he once asked William Leuchtenberg.[19]

On the other hand, Hofstadter encouraged innovative interdisciplinary work by his students; he took female graduate students seriously at a time when many in the profession did not, and worked very hard on behalf of his students after they graduated. He helped Dorothy Ross get her dissertation published by the University of Chicago Press, and he introduced Alfred Knopf to Christopher Lasch's work, thereby beginning a long and productive relationship between Lasch and the distinguished publisher. And he helped place three of his best students, Lawrence Levine, Robert Dallek, and Richard Weiss, all promising Jews, at west coast universities, where Jews had not always been welcome.[20]

Eric Foner, a Hofstadter student in the sixties, offers perhaps the most balanced appraisal. Foner conceded that Hofstadter, lacking a true love of the classroom, was not a great undergraduate teacher. More tellingly, Foner also suggested that in his lectures Hofstadter even went out of his way to be dull, perhaps to discourage some of the hero-worshippers who flocked to his courses.[21]

But in his seminars and individual conferences, and in his comments on written work, Hofstadter was a much different and better teacher, open, suggestive, and thought-provoking. In these areas, his erudition, his intelligence, and willingness to help emerged, although, as we have seen, not all of Hofstadter's graduate students would have agreed with this appraisal.

Not all of the Columbia history faculty, however, were celebrated Americanists with graduate students pounding on their doors. The brief Columbia career of Norman Cantor offers insight about life in the department from another angle. In 1960 Richard Morris, who had become department chair, approached Cantor, a junior faculty member at Princeton, about coming to Columbia. Morris needed someone to teach a popular class in legal history. Legal history had been taught for decades at Columbia, by Robert Livingston Schuyler, who had retired. Morris' son had taken Cantor's course at Princeton and returned with favorable reports. Morris invited Cantor to lunch at the Columbia faculty club, and, within an hour, had offered Cantor a tenured position at Columbia.[22]

At the time Cantor was more interested in staying at Princeton, but, when the Princeton history department declined to make an early decision on his tenure there, he decided to accept Morris' offer. Joseph Strayer, Cantor's mentor at Princeton, took the news of Cantor's departure from Princeton hard, and the two did not speak for nearly a decade. As Cantor was cleaning out his office at Princeton, Elmer Beller, another member of the Princeton department, stopped by to wish him well. "I am very sorry to see you leave," Beller said, "you are a very good teacher and a good scholar even if some of my colleagues do not think so. I am sure in a few years we will invite you back."

What Cantor did not know was that his appointment at Columbia had been secured by somewhat highhanded means. Morris appointed him without the review of the other tenured faculty in the department, although he got the support of Jacques Barzun, a historian who also served as the university's provost, and who was empowered to decide upon tenured appointments. Normally, Columbia required not only the approval of the department's tenured faculty but an *ad hoc* committee of five full professors from outside the history department, for its promotions and appointments to tenure. Barzun followed this protocol, but apparently stacked the deck by appointing faculty likely to approve most appointments.

While the circumstances of the appointment were somewhat irregular, Cantor was not an unworthy candidate. He had established an excellent reputation for his teaching at Princeton and had published a book on the medieval church. He also had an article coming out on medieval monasticism in the *American Historical Review*, which did not publish very many articles in medieval history.

Yet the irregular nature of his appointment came back to haunt him. After his arrival several department members, including John Hine Mundy, the senior medievalist at Columbia, asked him who he was and how he had been appointed. Surprised, Cantor realized only after his arrival the unusual nature of his appointment and that he had been thrust upon the department without its having the opportunity to evaluate his candidacy.

Despite the uncomfortable transition, Cantor's first few years at Columbia were successful. He was a popular teacher and finished a book, *The Civilization of the Middle Ages*, which has gone through forty printings and become the best-selling survey of medieval history published in the United States. Morris also arranged for him to teach medieval history at Barnard. In 1963 Columbia's senior faculty were impressed when Cantor was recommended by an ad hoc committee at Harvard for a senior appointment in medieval history, although the job eventually went to Giles Constable.

While at Columbia, Cantor enjoyed another one of the university's delights, unprecedented access to first-rate scholars in many disciplines. On his first day in Morningside Heights, he lunched at the faculty club with the sociologists Robert Merton and Paul Lazarsfeld. The next week he was joined by the anthropologists Margaret Mead and Marvin Harris. He sat in on lectures by Meyer Shapiro in art history, Lionel Trilling on literature, and Jacques Barzun on intellectual history. One day Trilling stopped him as he walked across campus to tell him that he had read Cantor's book on medieval civilization and liked it. On another occasion, Terence Hopkins, a rising star in the sociology department, appeared at Cantor's office door to suggest that he apply for a research grant handed out by a committee Hopkins chaired. The sociologists, Hopkins informed him, had noticed Cantor's promise.

But teaching at Columbia also posed problems. Cantor could not afford to raise a family on Columbia's salary, so he had to live in apartments far from campus. Every morning at six o'clock, he would leave a tiny apartment in north Manhattan or the Bronx, emerge from the IRT subway at 116th and Broadway to pick up three sugar donuts and a small black coffee at the Chock Full O'Nuts on that corner. He spent an hour in his office at Fayerweather Hall preparing to teach and then walked across Broadway to teach his medieval history course at Barnard.

Money was a constant problem at Columbia and not just for the junior faculty. Many of the senior faculty wrote textbooks or taught elsewhere to raise money. Richard Morris recorded American revolutionary songs. In 1961 money was so scarce at Columbia that Provost Jacques Barzun cut off off-campus telephone service from professors' offices. For several months, Columbia faculty, including several Nobel and Pulitzer Prize winners, lined up to use the pay phones between classes.

The second problem for Cantor at Columbia was, in his judgment, was departmental politics, especially after Richard Morris stepped down as chair in 1963. Having been hired by Morris, Cantor had his back covered while Morris remained as chair. But, when Morris left, Cantor, like Cardinal Wolsey, lay naked before his enemies, in particular, the senior medievalist John Mundy. Mundy thought that Cantor was not a serious scholar and should not be supervising dissertations. With Mundy and, soon, Peter Gay, arrayed against him, Cantor found himself isolated and assigned to teaching in Columbia's evening program for adult education. Fearing this was his long-term future at Columbia, Cantor accepted an offer from Brandeis in 1966.

Cantor's experience at Columbia is both confirmed and challenged by that of other faculty at Columbia during the sixties. Most would agree that among Columbia's strengths, both in the university and history department, was its strong interdisciplinary orientation. When Stanley Elkins wished to work on a broad-based interpretation of slavery, based on psychological and sociological approaches, he found a sympathetic audience in the history, including his advisor, Richard Hofstadter. But, when he moved to the University of Chicago as a junior faculty member in 1955, he found a less sympathetic reaction. He was told he shouldn't try to substitute theory for research in original sources and that his work was soft.[23]

On the other hand, not everyone found the financial problems that Cantor did. Henry Graff had no problem buying a house in the suburbs and raising a family on his Columbia salary. But it was true that many history faculty supplemented their incomes. Graff and Jacques Barzun wrote a popular textbook on research techniques, *The Modern Researcher.* John Garraty was a prolific writer of textbooks. There were also roughly ninety colleges in the greater New York City area, so there were plenty of opportunities for extra teaching and lecturing. History faculty often made more money outside of Columbia than from it.[24]

But, whatever the salary situation, it is clear that the department had very little turnover. In fact several faculty members turned down offers to move elsewhere. Both Graff and Hofstadter turned down Harvard, as did Lionel Trilling in the English department.

One departure, however, that of Peter Gay, was quite serious. Gay was a Columbia Ph.D. in European intellectual history who had earned the respect of Richard Hofstadter as a graduate student. After teaching in Columbia's political science department for several years, he joined the history department in 1955 and emerged as one of the department's leading scholars. Gay was an advocate of what he called the "social history of ideas," by which he meant the notion the intellectual developments could not be understood apart from their social and economic context. The book where his methodology was most boldly arrayed was the first volume of his two-volume study, *The Enlightenment: An Interpretation*, which won the National Book Award in 1967. But, just as he reached the pinnacle of the profession, he left Colubmia for Yale in 1970.

At about the same time, Richard Hofstadter was also tempted by an outside offer. Hofstadter was not upset with the department, but, while he was mulling an offer from Harvard's education school, his wife was held up outside their apartment. Fearing for the security of his family, Hofstadter seriously considered taking the Harvard post, but, eventually decided to stay at Columbia. In 1970, his death from cancer at 54 deprived the department of its most renowned member.[25]

As the discipline of history changed in the sixties, the department made some attempts to change with it. In 1966, the Ford Foundation approached the department with a proposal to support the hiring of three Africanists for a five-year period. Its generosity allowed the department to have extensive coverage of an emerging area of importance in the profession and enabled it to hire Graham Irwin, Hollis Lynch, and Marcia Wright. A few years later, the department hired Nathan Huggins to teach black history, so the department had its first blacks, Lynch and Huggins.

But, if the department had succeeded in adding qualified blacks to its ranks, it struggled to add women. While women, such as Annette Baxter, taught at Barnard, the graduate wing of the department did not have a woman until Marcia Wright's appointment.[26] In the fifties, David Donald had already noticed the ambivalent and sometimes hostile attitudes toward women. In addition Shepherd B. "Shep" Clough, the department's economic historian, echoing George Pierson at Yale, had once announced that the department would hire a woman "over his dead body."[27]

But the department had been admitting women into its graduate program for sometime. When Gerda Lerner, at age forty-three, decided, after raising two children, that she wanted a career as a historian and finish the work begun by Mary Beard a half-century earlier, Columbia was the only place she could find willing to accept her. She found a sympathetic faculty member in Carl Degler, a Columbia Ph.D. who was teaching at Vassar College, but who taught a graduate seminar in American social history at Columbia in the early sixties. Working with Degler, and, later, Eric McKitrick, Lerner explored the links between race, class, and gender in the abolitionist movement through the lives of the Grimke sisters.

Other women encountered difficulty. When Carol Berkin expressed her interest in pursuing a doctoral degree at Columbia, she was told that "a pretty girl like you will be married and pregnant before you know it." At one point the female graduate students in history called for a meeting with the department to air their concerns. Each woman present had written out on a note card a "horror story" about their treatment at Columbia. The cards were shuffled to disguise the identities of the authors and read aloud. One report described a scene in which a member of the department defended the Columbia's retention of the M.A. degree on the grounds that it was beneficial to those women who leave graduate school after a year or two. Another described finding out that a faculty letter of recommendation about her said that she was not very mobile because she was married.

At the end of the reading, several faculty members expressed doubts that the situation was as bad as it was described and assured the groups that there was no bias in the department against women. But the Russian historian Loren Graham affirmed that there was reason to believe that women were not always treated fairly, and, according to one observer, that comment seemed to silence the dissent.

Despite the claims of an unpleasant atmosphere for women, an impressive list of women earned Columbia Ph.D.s in the sixties and early seventies, including Linda Kerber, Carol Berkin, Regina Morantz-Sanchez, Estelle Freedman, Jacquelyn Dowd Hall, Joan Kelly-Gadol, Renate Bridenthal, Bonnie Anderson, Mary Nolan, and Paula Hyman. In 1973 Marcia Wright was granted tenure in the department, even though the administration had announced that there was a tenure freeze, and three women were offered temporary appointments in the history department.[28]

The temporary appointments reflected the fact that Columbia had fallen on difficult economic times, and the career of Eric Foner represents an interesting example of what a career at Columbia as both a graduate student and faculty member could be like.[29] In 1959 Foner entered Columbia as an undergraduate. Like Hofstadter in the thirties, Foner thrived on the intellectual energy of Columbia and New York in the sixties. He participated in the famous Freedom March of 1963 and the less famous march of 1957. At Columbia he was president of ACTION, a student political organization, and spent a great deal of time picketing Woolworth stores on behalf of the Civil Rights Movement.

He came to history only by accident, having entered Columbia fully intending to major in astronomy. During his junior year, however, he talked his way into James Shenton's senior seminar on the Civil War era. By the end of the year, Foner had become a history major and developed a lifelong passion for the subject and Civil War period.

His seminar paper for Shenton was a study of the Free Soil party in 1848, his first excursion into archival research. The paper became the subject of his senior thesis, directed by Richard Hofstadter, who eventually would supervise Foner's dissertation. Early on Hofstadter related to Foner how he got his first full-time teaching job. In the fall of 1941 a position opened up at a downtown branch of City College after a professor had been fired for being a Communist. That professor was Jack Foner, Eric Foner's father.

Whatever ironies Hofstadter might have held about replacing Foner's father, he played the mentor role to perfection. He helped Foner win a Kellett Fellowship to study at Oriel College, Oxford, and learn the Oxford art of the weekly tutorial essay. More importantly, he directed Foner toward the subjects which Foner pursued during his own career, the history and importance of political ideologies and the interconnections between social development and political culture.

When Foner returned to Columbia after his year at Oxford, he found Columbia completely changed. Like students at Harvard, Columbia's students were sensitive to the atmosphere of polarization surrounding the war in Viet Nam, race riots in American cities, and the assassination of Martin Luther King. At the same time, students also felt alienated from Columbia's administration and to a certain extent by the aloof nature of some of the faculty.

The student troubles at Columbia began when the Action Faction of Columbia's Students for a Democratic Society, under the leadership of Mark Rudd, launched a protest against the university's plan to construct a gymnasium next to a minority neighborhood. Like protestors at Harvard and elsewhere, Columbia's students decided to occupy administrative offices on campus, even Fayerweather Hall, and anger on several levels spilled out over the campus.[30]

The protest expanded as students expressed their resentment over Columbia's tacit support of the racism and, in other ways, the militarism which they saw destroying America. Their anger emerged in unexpected ways. Eugene Rice was frequently accosted by angry students and repeatedly called a "motherfucker" by them during this period, and the elderly Renaissance scholar Paul Oskar Kristeller was once surrounded by a group of threatening students.[31]

Mark Naison, a graduate student of Richard Hofstadter's, was scheduled to take his comprehensive exams during the middle of Columbia's student troubles in 1968. On the day in question, with Columbia's administrative offices occupied by students, a battle raged across the campus. Naison's examination, held in Fayerweather, began amidst the sounds of breaking furniture, shouts of rage, fragments of falling plaster, and chants of "Shut it down." Naison noticed that the behavior of Hofstadter and the other Columbia faculty was curious. Normally Ph.D. oral exams are intended to be rigorous and to test the candidate's mettle and intellectual depth. But Naison sensed that rather than testing him or even resenting him, the faculty were more interested in their own performance than in his. Their goal that day was not to examine him, but to see if they could maintain their own dignity and sense of decorum, which they did, even though they were aware that Naison supported everything that was "happening in that bldg, from the breaking of furniture to the slugging of professors." The conclusion of his examination saw Naison, in a suit and tie, "leading rh, Dwight Miner, equally attired, out of an occupied building in front of 2000 people." As he saw his comrades in protest, Naison raised his fist in triumph, "feeling at once overjoyed at having the whole fucking mess over with, and guilty at deserting my brothers inside…SCHIZOPHRENIA! You better believe it."[32]

Grayson Kirk, Columbia's president, after a long and Hamlet-like deliberation, ordered riot squads from the New York City Police Department to clear the buildings, resulting in a riot. The riot squads appeared to take the order to clear the buildings as an opportunity to take revenge on what they saw as spoiled, privileged students, resulting in numerous injuries and radicalizing people who were previously moderate. Final exams were cancelled, and Columbia was effectively shut down. Kirk soon announced his early retirement.

Like other departments confronted with student outrage, the Columbia history department was divided. Several of its members, including Fritz Stern, Hofstadter, and William Leuchtenberg, had met informally to discuss the issues raised by war in Viet Nam and had already expressed their opposition well before the student protests erupted. By the time the protests began, most of the Columbia history faculty thought the war in Viet Nam was a mistake, even if they also believed that the university was the wrong place to protest against it. There were, inevitably, a few hard liners, deeply offended by the students and who believed that values of the academy needed to be defended from the Philistines, whatever the cost. John Mundy, who was chair during the student troubles, had been a Trotskyite in his youth, generally eschewed confrontation with the radicals. His strategy was simply to hold on until the all the madness passed and reason returned.[33]

Foner was in the middle of these events, writing his dissertation while participating in the Columbia student rebellion of 1968. But he also seemed destined for glory in the Columbia history department. In 1969 he was offered a job as an instructor in the department. When, during the following year, he published his dissertation as *Free Soil, Free Labor, Free Men*, the way seemed cleared for his entry into the ranks of the Columbia senior faculty.

There were, however, some bumps along the road. He had been hired to teach the department's first course in African American history, where, having published on free soil and race, he was an authority. Understandably, however, black students believed that the course should be taught by a black instructor.

But Foner was committed to teaching the course and prepared intensively for it. During the first few weeks of the course, he was able to keep his critics at bay. But as time passed, a group of black students began demonstrating against his class, organizing walkouts and disruptions.

Most of the one-hundred and fifty students registered for the class continued to attend and seemed to be eager to hear Foner's wisdom. Even the troublemakers told him privately that they had nothing against him personally and actually liked his lectures. Since that course, Foner has taught black history many times with little problem, but in 1969 it was a difficult baptism under fire for any beginning teacher.

More seriously for his Columbia future, 1972 was the beginning of a decade of financial austerity. The dramatic growth of the sixties collapsed; student enrollments declined. The university administration had no choice but to cut back. Those, such as Kenneth Jackson, hired a few years before, were tenured before the crunch came. But those, like Foner, who came just a little later, were trapped. Even though he had been told not to expect tenure, the news still came as a shock.

Not only was the department not permitted to make senior appointments, but even assistant professor appointments were terminal. It fell to Eugene Rice, chair in the early seventies, to deliver the bad news to Eric Foner that his position was being terminated. When it came to new appointees in the future, Rice believed that it would be wrong to delude them about their futures at Columbia. "You have a good address," he would say to new appointees, "and you will be a member of an excellent and interesting department with access to a great library, good students, and job security for seven or eight years. But it is almost certain that there will be no job for you at the end of your contract.

As soon as you are settled into your teaching at Columbia, you should begin looking for another job."³⁴

Financial difficulties made hiring female faculty more difficult. By 1970 the federal government was exerting pressure on Columbia to hire women and had revoked its federal aid, in part because Columbia had few women and in part because their record keeping was so bad. Female graduate students in the department had also advocated that more female faculty be hired and that courses in women's history be offered. After Marcia Wright, the department had not hired additional women on a full-time basis, although Nina Garosian taught Middle Eastern history as a part-time faculty member. In the early seventies, the department approached Ann Scott and Willie Lee Rose about coming to Columbia, but both decided against it.³⁵

In 1974 the department was allowed to hire three new assistant professors in American history, all of them terminal appointments, and it decided that one of them should go to a woman. With that appointment, the department hired Rosalind Rosenberg, who was finishing her Ph.D. at Stanford.³⁶

Rosenberg was aware that she got the job because Columbia was under pressure to hire women and that the appointment was terminal. She and several of the others who came in with her referred to themselves as the "revolving door" generation. But, since they were aware that the appointment was terminal, they spent little time worrying about their prospects at Columbia. They were also were treated sympathetically by the senior faculty, who understood their plight and were also relieved that they would not have to make decisions on who would receive the grace of tenure at Columbia and who would not.

There was another unusual component of Rosenberg's teaching at Columbia. In the seventies, the university was taking steps to break down its traditional division between Columbia College and the graduate school. Thus, in her first year at Columbia, Rosenberg taught both graduate students and Contemporary Civilization, the great books course required of all Columbia undergraduates. Of the two, "C.C." presented the greatest challenge for her. She was an Americanist, and "C.C." was a course in the great books of the western Europe from Plato to Freud, very few of which she had actually read. In her first year, she taught six different courses, all of them new to her.

There were other quirks. On one hand, she sensed that there was lingering antagonism over the student protests among certain of the senior faculty, and that some of them were waging the battles of the past. On the other hand, she very much enjoyed her time at Columbia. She and the other junior faculty enjoyed a close bond, and the senior faculty were for the most part congenial. Junior faculty were regularly invited to the homes of the senior faculty and to the regular round of department social gatherings. Also, between her junior faculty colleagues, the graduate students, and across the street at Barnard College, there were plenty of women around, as well as some sympathy for women's issues. When she gave birth to her first child in her second year at Columbia, she was allowed to teach part-time, which enabled her to take care of the baby and revise her dissertation into a book.

As the department limped through the seventies, there were some advantages to financial austerity. Since there was no money for expansion, there was no point in discussing the long-term future of the department or who they should hire, and thus, no bitter arguments about those things.[37]

By the early eighties, Columbia's economic situation had improved, and the department could began to act like a department again, hiring faculty at all ranks and being able to think seriously about its direction and future. Among other appointments, the department was able to bring back Eric Foner at the senior level, and make other senior appointments, such as Yosef Yerushalmi in Jewish history. It also tenured several promising assistant professors, such as Barbara Fields and Betsy Blackmar.

The history of the Columbia history department is not easily summarized. In the decade or so after World War II, a very good department had to be rebuilt, which it was, with faculty such as Richard Hofstadter, William Leuchtenberg, Fritz Stern, Peter Gay, and a host of others. In the late sixties and early seventies, the department received a double blow; the student troubles were divisive, and hard financial times descended upon the university and department. While most departments across the country faced financial crises in the seventies, it was perhaps worse at Columbia, where they could only make terminal appointments. Thus, the department went for roughly ten years without making a permanent appointment, something that would be disastrous to any department that aspired, as Columbia did, to international prominence. The department was rescued only by the improved financial conditions of the eighties, which enabled it to again bring in promising persons at both the senior and junior levels.

---

[1] James Harvey Robinson, *The New History: Essays Illustrating the Modern Historical Outlook* (New York, 1912).

[2] Charles Beard, *An Economic Interpretation of the Constitution* (New York, 1935).

[3] William Palmer, "Interview with William Leuchtenberg," March 1, 2006; Idem., "Interview with Henry Graff," February 23, 2006.

[4] Carl E. Schorske, *A Life in Learning: The Charles Homer Haskins Lecture* (Washington, 1987), pp. 2–5.

[5] Fritz Stern, *Five Germanies I Have Known* (New York, 2006), pp. 162-3.

[6] Palmer, "Interview with Eugene Rice," March 4, 2006; Idem., "Interview with Leuchtenberg."

[7] Palmer, "Interview with Leuchtenberg."

[8] Ibid..

[9] David A. Brown, *Richard Hofstadter: An Intelletual Biography* (Chicago, 2006), p. 65.

[10] For Hofstadter as a graduate student, see William Palmer, *Engagement with the Past: The Lives and Works of the World War II Generation of Historians* (Lexington, Ky., 2001), pp. 47-9; Brown, *Richard Hofstadter*, pp. 18–27.

[11] Palmer, "Interview with David Donald," December 7, 2005; "Interview with Leuchtenberg."

[12] Alfred Kazin, *New York Jew* (New York, 1978), p. 17.

[13] Brown, *Richard Hofstadter*, p. 48

[14] For this and most of what follows, see Palmer, *Engagement with the Past*, pp. 187-90, which is based largely on Daniel Joseph Singal, "Beyond Consensus: Richard Hofstadter and American Historiography," *American Historical Review* 89!984): 976-1004. See also Brown, *Richard Hofstadter*, pp. 90-5.

[15] Palmer, "Interview with Leuchtenberg, March 1, 2006."

[16] Palmer, "Interview with Stern," November 13, 2006.

[17] For Donald's experience at Columbia, see Palmer, "Interview with Donald."

[18] Brown, *Richard Hofstadter*, p. 66.

[19] Palmer, "Interview with Leuchtenberg."

[20] Brown, *Richard Hofstadter*, pp. 66-7.

[21] Eric Foner, *Who Owns History: Rethinking the Past in a Changing World* (New York, 2002), p. 45.

[22] Cantor's Columbia career is recounted in Norman Cantor, *Confessions of a Medievalist* (Tempe, Ariz., 2002), pp. 75-80, 108–114.

[23] Palmer, "Interview with Stanley Elkins," December 12, 2005

[24] Palmer, "Interview with Kenneth Jackson," February 22, 2006.

[25] Palmer, "Interview with Leuchtenberg;" Brown, *Richard Hofstadter*, p. 225. (There is a minor difference in detail in the two accounts. Leuchtenberg remembers Hofstadter's wife being held up at "knifepoint;" Brown says at "gunpoint.")

[26] This statement represents the best recollection of several in the department at the time, including William Leuchtenberg. Marcia Wright did not answer my email.

[27] Rosalind Rosenberg, *Changing the Subject: How the Women of Columbia Shaped the Way We Think About Sex and Politics* (New York, 2004), p. 229.

[28] Ibid., pp. 232, 285.

[29] For the career of Eric Foner at Columbia, see Foner, *Who Owns History?*, pp. 9-12.

[30] For an interesting general account of the student uprising at Columbia, see Roger Kahn, *The Battle for Morningside Heights: Why Students Rebel* (New York, 1970).

[31] Palmer, "Interview with Eugene Rice," March 4, 2006.

32 Mark Naison is quoted in Peter Novick, *That Noble Dream: The "Objectivity Question" and the American Historical Profession* (Cambridge, 1987), pp. 428-9.

33 Palmer, "Interview with Rice."

34 Palmer, "Interview with Rice."

35 Palmer, "Interview with Leuchtenberg."

36 Palmer, "Interview with Rosalind Rosenberg, September 4, 2006."

37 Palmer, "Interview with Leuchtenberg."

Conclusion
The Emergence of a More Professional Body

On a clear fall night, the campus of the University of California at Berkeley looks much as it did a half century ago. From the foot of the Sather Tower, one can see the Bancroft Library where Raymond Sontag had an office that was the envy of the rest of the department. One can also see Wheeler Hall, where most of the department was housed until about 1950, and Dwinelle Hall, where it is today and where the bitter departmental battles of the fifties were waged. With a few exceptions, the principals in those battles are long dead. It is no doubt fanciful, but, like walking the Gettysburg battlefield at twilight, someone who walks Dwinelle's halls today can feel their presence. The ghosts of Carl Bridenbaugh, Ray Sontag, and others still haunt the corridors of the Berkeley history department.

Dwinelle Hall was only one of many sites where the modernizing of history departments occurred in the fifties and sixties. Similar, though less controversial processes occurred at Yale, Princeton, Wisconsin, and Chicago as well as Berkeley. To a certain extent, several of the steps in the process of modernization had occurred somewhat earlier at Harvard and Columbia, but, by the fifties many of the faculty members involved in them were nearing retirement, and it was time to rebuild again.

The process of modernization was triggered by several forces. The most obvious was the demographic transformation that followed World War II. The end of the war brought thousands of veterans, who had their studies interrupted by military service, back to college or graduate school, and the passage of the so-called "G.I. Bill" would bring still more. Their presence both increased the revenues flowing into American colleges and required more instructors to teach them. Moreover, as the post-war economy boomed in the fifties, more families could afford to send their children, male and female, to college, and a college education ceased to be regarded as something simply for the children of the affluent and increasingly as something that should be open to everyone.

The staggering numbers of students stampeding onto college campuses in the decade following World War II provided the money necessary to hire more faculty. But the kinds of faculty members who would be hired was determined by several visionary departmental chairs and distinguished senior members. In the category of visionary chairs, the most conspicuous of these were George Pierson at Yale and Joseph Strayer at Princeton, and, slightly later, William McNeill at Chicago. In the category of distinguished senior members, the most conspicuous of these was Carl Bridenbaugh at Berkeley.

All of these men wished to upgrade the quality and reputation of their departments by placing more emphasis on research and graduate education. But each of them had a distinctive sense of how to do it, which in the cases of Pierson, Strayer, and Bridenbaugh, at least partially involved chasing the elusive ideal of Harvard. Pierson wanted the Yale history department to rival Harvard's, and he thought that recruiting Harvard men was the surest way to make it happen. Strayer, a Harvard Ph.D., wished to hire faculty members who excelled in research and teaching, and he thought that those who held degrees from Harvard comprised the most likely, though not the only, group in which to find these qualities. At Berkeley, Bridenbaugh, who also held a Ph.D. from Harvard, wished to take what he regarded as an inferior department and make it the Harvard of the West. At Chicago, people holding Harvard degrees were certainly respected, but their superiority was not assumed. "I can read, and I can tell this guy isn't any good," McNeill remarked about one candidate.

How smoothly the process unfolded depended to a large extent upon the main person leading it. Pierson, Strayer, and McNeill were all insiders at their institutions. All three had also been undergraduates at the institutions where they taught. By the time they assumed the position of chair, they were closely connected to institutional power structures and were persons who could be trusted by administrators and older faculty to reform their departments without leaving devastation in their wake or bruising too many egos. The process proceeded smoothly in most cases at their institutions.

By contrast, Bridenbaugh was an outsider, contemptuous of almost anything connected to the "Old Berkeley." He was determined to reform the department whatever the cost, whoever's ego was bruised, and he treated the department's older faculty as if he were a German general and they were Polish stragglers in the way of *Wehrmacht* in 1939. The process of modernization therefore was much rougher at Berkeley than it was elsewhere.

At the same time, it became clear that any department that aspired to be the best would have to hire Jews, in part because Harvard, Columbia, and other schools had been admitting Jewish graduate students for several decades, and many of these students had established themselves as candidates with superior ability. Selection as a member of Harvard's Society of Fellows was (and still is) regarded as an unmistakable sign of the highest distinction. And the hiring of Harvard-trained Jews, such as Joseph Levenson and Thomas Kuhn at Berkeley, both of whom had been fellows of the Society, were breakthrough appointments at an institution which, in the fifties, had a reputation for anti-Semitism. At roughly the same time, hiring John Morton Blum at Yale and George Mosse at Wisconsin, signaled that Jews of ability could find jobs in history departments at two other American universities also known to possess an anti-Semitic strain.

A closely related component of modernization was the expansion of departments to include more faculty members teaching in non-western areas. While several departments had Latin Americanists and Asianists before the fifties, most departments still maintained highly western-centered curricula. World War II exposed American ignorance of areas outside the West, and the fifties saw a striking expansion of the number of people teaching in non-western areas. By the sixties, it was not enough to have one person in, say, Chinese history, and claim you had the field covered. It was the realized goal of William McNeill at Chicago to have the major areas of the world covered at least two people with linguistic competence.

The addition of faculty to teach in non-western areas was not always achieved easily. At most institutions non-western history needed a tireless advocate to reach the unconverted. At Harvard it was John King Fairbank, an Asianist, and at Wisconsin it was the Africanist Philip Curtin. While both, especially Curtin, succeeded in upgrading the coverage of areas of the outside of Western Europe and the United States, at the end of their careers, both reflected upon the difficulty they had particularly in convincing their Americanist colleagues to see the value in non-western courses. At Harvard, Fairbank remarked ruefully at the end of his career, "the faculty was not organized to accommodate an increase of tenured professors in East Asian history."

In several cases, the modernizing of the history department required more than one visionary. While Pierson and Strayer took the initial steps at Yale and Princeton, the remaking of their departments was not complete until a second stage in recruitment had occurred. After Pierson's initial steps, the Yale department was vastly better by the early sixties than it had been a decade before, but the final steps in its emergence were not taken until the "class of 69" had been recruited largely under the leadership of Howard Lamar.

Even with the impressive recruiting of Joseph Strayer in the fifties, the Princeton department had reached a crossroads in the mid-sixties, until Lawrence Stone injected some new life into its ranks. His main contribution to the process was to take the lead in appointing several new faculty, distinguished in part by their interdisciplinary orientations, including Carl Schorske and Robert Darnton.

A second demographic force driving the modernization of history departments was the impact of the arrival of the "Baby Boom" generation on campus in the early sixties. Their arrival injected even more money into university budgets and required departments to hire still more instructors. Benefiting from an economy that continued to expand, generous state legislatures, granting agencies eager to help fund non-western areas, and new methods of reckoning available funds from endowments, American colleges and universities enjoyed a period of prosperity and expansion they had never previously experienced and are unlikely to see again.

It is also clear that increased revenue did not necessarily mean increased salaries, and financial incentives appear to have played little role in attracting new faculty. Oscar Handlin turned down a salary offer from the University of Chicago that was four times higher than his Harvard salary to stay in Cambridge. Stuart Hughes found that Harvard salary in the sixties was barely enough to survive. Yale initially offered John Blum less money to come to Yale than he was making at M.I.T. Members of the Columbia history department often had to find other means of making money, such as writing textbooks or teaching at other New York City colleges, to make ends meet. In most cases, it was the prestige of working in an elite department that motivated new faculty to come. Stanley Kutler recalled that when he was offered a job at the University of Wisconsin, he would have "walked to Madison to take it," regardless of the salary.

But the arrival of the Baby Boom generation eventually produced difficulties for departments. For a variety of reasons, they tended to be more skeptical of authority than previous generations and more willing to question the wisdom of their elders. Their arrival also corresponded to a time when the Viet Nam War, the Civil Rights and Women's Movements, and the increasingly impersonal nature of the higher education in the United States raised fundamental questions about the nature of American society and the place of the university in it.

To express their misgivings, student leaders often determined that peaceful demonstration was insufficient to their purposes, and they occupied buildings, destroyed university properties and records, and terrorized administrators and faculty members. At Wisconsin a bomb planted in a laboratory and designed to go off in the early morning hours when it was thought that no one would be around, actually killed a graduate student in physics who happened to be working when it went off.

Dealing with the students proved to be a divisive issue. Many faculty members of that era sympathized with the students, opposing the war and supporting the various equality movements. But they doubted that the university was the proper place for the students to voice their protests and objected to the violence directed at buildings, administrative offices, records, and, sometimes, faculty. Angry debates erupted in several departments about how protesting students should be handled, and, in many cases, ill feelings among members lasted far beyond the end of student unrest.

On the other hand, student protest expedited the next phase of modernization. By the sixties, most departments were more professional, but remained for the most part all-white and all-male conclaves. Protesting students often demanded the hiring of more blacks and females and the teaching of courses in black and women's history. While several departments were already moving in this direction before the students began to protest, angry protestors clearly forced lagging departments to take action.

Of the various groups that fought their way into leading history departments in the fifties and sixties, women were the group that probably had the most difficult time. Even faculty members who believed that hiring of women was long overdue were unsure about how to behave towards them. Other male faculty displayed outright hostility. Most of the women who were hired in the sixties and seventies faced a wide range of reactions from male faculty. Some welcomed their presence and went out of their way to make them feel welcome; others were hostile. Still others ranted about the declining standards that compelled them to hire women.

It is stunning to note how quickly the boom came to an end. Approximately a quarter century of expansion halted abruptly around 1970 and 1971. In contrast with the free flow of money after World War II, the seventies brought economic hard times. The impact was harder on some departments than others. Yale, which, during the presidency of Kingman Brewster, had spent quite liberally, found itself facing a long period of hard financial times. At Columbia the history department went roughly a decade without tenuring a junior faculty member. At other places, such as Berkeley and Wisconsin, austerity simply meant fewer tenure-track appointments and no senior ones.

At some places, austerity meant that there was at least less departmental acrimony. With few or no new hires, there weren't as many job descriptions and appointments to fight about and no need to argue about the direction of the department. The great exception here was Harvard where the senior faculty appeared to fear that expanding the size of the department meant that they would be compelled to appoint inferior candidates, thereby compromising the department's quality and reputation. Expectations for tenure among the junior faculty at Harvard, already high, were driven still higher in the sixties and seventies, to the point where scarcely any junior faculty were tenured after 1970, not by lack of funding, but by the choice of senior faculty. The department which survived the austerities of the seventies the best was probably Princeton where the Davis Center provided intellectual excitement, and the department continued to make superb appointments, especially in European history.

The changes that occurred in history departments from 1940 to 1980 were about several things. On one hand they were about equalizing opportunity, that is, changing the composition of the waspish, heavily male departments that characterized the first century or so of the profession's history to include other deserving groups such as Jews, Catholics, blacks, and women. This process in American academic life, not limited just to history departments, is an often neglected part of the general movement to ensure civil rights for all in the years after World War II. At the same time excellence in research became the defining characteristic of what constituted the best candidates, and, with a few exceptions, the reformers usually wanted the best scholars, regardless of race, creed, or gender.

But the transition of history departments from gentleman's clubs to professional bodies was also about approach. Like history itself, historical trends and fashions move in phases. New light flashes across the eastern sky heralding the coming of an exciting new theory or approach with a flock of acolytes eager to plead its case. But, after many a summer dies the swan, and in time what was once fresh and innovative may seem stale and obsolete. It is possible to view the changing imperatives of the historical profession through the lens of the history department.

For much of the first half of the twentieth century, historians focused on writing the grand narratives of political and diplomatic history, and most history departments were composed of men who either taught or wrote in this fashion. By the thirties, under the influence of a variety of figures, including Marx, Weber, Charles Beard, James Harvey Robinson and the "New History," and the French *Annaliste* historians, historians began to recognize the inadequacies of this approach. It attended mainly to elites and took little account of the social and economic contexts in which political and diplomatic activities took place.

In the United States it was mainly the "World War II Generation of Historians," those born between 1908 and 1922, who were most affected by this change. Whether it was Edmund Morgan writing about the Puritans, C. Vann Woodward writing about the post-Reconstruction South, or Richard Hofstadter writing about the Populists, the historians of this generation still often wrote political history, but what they wrote most often was intellectual, religious, and political history placed in its social and economic context. By the mid-fifties, persons of this generation, usually men, writing this kind of history were the innovative young scholars of most leading departments.

Within a decade, however, there were evident flaws in this approach. With significant exceptions, such as Kenneth Stampp's *The Peculiar Institution*, it was still a history which dealt mainly with white, male, western elites. And, next to Braudel's *The Mediterranean World in the Age of Philip II*, E.P. Thompson's, *The Making of the English Working Class*, even the best intellectual and political history placed in context, looked somewhat narrow.

A new generation slouched toward Bethlehem, or at least toward New Haven and the other campuses of major departments. They preferred the history of disadvantaged groups, particularly slaves, women, and the working classes, and they needed new theories and approaches, borrowed from other disciplines to study them. To a large extent, the cutting edge of the discipline reflected the histories and of the groups, blacks, women, and working-class Jews and Catholics who had just been hired. In time, the western focus of much of this history would also be challenged.

In this sense, the transformation of history department reflected a process already at work in society as well as a defining moment for the profession. What history departments are today largely follows the processes and values established during the fifties and sixties. During the eighties and nineties, another seismic shift would occur as, among other things, cultural history vaulted to the forefront of the profession, and many departments confronted the challenge of post-modernist thought, but that is the subject of another book.

Illustrations

Bernard Bailyn and Donald Fleming

Carl Bridenbaugh

George Pierson

Joseph Strayer

Paul Knaplund

Lawrence Stone

Raymond Sontag

Richard Hofstadter

WILLIAM H. McNEILL
Assistant Professor and Chairman of History

William H. McNeill

Bibliography:

Archives:
University of California at Berkeley, Regional Oral History Office, Bancroft Library
Ann Lage of the Regional Oral History Office has interviewed several members of the Berkeley history department. Her interviews include:
Kenneth Stampp, 1996
Delmer Brown, 1996
Carl Schorske, 1996-7
Nicholas Riasinnovsky, 1997
Henry May, 1999
William Bouwsma, 2000
Gene Brucker, 2001
Beverly Bouwsma, 2001
Natalie Davis, 2003
Leon Litwack, 2004

Yale University, Department of Manuscripts and Archives, Sterling Library
Wallace Notestein Papers
George Pierson Papers
C. Vann Woodward Papers

Books:

Abelove, Henry, et al, eds. *Visions of History*. New York: Pantheon Books, 1983.

Agnew, Jean Christophe. *Worlds Apart: The Market and the Theatre in Anglo-American Thought, 1550–1750*. Cambridge: Cambridge University Press, 1986.

Ayers, Edward L. *What Caused the Civil War? Reflections on the South and Southern History*. New York: Norton, 2005.

Bailyn, Bernard, ed. *Glimpses of the Harvard Past*. Cambridge: Harvard University Press, 1986.

____. *The Ideological Origins of the American Revolution*. Cambridge, Mass.: The Belknap Press of Harvard University Press, 1967.

Baker, Susan Stout. *Radical Beginnings: Richard Hofstadter and the 1930s*. Westport, Conn.: The Greenwood Press, 1985.

Bannon, John Francis. *Herbert Eugene Bolton: The Historian and the Man, 1870–1953*. Tucson: University of Arizona, 1978.

Beard, Charles. *An Economic Interpretation of the Constitution*. New York: MacMillan, 1912.

Beier, A.L., David Cannadine, and James Rosenheim., eds. *The First Modern Society: Essays in Honour of Lawrence Stone*. Cambridge: Cambridge University Press, 1989.

Bender, Thomas, ed. *The Anti-Slavery Debate: Capitalism and Abolitionism as a Problem in Historical Interpretation*. Berkeley: University of California Press, 1992.

Blassingame, John. *The Slave Community: Life in the Antebellum South*. New Haven: Yale University Press, 1972.

Blum, John Morton. *A Life with History*. Lawrence: University of Kansas Press, 2004.

____. *V Was for Victory*. New York: Harcourt, Brace, and Jovanovich, 1976.

Billington, Ray Alan. *Frederick Jackson Turner: Historian, Scholar, Teacher*. New York: Oxford University Press, 1973.

Boorstin, Daniel. *The Genius of American Politics*. Chicago: University of Chicago Press, 1953.

____. *The Lost World of Thomas Jefferson*. Chicago: University of Chicago Press, 1948.

Bouwsma, William. *Concordia Mundi: The Career and Thought of Guillaume Postel, 1510–1581.* Cambridge, Mass.: Harvard University Press, 1957.

Boyer, John. *The Organization of the College and the Divisions in the 1920s and 1930s.* Occasional Papers on Higher Education, VIII, published by the College of the University of Chicago, 2001.

____. *Three Views of Continuity and Change at the University of Chicago.* Chicago: University of Chicago Press, 1999.

Brown, David. *Richard Hofstadter: An Intellectual Biography.* Chicago: University of Chicago Press, 2006.

Brown, Norman O. *Life Against Death: The Psychoanalytic Meaning of History.* Middletown, Conn.: Wesleyan University Press, 1959.

Brucker, Gene A., Henry F. May, and David Hollinger. *History at Berkeley: A Dialogue in Three Parts.* Berkeley: University of California Press, 1998.

Buhle Paul, ed. *History and the New Left: Madison, Wisconsin, 1950–1970.* Philadelphia: Temple University Press, 1990.

Buhle, Paul and Edward Rice-Maximin. *William Appleman Williams: The Tragedy of Empire.* New York and London: Routledge, 1995.

Bushman, Richard, ed., *Uprooted Americans: Essays to Honor Oscar Handlin.* Boston: Little Brown, 1979.

Cantor, Norman. *Inventing Norman Cantor: Confessions of a Medievalist.* Tempe: Arizona Center for Medieval and Renaissance Studies, 2002.

____. *Inventing the Middle Ages: The Lives, Works, and Ideas of the Great Medievalists of the Twentieth Century* (New York: William Morrow, 1991).

Curtin, Philip. *On the Fringes of History* (Athens: Ohio University Press, 2005).

Curtis, L. Perry. *The Historian's Workshop: Original Essays by Sixteen Historians.* New York: Alfred Knopf, 1970.

Darnton, Robert. *The Literary Underground of the Old Regime.* Cambridge, Mass.: Harvard University Press, 1982.

Davis, David Brion. *The Problem of Slavery in the Age of Revolution.* New York and Oxford: Oxford University Press, 1975.

Davis, Natalie Zemon. *Society and Culture in Early Modern France.* Palo Alto: Stanford University Press, 1975.

Duberman, Martin. *Cures: A Gay Man's Odyssey.* Boulder, Colo.: Westview Press, 2002.

Fairbank, John King. *Chinabound: A Fifty-Year Memoir.* New York: Harper and Row, 1982.

Fitzpatrick, Ellen. *History's Memory: Writing America's Past, 1880–1980.* Cambridge, Mass.: Harvard University Press, 2002.

Foner, Eric. *Who Owns History?: Rethinking the Past in a Changing World.* New York: Hill and Wang, 2002.

Franklin, John Hope. *A Life in Learning: The Charles Homer Haskins Lecture.* New York: American Council of Learned Societies, 1988.

____. *Mirror to America: The Autobiography of John Hope Franklin.* New York: Farrar, Strauss, and Giroux, 2005.

Freedman, Estelle. *Feminism, Sexuality, and Politics: Essays by Estelle B. Freedman.* Chapel Hill: University of North Carolina Press, 2006.

Frye, Richard. *Greater Iran: A Twentieth-Century Odyssey.* Costa Mesa, California: Mazda Publishers, 2005.

Genovese, Eugene. *Roll, Jordan, Roll: The World the Slaves Made.* New York: Vintage, 1972.

Gaddis, John Lewis, *The United States and the Origins of the Cold War.* New York: Columbia University Press, 1972.

Gay, Peter, *The Bourgeois Experience: The Education of the Senses.* Oxford: Oxford University Press, 1985.

Gutman, Herbert. *The Black Family in Slavery and Freedom, 1725–1925.* New York: Pantheon, 1976.

____. *Work, Culture, and Society: Essays in American Working Class and Social History.* New York: Alfred Knopf, 1976.

Hahn, Steven. *The Roots of Southern Populism: Yeoman Farmers and the Transformation of the Georgia Upcountry, 1850–1890.* New York: Oxford University Press, 1983.

Hamerow, Theodore S. *Reflections on History and Historians.* Madison: University of Wisconsin Press, 1987.

Handlin, Oscar. *Truth in History.* Cambridge: Harvard University Press, 1979.

Hicks, John D. *My Life as a Historian*. Lincoln: University of Nebraska Press, 1968.

Hollinger, David A., *Science, Jews, and Secular Culture: Studies in Mid-Twentieth Century American Intellectual History* (Princeton: Princeton University Press, 1996.

Hughes, H. Stuart. *Gentleman Rebel: The Memoir of H. Stuart Hughes*. New York: Ticknor and Fields, 1990.

Hunt, Lynn, ed. *The New Cultural History*. Berkeley: University of California Press, 1989.

Johnson, Paul, *A Shopkeeper's Millenium: Society and Revivals in Rochester, New York, 1815–1837*. New York: Hill and Wang, 1978.

Kabaservice, Geoffrey. *The Guardians: Kingman Brewster, His Circle, and the Rise of the Liberal Establishment*. New York: Henry Holt and Company, 2004.

Kahn, Roger. *The Battle for Morningside Heights: Why Students Rebel*. New York: William Morrow, 1970.

Kazin, Alfred. *New York Jew*. New York: Alfred Knopf [distributed by Random House], 1978.

Keller, Morton, and Keller, Phyllis. *Making Harvard Modern: The Rise of America's University*. Oxford: Oxford University Press, 2001).

Kernan, Alvin. *In Plato's Cave*. New Haven and London: Yale University Press, 1999.

Kuhn, Thomas S. *The Structure of Scientific Revolutions*. Chicago: University of Chicago Press, 1962.

Langer, William. *In and Out of the Ivory Tower*. New York: Watson Academic Publications, 1977.

Lears, T.J. Jackson. *No Place of Grace: Anti-Modernism and the Transformation of American Culture, 1880–1920*. New York: Pantheon, 1983.

Lears, Jackson, and Fox, Richard Wightman, eds. *The Culture of Consumption: Critical Essays in American History, 1880–1980*. New York: Pantheon, 1983

Lemisch, Jesse. *On Active Service in War and Peace: Politics and Ideology in the American Historical Profession*. Toronto: New Hogtown Press, 1978.

Levenson, Joseph. *Confucian China and its Modern Fate.* Cambridge, Mass.: Harvard University Press, 1971.

Limerick, Patricia. *The Legacy of Conquest: The Unbroken Past.* New York: W.W. Norton, 1987.

Maddox, Robert J. *The New Left and the Origins of the Cold War.* Princeton: Princeton University Press, 1973.

Major, J. Russell. *The Estates General of 1560.* Princeton: Princeton University Press, 1950.

____. *Representative Institutions in Renaissance France.* Madison: University of Wisconsin Press, 1960.

Mannheim, Karl. *Ideology and Utopia: An Introduction to the Sociology of Knowledge.* Trans. Louis Wirth and Edward Shils. New York: Harcourt, Brace, 1936.

Marks, Patricia, ed. *Luminaries: Princeton Faculty Remembered.* Princeton: Association of Princeton Graduate Alumni, 1996.

May, Henry F. *Coming to Terms: A Study in History and Memory.* Berkeley: University of California Press, 1987.

McNeill, William H. *Hutchins' University: A Memoir of the University of Chicago, 1929–1950.* Chicago: University of Chicago Press, 1991.

____., *The Pursuit of Truth: A Historian's Memoir.* Lexington: University Press of Kentucky, 2001.

____. *The Rise of the West.* Chicago: University of Chicago Press, 1963.

Morgan, Edmund. *American Slavery, American Freedom: The Ordeal of Colonial Virginia.* New York: W.W. Norton, 1975.

Morgan, Edmund S., and Morgan, Helen M., *The Stamp Act Crisis: Prologue to Revolution.* Chapel Hill, N.C., 1953).

Mosse, George. *Confronting History: A Memoir.* Madison: University of Wisconsin Press, 2000.

Novick, Peter. *That Noble Dream: The Objectivity Question and the American Historical Profession.* Cambridge: Cambridge University Press, 1987.

Oren, Dan A. *Joining the Club: A History of Jews at Yale.* New Haven and London: Yale University Press, 1985.

Palmer, William, *Engagement with the Past: The Lives and Works of the World War II Generation of Historians* (Lexington: University Press of Kentucky, 2001.

Pipes, Richard. *Vixi: Memoirs of a Non-Belonger.* New Haven: Yale University Press, 2004.

Potter, David. *People of Plenty: Economic Abundance and the American Character.* Chicago: University of Chicago Press, 1954.

Reischauer, Edwin O. *My Life between Japan and America.* New York: Harper and Row, 1986.

Robinson, James Harvey. *The New History: Essays Illustrating the Modern Historical Outlook.* New York: MacMillan, 1912.

Rorabaugh, William J. *Berkeley at War: the 1960s.* Oxford: Oxford University Press, 1989.

Rosenberg, Rosalind. *Changing the Subject: How the Women of Columbia Shaped the Way We Think About Sex and Politics.* New York: Columbia University Press, 2004.

Rutland, Robert Allan, ed. *Clio's Favorites: Leading Historians of the United States, 1945-2000.* Columbia: University of Missouri Press, 2000.

Schlesinger, Arthur M., Jr. *A Life in the Twentieth Century.* New York and Boston: Houghton Mifflin, 2000).

Schlesinger, Arthur M., Sr. *In Retrospect: The History of a Historian.* New York: Harcourt, Brace, and World, 1963.

Schorske, Carl. *A Life in Learning: The Charles Homer Haskins Lecture.* Washington: American Council of Learned Societies, 1987.

____. *Fin-de-Siecle Vienna: Politics and Culture.* New York: Vintage, 1981.

Schrecker, Ellen W. *No Ivory Tower: McCarthyism and the Universities.* Oxford: Oxford University Press, 1986.

Sewell, William. *Work and Revolution in France: The Language of Labor from the Old Regime to 1848.* Cambridge: Cambridge University Press, 1980.

Stansell, Christine. *City of Women: Sex and Class in New York City, 1789–1850.* Urbana: University of Illinois Press, 1983.

Stern, Fritz. *Five Germanys I Have Known*. New York: Farrar, Strauss, and Giroux, 2006).

Susman, Warren. *Culture as History: The Transformation of American Society in the Twentieth Century*. New York: Pantheon Books, 197e.

Thompson, E.P. *The Making of the English Working Class*. New York: Vintage, 1963.

Tuchman, Barbara. *Practicing History: Selected Essays by Barbara Tuchman*. New York: Alfred Knopf, 1981.

Wilentz, Sean. *Chants Democratic: New York City and the Rise of the American Working Class, 1788–1850*. New York: Oxford University Press, 1984.

White, Theodore H. *In Search of History: A Personal Adventure*. New York: Harper and Row, 1978.

Williams, William Appleman. *The Contours of American History*. Cleveland: World Publishing Company, 1961.

_____. *The Tragedy of American Diplomacy*. Cleveland: World Publishing Company, 1959.

Woodward, C. Vann, *The Strange Career of Jim Crow*. New York: Oxford University Press, 1955.

Articles:

Bynum, Caroline Walker. "Curriculum Vitae: An Authorial Aside." *Common Knowledge* 9 (2003): 1–12.

Bridenbaugh, Carl. "The Great Mutation." *American Historical Review* 68 (1963): 315-31.

Courtwright, David. "Fifty Years of American History: An Interview with Edmund S. Morgan." *William and Mary Quarterly*, 3rd Series, 44 (1987): 336-69.

Darnton, Robert. "In Search of Enlightenment: Recent Attempts to Create a Social History of Ideas." *Journal of Modern History*. 43(1971): 113-32.

Gillispie, Charles. "*Apologia Pro Vita Sua*." *Isis*. 90 Supplement (1999): 584-94.

Gorn, Elliott. "Gouge and Bite, Pull Hair and Scratch: The Social Significance of Fighting in the Southern Backcountry." *American Historical Review*. 90 (1985): 18–48.

Handlin, Oscar. "A Career at Harvard." *American Scholar*. (Winter, 1996): 47–58.
Hexter, J.H. "Call Me Ismael, or, A Rose by Any Other Name." *American Scholar* (Summer, 1983): 191–216.
Lears, T.J. Jackson. "The Concept of Cultural Hegemony: Problems and Possibilities." *American Historical Review*. 90 (1985): 567–93.
Lemisch, Jesse, "If Howard Cosell Can Teach Yale, Why Can't Herbert Aptheker?" *Radical History Review*. 3 (1976): 46–8.
Lynd, Staughton. "Academic Freedom: Your Story and Mine." *Columbia Forum*. (Fall, 1967): 23–8.
Lynn, Kenneth S. "F.O. Matthiessen: *American Scholar*. (Winter, 1976-77): 86–93.
____. "Perry Miller." *American Scholar*. (Spring, 1983): 221–27.
Singal, Daniel J. "Beyond Consensus: Richard Hofstadter and American Historiography," *American Historical Review*. 89 (1984): 976–1004.
Weber, David J. "Turner, the Boltonians, and the Borderlands," *American Historical Review*. 61 (1986): 66–81.
Wiener, Jon, "Radical Historians and the Crisis in American History, 1959–1980," *Journal of American History*. 72 (1989): 399–434.

Reference Works:
American Historical Association. *Guide to Departments of History, 1982-3*. Washington, D.C.: American Historical Association, 1982.
American Historical Association. *Directory of History Departments, Historical Organizations, and Historians, 2002–3*, Washington, D.C.: American Historical Association. 2002.

Newspapers:
Boston Globe, "Tenure System Comes Under Fire," June 2, 1998, Metro, p. A1.
New York Times. June 7, 1968.
Silk, Mark. "The Hot History Department." *New York Times Magazine*.

Interviews:
Edward Ayers, February 21, 2002.
Bernard Bailyn, December 15, 2004.
James Banner, February 26, 2005.
Thomas Barnes, October 28, 2005.
Allan Bogue, September 13, 2005.
Gene Brucker, October 25, 2005.
Caroline Bynum, May 27, 2005.
Maureen Callahan, April 19, 2005.
Nancy Cott, July 4, 2005.
Gordon Craig, January 4, 1996.
David Cronon, February 8, 2005.
David Davis, February 13, 2004.
David Donald, December 9, 2004.
Martin Duberman, October 17, 2004.
Stanley Elkins, December 20, 2005.
Eric Foner, March 23, 2006.
Richard Fox, March 20, 2002; July 16, 2005.
Richard Frye, February 16, 2005.
John Gillis, June 24, 2004.
Charles Gillispie, June 4, 2004.
Elliott Gorn, March 23, 2002.
Henry Graff, February 23, 2006.
Hannah Gray, December 8, 2005.
Raymond Grew, July 7, 2004.
Steven Hahn, December 15, 2003.
Theodore Hamerow, January 19, 2005.
Richard Hellie, December 12, 2005.
J.H. Hexter, December 19, 1995.
Kenneth Jackson, February 22, 2006.
William Chester Jordan, May 27, 2004.
Donald Kagan, June 16, 2005.
Morton and Phyllis Keller, January 15, 2005.
Robert Kingdon, September 6, 2005.
Philip Kuhn, May 3, 2005.
Stanley Kutler, September 10, 2005.
Howard Lamar, January 8, 2004.

David Landes, March 1, 2005.
Emmett Larkin, February 4, 2006.
Jesse Lemisch, December 15, 2004.
William Leuchtenberg, March 1, 2006.
Diane Lindstrom. September 25, 2005.
Christine Lunardini, April 20, 2005
Charles Maier, March 21, 2005.
Pauline Maier, March 22, 2005.
Nancy Malkiel, December 14, 2004.
William McNeill, December 22, 1995.
James McPherson, September 15, 2004.
John Merriman, June 29, 2005.
Edmund Morgan, December 22, 2003.
Karl Morrison, January 24, 2006.
John Murrin, May 24, 2004.
Gary Nash, July 13, 2004.
Peter Novick, December 9, 2005.
Richard Pipes, February 3, 2005.
Theodore Rabb, June 19, 2004.
Eugene Rice, March 4, 2006.
Rosalind Rosenberg, September 4, 2006.
Cynthia Russett. June 23, 2005.
Jonathan Schneer, July 6, 2005.
Carl Schorske, November 5, 2005.
Richard Sewell, September 7, 2005.
William Sewell, February 2, 2006.
Jerrold Siegal, July 20, 2004.
John Shy, July 3, 2004. (by email)
Gaddis Smith, December 16, 2003.
Jonathan Spence, July 6, 2005.
Jonathan Sperber, January 18, 2006.
Fritz Stern, November 13, 2006.
Lawrence Stone, June 5&8, 1996.
Stephan Thernstrom, April 8, 2005.
Robert Tignor, June 19, 2004.
Robert Westbrook, March 13, 2002.
James Wilkinson, April 28, 2005.
John Womack," March 25, 2005.

Index

Abrams, Richard 137
Adair, Douglas 53
Adams, Herbert Baxter 160
Adams, John Quincy 162, 170
Adler, Mortimer 191
Administration of Normandy 90
African Studies 43, 66, 140, 147, 149-50
Age of Democratic Revolution 98, 103
Age of Jackson 20
Age of Reform 299-300
Agnew, Jean-Christophe 80
Alexander, John 206
Alpers, Svetlana 151
American Baptist Education Society 189
American Council of Learned Societies 205
American Historical Association 53, 90, 99, 126, 135, 143, 150 191, 217, 223
American Historical Review 118, 212, 227, 237
American Political Tradition 15, 229
American Renaissance 10
Americans: The Colonial Experience 203, 206
Americans: The Democratic Experience 203
Americans: The National Experience 203
American Studies 79, 82
Anderson, Bonnie 241
Andrews, Charles McLean 52
Annales School 1, 107, 109, 121, 147, 258
Anti-Federalism in Duchess County, New York 61-2
Anti-Intellectualism in American Life 221, 232
Anti-Semitism xix, xv, 6, 10, 15, 54, 64, 132, 142, 190, 228, 230, 253
Aptheker, Herbert 62, 63, 145

Agulhon, Maurice 109
Aristotle 193
Article 39 7
Asia and the Making of Europe 199
Austen, Ralph 216
Ayers, Edward 79, 80

Bailyn, Bernard xiv, 18-22, 24, 40, 41, 46, 141, 148
Bainton, Roland, 169
Baker, Jean 44
Baker, Keith Michael 213, 216
Bancroft, Elizabeth 233
Bancroft Library xxiv, 128
Bancroft Prize 20, 47, 78, 98
Banner, James 97
Barnard College 237, 247
Barnes, Thomas G. 134, 146
Baron, Salo 228
baroni 129
Barzun, Jacques 222, 224, 225, 233, 236, 238, 239
Bay of Pigs 61
Beadle, George 199
Beale, Howard K. 161, 165
Bean, J.M.W. 232
Bean, Walton 126, 128
Beard, Charles A. 161, 221-2, 223, 230, 258
Beard, Mary 161
Becker, Carl 194
Beckert, Sven 48
Beeman, Richard 205
Beller, Elmer 96, 97, 103, 236
Bemis, Samuel F. ix, x, 52, 55

Benson, Lee 161
Berger, Peter 80
Berkin, Carol 241
Beveridge Prize 78
Bielenstein, Hans 232
Bien, David xviii, 97, 101
Big Red Machine 176, 183
Bingham, Woodbridge 132, 140
Black, Cyril 89, 95, 112
Black Family in Slavery and Freedom 74
Black Panthers 66, 211
Blackmar, Elizabeth 80
Blair, Ann 48
Blassingame, John xix, 70, 75, 150
Blum, Jerome 92, 95, 97, 98, 103, 105, 112, 253, 255
Blum, John xi, xiii, 6, 18, 51, 52, 54, 55, 58, 59 62, 67, 68, 73, 97, 111, 120
Boardman, Eugene 177
Boas, Franz 223
Bogue, Allan G. 169, 176, 177, 179
Bolton, Herbert Eugene 126, 132
Boltonians 126, 128, 138
Boorstin, Daniel 9, 190, 192, 194, 202-7, 208, 210, 211
Boorstin, Ruth 210
Borah, Woodrow 132, 140
Boss Reuf's San Francisco 128
Boston's Immigrants 13
Bouwsma, Beverly 139-40,

146, 152
Bouwsma, William xxvi, 133-7, 139, 147, 149, 150, 151, 152, 153
Boyd, Julian 96
Boyer, John 213, 217
Brandeis University 22, 42, 238
Branford College ix, 59
Braudel, Fernand 213, 259
Brentano, Robert 132, 133, 135
Brewster, Kingman xxi, 52, 57, 62, 63, 66, 70, 257
Bridenbaugh, Carl 28, 128, 129, 130, 133-7, 138, 141, 143, 144, 153, 251
Bridenthal, Renate 241
Brinkley, Alan 47
Brinton, Crane 2, 3, 12, 13, 21
Brooklyn Bridge 76
Brooklyn College 6, 11, 208, 228
Brown, Delmer 140, 142, 143
Brown, J. Douglas 98, 113
Brown, L. "Pat" xvi, 145, 148
Brown, Norman O. xviii
Brown, Peter 120
Brown University 8, 42, 43, 55, 57, 138
Brown, William xix, 180
Brucker, Gene 132, 135, 136, 146, 149, 151, 152
Buck, Paul 5, 15, 29
Bundy, McGeorge xvi, 23, 27, 31, 52, 60
Bushman, Richard 22-3

Butler, Nicholas Murray 223
Bynum, Caroline 43, 44-5

Cam, Helen Maud 43, 44
Cambodia 36-7, 147
Cameron, Rondo 169
Cantor, Norman 92, 99, 100, 103, 236-9
Carmen, Harry 222
Carr, E.H. 21
Carstensen, Vernon 179
Center for Advanced Study in the Behavioral Sciences 31
Central Intelligence Agency 35, 92
Channing, Edward 1, 6
Cheese and the Worms 109
Chicago Laboratory School 208
Chinabound: A Fifty-Year Memoir 38
Christ Church, Oxford 104, 105
City University of New York 231, 242
Civilization in the Middle Ages 236
Civil Rights Movement 210, 211, 242, 255
Clarke, Arthur C. 170
Clemens, Diane 152
Clive, John 28, 52
Clough, Shepherd B. 22, 225, 233, 240
Coatsworth, John 216, 218
Cochrane, Eric 194

Cohen, Lizabeth 48
Cohn, Bernard 200
Cole, Arthur 18
Colonial Merchants and the American Revolution 2
Columbia University ix, xix, 1, 15, 39, 150, 163, 221-250
Commager, Henry Steele 229
Committee on Academic Freedom 146
Commons, John R. 175
Conant, James B. xii, xiii, xx, 3, 4, 5, 13-14, 24
Constable, Giles 237
Connections 180
Consciousness and Society 31
Contemporary Civilization 224, 246
Conzen, Kathleen N. 217
Coolidge, Archibald Cary 1, 6
Confucian China and its Modern Fate 141
Conkin, Paul 179, 185
Constance, Lincoln 136
Contours of American History 171-3
Copenican Revolution 142
Cornell University 70, 102, 192, 233
Cosell, Howard 63
Cott, Nancy 71, 75
Cox, Archibald 35-6
Craig, Albert 16
Craig, Gordon 53, 92, 93, 94, 97, 103
Craven, Avery 191

Craven, Frank 90, 92, 96, 97, 99, 102, 106, 110, 113, 114
Crisis of the Aristocracy 105
Cronon, E. David 54, 174, 179, 180
Culture of Consumption 81
Current, Richard N. 164, 166, 167, 174
Curtis, L. Perry 143
Curti, Merle 128, 133, 161, 162, 163, 169, 176, 178, 179, 185, 222, 226
Curtin, Philip D. xvi, 185, 186, 254

Da Costa, Emilia 81
Dallek, Robert 235
Dante Aligheri 126
Darcy, Elizabeth 100
Darnton, Robert 45, 108, 118, 119, 120, 255
Davis Center, Princeton 109-10, 116, 120
Davis, Chandler 150-1
Davis, David B. 58, 76-80, 139
Davis, Natalie 108, 110, 119, 120, 150-2
Davis, Shelby Cullom 109
Deak, Istvan 232
Degler, Carl 270
De Monarchia 126
DeNovo, John 179
Detroit riots 67
Diamond, Sigmund 232

Dinners of the Ephermal Faculty 41
Dixon, Marlene 210
Dodd, William E. 191
Donald, David 4, 62, 111, 120, 232, 233, 234, 240
Douglas, Mary 151
Dow Chemical Company 34, 180
Duberman, Martin 97, 100, 120
Duke University 89
Dulles, Allen 92
Duncan, Bentley 200
Dunwalke Chair 41
Dupree, A. Hunter 142, 143

Economic History Review 104
Economic Origins of the Constitution 222
Edson, Charles 162
Eliot House 3
Elkins, Stanley 204, 238
Embree, Ainslee 232
Engagement with the Past xxv
English Civil War 17
English Revolution 104, 107
Enlightenment: An Interpretation 76, 119, 239

Fairbank, John King xv, xvi, 5, 8-9, 13, 15, 16, 31, 38, 39, 40, 46, 131, 254
fame deficit 120
Fasolt, Constantin 217
Feldman, Gerald xv, 137

Ferguson, William Scott 2, 5, 8
Fields, Barbara 247
Fin-de-Siecle Vienna 31, 118
Fleming, Donald 32, 36, 40, 41, 48,
Foner, Eric 120, 235, 241-5, 247
Foner, Jack 242
Ford Foundation 16, 60, 199
Ford, Franklin xvi, 30, 34, 35, 36
Fowles, John 21
Fox, Dixon Ryan 221
Fox, Richard xi, 80, 81
Frankfurt School 175
Franklin, Benjamin 138
Franklin, John Hope 10, 11, 200, 207-10
Fred, E.B. 165
Freedom From Fear 59
Free Soil, Free Labor, Free Men 244
Free Speech Movement 42, 145
Freidel, Frank 17, 29-30, 114, 166, 167, 228
French Lieutenant's Woman 21
Freedman, Estelle 115, 241
Friendly, Judge Henry 34
From Slavery to Freedom 207
Frye, Richard xiii, 15, 46
Furet, Francois 213

Gaddis, John Lewis 173
Gallagher, Katherine 151

Gargan, Edward 169
Garosian, Nina 246
Garraty, John 232
Gates, Paul 161
Gatzke, Hans 56
Gay, Peter 58, 76, 119, 238, 239, 247
Gauss, Christian 89
Geertz, Clifford 117, 151, 217
Geneva and the Coming of Wars of Religion in France 168
Genius of American Politics 202
Genovese, Eugene 75, 78, 82, 170
German Social Democracy 30
Gerth, Hans 175
Giamatti, A. Bartlett xxiii, 70
Gibbon, Edward 9
Gilbert, James 226
Gillispie, Charles 92, 93, 94, 97, 143
Gilmore, Myron 29
Ginsberg, Carlo 109
Ginsberg, Alan 224
Giveness 202
Goheen, Robert 112
Goldberg, Harvey 162, 167, 169, 174, 176, 180
Goldman, Eric 89, 94, 96, 97, 111, 112
Goldstein, Jan 217
Goodrich, Carrington 222
Gordon, Peter 48
Gorn, Elliott 79, 80
Gottschalk, Louis 190, 191, 194, 195

Goubert, Pierre 109
Goucher College 44
Graff, Henry 223, 232, 238
Graham, Loren 241
Gramsci, Antonio 81
Gray, Charles 114
Gray, Hannah 43, 194-5, 210-1, 215, 217
Grew, Raymond 97, 99
Griswold, A. Whitney 56, 63
Gross, Charles 3, 5
Growth of American Thought 162, 227
Gutman, Herbert 79, 81, 82, 120, 166
Guttridge, George 130, 136

Haber, Samuel 137
Hackney, Sheldon 97
Hahn, Steven 81
Hall, Jacqueline Dowd 241
Hall, Walter 89
Haller, Mark 209
Hamerow, Theodore 166-7
Hammond, George 126, 128
Hammond, Mason 3
Handbook of Western Civilization 192
Handlin, Oscar xiv, 2, 5, 6, 11-13, 14-15, 19, 22-3, 24, 27, 30, 36, 38, 40, 150, 173, 255
Hankins, James 48
Harbison, E. Harris 89, 92, 96, 99, 103, 133
Harding, Robert 80

Haring, Clarence xv, xvi, 2, 15
Harper, William Rainey 189-90
Harrington, Fred 162, 163, 167, 169, 171, 175, 177, 178
Harris, Marvin 236
Harris, Neil 200, 216
Hart, Albert B. 1
Hartz, Louis 203
Harvard University xi, xiv, xx, xxii, xxv, 1-50, 89, 90 141, 148, 150, 160, 174, 211, 217, 221
Harvard University Press 19
Haskins, Charles H. 2, 5, 6, 11, 18, 30, 89, 160
Hayes, Carlton J.H. xiv, 42, 43, 169, 184
Hedges, James B. 57
Hellie, Richard 214, 216
Herlihy, David 42, 43, 169, 185
Herr, Richard 137
Herzen, Alexander 21
Hesseltine, William xix, 161, 162, 163, 164, 165, 178, 179
Hexter, Jack H. 10, 54, 57, 58, 68, 69, 70, 80, 134, 139, 213
Hicks, John D. 128, 129, 130, 132, 134, 136, 162, 162
Higham, John 166
Higonnet, Patrice 17-18, 40
Hill, Bennett D. 113
Histoire totale 197, 221
History and Literature 3, 28
History of the Americas 126

Ho, Ping-ti 200
Hobbes, Thomas 170
Hofstadter, Richard 15, 29, 60, 128, 145, 204, 209 225, 226, 228, 233, 234-5, 238, 239, 240, 243, 244, 246
Holborn, Hajo ix, 52
Hollinger, David xiv
Homeless Mind 80
Hoover Institution 56
Hopkins, Terence 237
House Un-American Activities Committee (HUAC) 171, 212
Huggins, Nathan I. xix, 43, 150, 240
Hughes, H. Stuart 10, 31-2, 33, 43-4, 92
Hughes, Judith 43-4
Hunt, Lynn 152
Hurewitz, Jacob 232
Hutchens, Robert Maynard 190-2, 193, 194
Hyman, Paula 241

Ideological Origins of the American Revolution 19-21
Ideology and Utopia 229
Inden, Ronald 216
Institute for Advanced Study 105, 116, 131, 217
Institute for Research in the Humanities 182
Intellectual Origins of American Radicalism 62
Irschick, Eugene 140
Irwin, Graham 240

Irye, Akira 218

Jackson, Kenneth 245
Jameson, J. Franklin 189
Jansen, Marius xvi, 108, 111, 113
Jaures, Jean 167
Jefferson, Thomas, Papers of 96
Jelavich, Charles 134
Jensen, Merrill 161, 162, 163, 176
Johns Hopkins University, The xiii, 41, 89, 98, 106, 159, 160
Johnson, Dale 199
Johnson, Lyndon 112
Johnson, Paul 80
Johnson, Walter 194, 208, 209, 211
Jones, Howard Mumford 10
Jordan, William Chester xix, 113, 147
Jordan, Winthrop 120, 137, 138
Journal of Interdisciplinary History 117
Journal of Modern History 212

Kagan, Donald 58, 68, 69, 70
Kantorowicz, Ernst xiv, 127, 130, 131
Karl, Barry 200
Karlsen, Carol 81
Karpat, Kemal 178
Karpovich, Michael 2, 5, 11, 12, 17, 29
Katz, Friedrich 216

Katz, Stanley 179
Kazin, Alfred 226
Keenan, Edward 17, 40
Keeney, Barnaby
Keightly, David 141
Kelly, Suzanne 115
Kelly-Gadol, Joan 241
Kennedy, Donald 59
Kennedy, John xvi
Kennedy, Paul 201
Kent, Raymond 141
Kerber, Linda 241
Kernan, Alvin xxiii
Kerner, Robert 29, 129
Kerr, Clark 144, 145, 147
King, James 126, 130, 134
King, Martin Luther 75, 209, 242
Kingdon, Robert 168, 183
Kinnard, Lawrence 126
Kirby, William 32
Kirk, Grayson 244
Kirkendall, Richard 166
Kirschner, Julius 213, 216
Kishlansky, Mark 218
Klein, Julius 3, 5
Knaplund, Paul xiv, 161-2, 163, 165, 177
Knight, Walter 147
Knopf, Alfred 235
Koch, Adrienne xx, 137-8, 151
Kolchin, Peter 184
Krieger, Leonard 54, 200
Kristeller, Paul O. 243
Kroeber, Clifton 177
Kuhn, Philip 32, 46
Kuhn, Thomas xv, xxvi, 94,

103, 137, 142-3, 253
Kutler, Stanley 179, 255

Lach, Donald 199
Ladurie, Emmanuel Le Roy 109
LaFeber, Walter 174
Laiou, Angelike xx, 44
Lamar, Howard 53, 58, 59, 69, 76, 82, 254
Landes, David xv, 18, 28, 42, 43, 137, 146
Langer, William 2, 5, 12, 30, 90, 92
Lapidus, Ira 141
Laqueur, Thomas 151
Larkin, Emmett 200
Lasch, Christopher 75, 235
Lazarsfeld, Paul 223, 236
Lears, T.J. Jackson 79, 80
Lefeber, Walter 174
Legacy of Conquest 47
Lemisch, Jesse 60, 61, 63, 204-5, 212
Lepore, Jill 48
Lerner, Gerda 240
Leuchtenberg, William 225, 232, 233, 234, 235, 244, 246
Levenson, Joseph xiv, 131, 132, 140, 142, 147, 149, 253
Levenson, Rosemary 140
Levi, Edward 190, 197, 210
Levine, Lawrence xv, 137, 145, 147, 235
Life Against Death xviii
Limerick, Patricia 47-8
Lindstrom, Diane 192-3

Link, Arthur S. 96-7, 113
Literature Humanities 224
Little, Lester 103
Litwack, Leon xiii, 137, 147
Liuzzo, Viola 209
Lopez, Robert 73, 97
Lord, Robert Howard 2
Lost World of Thomas Jefferson 202
Lowell, A. Lawrence 3, 4
Luther, Martin 192
Lynch, Hollis 240
Lynd, Helen 61
Lynd, Robert 61
Lynd, Staughton xiv, 61-3
Lyon, Bryce 143

MacArthur Foundation 31, 118, 178
MacCaffrey, Wallace 32
Mackauer, Christian 193
MacMullen, Ramsay 70
Maddox, Robert J. 173
Magna Carta 7, 16
Maier, Charles 17, 32
Maier, Pauline 22, 43
Main Currents of American Thought 206
Main, Jackson Turner 166
Major, J. Russell 135
Making of the English Working Class 74, 259
Malia, Martin 17, 28, 29, 137, 146
Malkiel, Nancy xx, 114, 115
Malone, Dumas 222
Mann, Arthur 200

Mann, Herbert Mann 149
Mannheim, Karl 229, 230
Martin, Waldo xix, 156
Massachusetts Institute of Technology 51, 52, 57 106, 117, 134, 200
Matthiessen, F.O. 9-10
Mattingly, Garrett 222, 225
May Day 66-8
May Day at Yale 68-9
May, Ernest O. xvii, 23, 40, 48
May, Henry 132, 137, 140, 142, 153
Mayer, Arno 113
McCarthy, Joseph 129-30
McCormick, Thomas 174, 179
McIlwain, Charles 7, 11, 87
McKay, Donald 18
McKeon, Richard 192
McKitrick, Eric 204, 225, 234, 240
McNamara, Robert 34
McNeill, William 191, 192-201, 205, 208, 210, 212 214, 252, 253, 254
McPherson, James 97, 101, 120
Mead, Margaret 236
Mediterranean and the Mediterranean World in the Age of Philip II 259
Mellon Foundation 56
Mencken, H.L. 227, 231
Merk, Frederick 2, 5, 6, 7, 16, 24, 30
Merriman, John 54, 72, 73, 79

Merriman, Roger 3, 7-8, 16
Merton, Robert K. 22, 236
Mesmerism and the End of the Enlightenment 45
Metcalf, Thomas 140
Metzger, Walter 225
Mickey Mouse 76
Middlekauff, Robert 137, 138
Middletown 61
Miller, Perry 3, 9-10, 18, 30
Mills, C. Wright 175, 203, 205, 228, 229
Miner, Dwight 243
Mississippi Valley Historical Association 54, 163, 172
Mississippi Valley Historical Review 172
Modern Researcher 239
Mommsen, Theodore 53, 92, 97
Montgomery, David 75
Morantz-Sanchez, Regina 241
Morgan, Edmund S. xii, xiii, 9, 10, 28, 52, 53, 55, 56, 58, 59, 61, 62 63, 68, 73, 75, 141, 192
Morison, Samuel E. xiv, 1, 3, 5, 12, 24, 28, 30, 141
Morris, Richard B. 234, 236, 238
Morris, William 172
Morrison, Karl 200, 214
Mory's 52
Mosse, George 11, 162, 165, 168, 169, 171, 259
Mote, Fritz xvi

Mundy, John Hine 232, 236, 238, 244
Munro, Dana C. 89
Munro, Dana G. 89, 94
Murderer's Row 165, 178, 182
Murdock, Kenneth 4, 12

Naison, Mark 213-4
Nangle, Benjamin 55
National Book Award 239
National Endowment for the Humanities 71
National Experience 73
Nef, John U. 191
Nettels, Curtis 163
Nevins, Alan 222, 233
New England Merchants in the Seventeenth Century 19
New England Mind 10
New History 1, 258
New history 221, 258
New Left and the Origins of the Cold War 173
New Viewpoints in American History 2
New York City 81, 234
New York Historical Society 234
New York Public Library 234
New York Review of Books 120, 170
New York Times 63, 112, 170, 181
New York Times Magazine 123
Nixon, Richard 36
Noble, David 166

Nolan, Mary 241
non-western history xv, xvi, 6, 55, 60, 131-2, 140, 141, 177-8 199-200
Northwestern University 254
Norton, Marybeth 43
Notestein, Wallace ix, x, 6, 52, 104
Novick, Peter xxiii, 200, 216

Office of Strategic Services 92
Oregon State University 17
Oriel College, Oxford 242
Oriental Studies Department 8, 95
Origins of the Cold War 173, 185
Origins of the Modern State 90
Osgood, Herbert 221
Owen, David 11, 17
Oxford University, x, 127

Palm, Franklin 129
Palmer, Robert R. 58, 73, 89, 92, 93, 94, 97, 98, 99, 102, 103
Pamphlets of the American Revolution 19-20
Parrington, Vernon L. 161, 206
Partisan Review 226
Paxon, Frederick 128, 133
Peculiar Institution 164
Pederson, Susan 48
Pennsylvania State University 70

People of Plenty xviii
Perkins, Elliott 6, 13
Perlman, Selig 162, 175
Perry, Ralph Barton
Phelan, John 182
Phillips, Ullrich B. 52
Pierce, Bessie Louise 195
Pierson, George xiii, xx, xxi, xxiii, 51, 52, 53, 54, 55 58, 59, 68, 82
90, 126, 148, 240, 252, 254
Pipes, Richard 17, 28-9, 33, 36, 46, 240, 252, 254
Pocock, John 139
Political Science Quarterly 178
Pollack, Norman 60, 61
Pomfret, John 112, 113
Porter, David 171
Potter, David M. xiii, xviii, 52, 53, 55, 58, 59, 90
Poverty and Progress 42
Preceptorial system 87-8, 111, 116
Princeton University xi, xviii, xx, xxi, 32, 45, 65, 87-124, 127
133, 143
Problem of Slavery in the Age of Revolution 77-9
Problem of Slavery in Western Culture 76
Progressive Movement 60, 61
Pulitzer Prize 5, 20, 41, 68, 163, 227, 229, 234
Pusey, Nathan 34, 35

Rabb, Theodore 97, 117
Radcliffe College 43, 150-1
Raeff, Marc 232
Rand, E.K. 2, 12
Ranke, Leopold von 159
Rappaport, Armin 136
Rawick, George 166
Reagan, Ronald 147, 148
Reischauer, Edwin 3, 5, 15, 37, 40
Representations 151
Reserve Officer Training Corps (ROTC) 35
Return of Martin Guerre 110
Rhodes Scholarship 9, 132, 133
Riasanovsky, Nicholas 29, 137 148
Rice, Eugene 225, 232, 243, 245
Riesman, David 203, 230
Rise of American Civilization 161, 222
Rise of the City 2
Rise of the West 195-8, 199
Robe and Sword 30
Robinson, J.H. 1, 221, 258
Rockefeller Foundation 16
Rockefeller, John D. 189, 227
Rodgers, Daniel 120
Roll, Jordan, Roll 78
Romantic Exiles 21
Roosevelt, Franklin D. x, 170
Rosenberg, Hans xv, 137, 215
Rosenberg, Rosalind 246-7
Rosovsky, Henry xv, 137, 146

Rose, Willie Lee 44, 246
Ross, Dorothy 115, 235
Rotberg, Robert I. 117
Rothblatt, Sheldon xv, 137
Rudd, Mark 242
Rudin, Harry 55, 57
Russett, Cynthia 59, 71
Rutgers University 175
Ryder, Arthur 125

Sachse, William 162
Salviemini, Gaetano 2
Sarton, George 2, 12
Savio, Mario 144, 145
Schaeffer, Paul 128, 136
Scheiner, Irwin 140
Schevill, Ferdinand 191
Schlatter, Richard 212
Schlesinger, Arthur M., Jr. 9, 13, 17, 24, 29, 50, 173, 207
Schlesinger, Arthur M., Sr. 1, 2, 5, 13, 24, 30, 163
Schmidt, Bernadotte 191
Schneer, Jonathan 71
Schoenberger, Howard 177
Schorske, Carl xv, 30, 92, 108, 117, 118, 120, 135, 137, 139 142, 146, 223-4, 228, 255
Schuyler, Robert 222, 236
Schumpeter. Joseph 3
Schurman, Franz 140
Schwartz, Benjamin 16, 28, 131, 139
Science and Polity in France 94
Science and Society 163
Science in the Modern World 9

Scott, Anne 23
Seale, Bobby 66
Seigel, Jerrold 97, 101
Sellers, Charles 137, 145, 146, 147
Serviceman's Readjustment Act (G.I. Bill) xvii, 252
Sewell, Richard 179
Sewell, William 215-7
Shannon, David 174
Shenton, James 225, 242
sherry hour xi, 72-3
Shopkeeper's Millenium 80
Shugg, Roger 209
Shy, John xviii, 54, 97, 101, 102, 113, 120
"Significance of the Frontier in American History" 160
Simpson, Alan 208
Slater, Miriam 115, 116
Sluiter, Engel 126, 130
Smalley, Beryl 234
Smit, Jacob 232
Smith College 163
Smith, Gaddis 53, 59
Smith, Michael 81
Smith, John 141
Smith, Thomas 140
Social Darwinism in American Thought 228
Social Science Research Council 233
Society and Culture in Early Modern France 119
Society of Fellows, Harvard 13, 18, 131, 142, 253

Sontag, Raymond 89, 127-8, 129, 130, 131, 133, 134, 135, 136 146, 251
Spence, Jonathan 46, 56, 60
Spengler, Oswald 195
Sproul, Robert 130
Stamp Act Crisis 72
Stampp, Kenneth 127, 130, 131, 132, 133, 135, 140, 141, 142 143, 145, 146, 147, 150, 153, 164, 165, 166, 228, 259
Stanford University 31, 56, 103
Stansell, Christine 79, 81
Starn, Francie 152
Starn, Randolph 151, 152
State University of New York at Albany x
Stearns, Peter 215
Stein, Stanley xvi, 92
Stella, Frank
Sterling Professorship 55
Stern, Fritz 224, 232, 233, 244, 246
Stevens, Henry Morse 125
Stevens Institute of Technology 90
Stone, Jeanne 116
Stone, Lawrence xxii, 97, 103, 104, 105, 106, 107, 108, 109, 110 113, 114, 116, 118, 120, 121, 254
Strange Career of Jim Crow 73, 75
Strayer, Joseph xiii, xx, xxi, 89, 90, 92, 93, 95, 98, 99, 103, 106 111, 112, 113, 120, 121, 126, 236, 252, 254
Structure of Scientific Revolution 94, 137, 142
Struggle for Sovereignty 11
Student Non-Violent Coordinating Committee 144
Students for a Democratic Society 34, 35, 61, 243
Studies on the Left 174
Study of History 195-7
Susman, Warren 76, 161, 166
Swados, Felice 227, 229

Tannenbaum, Frank 222, 229
Tawney, Richard H. 104, 107
Taylor, A.J.P. 213
Taylor Charles (Harvard) 18
Taylor, Charles (Yale) 62
Thernstrom, Stephan 32, 41, 42, 46
Thompson, Edward P. 74, 81, 110, 259
Thompson, Leonard 58
Thorndike, Lynn 222
Thrupp, Sylvia 193, 195, 217
Thucydides 68
Tignor, Robert xvi, 97, 101
Tilly, Charles 79
Tocqueville, Alexis 51
Total return 60
Toynbee, Arnold 195-6

Trachtenburg, Allan 76
Tragedy of American Diplomacy 170
Trevor-Roper, Hugh 104, 105, 107
Trilling, Lionel 223, 224, 225, 229
Troeltsch, Ernst 193
Tse-Ting, Mao 9
Tuchman, Barbara 7, 9, 233, 234, 239
Tudor, Frederick 203
Turner, Frederick Jackson xx, 1, 5, 30, 159, 161, 163, 169
Turner, Henry 59, 72

Ullrich, Laurel Thatcher 48
Unbound Prometheus 42
University College, Oxford 104
University of California at Berkeley xi, xiv, xv, xx xxvi, 27, 29, 32, 47, 64, 118, 125-58, 215
University of California at Los Angeles x, 42, 106
University of California at San Diego 44
University of Chicago xi, xx, 27, 89, 189-220
University of Colorado 233
University of Illinois xix, 135, 167
University of Iowa 166, 169
University of Kentucky x
University of Leningrad 17

University of Maine 177
University of Maryland 137, 278
University of Michigan 32, 42, 72, 79, 150, 217
University of Nebraska 136
University of Pennsylvania 127
University of Sao Paulo x
University of Toronto 150
University of Washington 45
University of Wisconsin xi, xiii, xiv, xvii, xix, xx, xxiv, xxvi 125, 128, 159-220
Uprooted 14-15, 20
Uses of the University 144
Usher, Abbott Payson 2, 18

V Was for Victory 73
Vance, Cyrus
Vanderbilt University 185
Van Doren, Mark 223
Vansina, Jan 178
Vassar College 65, 208
Veblin, Thorstein 189
Viet Nam War xvi, 36, 63, 67, 75, 112, 116, 145, 173, 180, 210, 211 242, 244, 255
Voices of Protest 47
Von Ranke, Leopold 159

Wade, Richard 200
Wadham College, Oxford 104
Walpole, Sir Robert 110
Warren, Annielouise Bliss 33
Warren Center, Harvard 33-4, 109

Warren, Charles 33
Warren Commission 61
Washington University 58, 103
Weber, Max 175, 258
Wector, Dixon 133
Wedgewood, C.V. 17
Weintraub, Karl 190, 194
Weisberger, Bernard 209
Weiss, Nancy (see Malkiel, Nancy) xx, 114, 115
Weiss, Richard 235
Wertenbaker, Thomas J. 88
Wesleyan University 139
West, Andrew Fleming 110
Westbrook, Robert 80, 81
Westerman, William 228
White, Lynn 89-90
White Over Black 138
White, Theodore H. 7, 8
Whitehead, Alfred North 9
Widener Library 11
Wilentz, Sean 79, 81
Wilkinson, James 17
Williams, William A. xvii, 162, 166, 169-74, 176, 177, 179, 180-1, 184
Wilson, Woodrow 87, 110, 172
Wilson, Woodrow, Papers of 96-7
Winks, Robin 59
Wisconsin Alumni Research Fund (WARF) 175

Wolff, Robert Lee 17, 29, 31, 36, 46
Womack, John xvi, 16, 23-4, 40
Women in history departments xix-xx, 42-5, 56, 70, 114-16 137-8, 150-2, 182-3, 195, 217, 240-1, 246-7
Women's movement 255
Woodside, Alexander 39-40
Woodward, C. Vann x, xii, xiii, xxiii, 29, 55, 57, 59 62, 68, 73, 76, 204
Work and Revolution in France 216
World War II Generation of Historians 73-4, 92
Wright, Arthur 55-7, 60
Wright, David 151
Wright, Marcia 240, 246
Wright, Mary xx, 54, 55, 70
Wyllie, Irvin 174

Yale University ix, xi, xviiii, xix, xx, xvii, xxi, xxix 32, 46, 47, 51-86, 200
Yerashalmi, Yosef 247
Young Turks 134, 136, 137, 153

Zappa, Frank 215

Made in the USA